radic

JOBS OF OUR OWN

Building a Stake-holder Society

Alternatives to the Market
and the State

RACE MATHEWS

jointly published

Pluto Press

SYDNEY · LONDON

First published in 1999
under the Radical Writing imprint, jointly by
Pluto Press Australia
Locked bag 199, Annandale NSW 2038, Australia
http://www.socialchange.net.au/pluto
and
Comerford and Miller
36 Grosvenor Road
West Wickham, Kent, BR4 9PY, United Kingdom

UK and Ireland distributors Central Books,
99 Wallis Road, London E11 5LN

Design and typesetting by Wendy Farley, Anthouse
anthouse@acay.com.au

Cover photographs are from *The Family of Man*
exhibition, Museum of Modern Art, New York.
Front: Howard Sochurek
Back: Arthur Lavine
Printed and bound by Alken Press

Australian Cataloguing in Publication Data
Mathews, Race, 1935 – .
Jobs of our own: building a stakeholder society:
alternatives to the market and the state.

Bibliography.
Aus ISBN 1 86403 064 X

1. Distribution (Economic theory.) 2. Cooperation –
Australia. 3. Cooperation – Great Britain. I. Title.

339.2

A catalogue record for this book is available at the
British Library
UK ISBN 1 871204 17 8

What people are saying about
Jobs of Our Own...

Race Mathews has produced an exciting, informative and visionary manuscript. As I read and re-read this work, I was continually struck by its relevance to the contemporary political scene here in Britain, as well as in other parts of the world. It is a scholarly study which reads as easily as a novel.

Peter Thomson, Anglican Priest, and, by Tony Blair's account, "the person who most influenced me".

In Britain, Canada, Spain and Australia, there have been on-going efforts to develop an alternative and kinder way of doing business – a Middle Way – dating back to and beyond the opening of this century. Race Mathews has uncovered a fascinating and unexpected linkage between these apparently unconnected reform movements. Are these the roots of a 21st century renaissance?

Father Greg MacLeod, Director of the Tompkins Institute, University College of Cape Breton, and author of From Mondragon to America: Experiments in Community Economic Development.

Race Mathews' book penetrates to the heart of the Mondragon Co-operative experience. There is a common factor in all three of his case studies: individual men – believers – who interpreted their mission in terms of responsibility to their natural community.

Sr. Jesus Larrañaga, former associate of Don José Maria Arizmendiarrieta, and one of the five founder members of the Mondragon co-operatives.

This is a remarkable social history that illustrates the influence of personalities on the course of events. Conscience and the rejection of poverty was the dynamic that led to insights into the necessity of equity in the distribution of wealth as a corrective. In England, intellectual debates and theories; in Antigonish, discussion and study issuing in social action; and in Mondragon insight, theory and action combined! And lastly, hope for the future.

Sister Irene Doyle, former Antigonish Movement field worker and associate of Father "Jimmy" Tompkins and Father Moses Coady.

RACE MATHEWS is a Senior Research Fellow in the International Centre for Management in Government at the Monash University/Mt Eliza School of Business and Government in Melbourne. He has been a state MP and minister, a federal MP and a municipal councillor. He was Principal Private Secretary to Gough Whitlam as Leader of the Opposition in the Australian Parliament 1967-1972 and to Opposition Leaders in the Victorian Parliament 1976-1979. His *Australia's First Fabians: Middle-Class Radicals, Labour Activists and the Early Labour Movement* was published by Cambridge University Press in 1994, and he is currently editing case study collections in public sector transparency and accountability and police and emergency services management. His E-mail address is race@netspace.net.au

Contents

*To the memory of Jimmy Tompkins, Moses Coady
and José Maria Arizmendiarrieta*

Foreword

by Peter Thomson

Peter Thomson is an Australian Anglican priest, currently working in Britain. Britain's Prime Minister, Tony Blair, describes him as 'the person who most influenced me'.

RACE MATHEWS has produced an exciting, informative and visionary manuscript. I am honoured to have been invited to write this foreword. As I read and re-read this work, I was continually struck by its relevance to the contemporary political scene here in Britain, as well as in other parts of the world. It is a scholarly study which reads as easily as a novel.

The scene is set deeply in that distinctive phenomenon of nineteenth-century British history, Christian socialism, and allows us to see the very wide meaning thinkers of the time gave to the term. Christian socialism had not then been subjected to the hijacking of its meaning and value by other groups on the Left, which so damaged its visionary warmth and appeal.

Subsequently, the sense of hope for a people dispossessed of a stake in the emergent industrialised world was shattered by ideologies of the Left and the Right that were barely a caricature of the reality of human existence. From that perspective, the book traces the rise of distributism, through Hilaire Belloc and Gilbert and Cecil Chesterton and their links with Catholic social thinking, especially the work of Cardinal Manning. Its account continues with the founding of the Antigonish initiative in Nova Scotia, through to the ongoing success of the collective Mondragon experience in northern Spain.

Both Antigonish and Mondragon owed their birth to the entrepreneurial work of visionary yet 'earthed' Catholic priests, eagerly seeking a way to deal with one aspect of the legacy of industrialised capitalism: poverty, and hence dispossession. That so shameful a disregard of our brothers and sisters had occurred was not only a failure of intelligence but, worse, a failure of the heart; of character, even morality. We had lost our way.

In our world of late twentieth-century capitalism, hope has now re-entered the political vocabulary with the advent of

New Labour, and its sweeping victory in the recent elections in Britain. A new symphony in a new key has been born, bearing the mark of a new and positive form of political democracy, where *fraternitas* — the common good — is seen to underpin the familiar tunes of equality and freedom. The name of the symphony is community. It is the Third Way. Together with hope, there has been a return of trust: another word which sears its way into the language of politics and the common good.

The political polarities of the past are seen to be transcended by the realities of the present, by an acknowledgement of the global economy and of the political possibilities of the global village. Our human condition cries out 'we long to belong', but it is also the paradoxical nature of humanity that the ongoing tension — and often open tribal conflict — between the 'I' and the 'we', with which even our families deal in the course of their daily round, can threaten the very fabric of our fragile social existence. If individualism is dying, collectivism in the form of state socialism is dead. Can we live with the understanding of that paradox within our political structures? The challenge is squarely before us. The future of our civilisation is at stake. The crisis is there to be met head-on.

The answer must be that change is possible. Critical analysis is of the utmost importance, but cynicism must be seen for what it is: the product of a lazy intelligence, unnatural in its cosy conservatism, fearful of risk, rejecting the power and energy of change. The new agenda of the Third Way, pioneered in Britain, has lit a flame that is spreading across Europe, and is finding its way into America. It is sharply focused. It is an investment in people. It is an admission that we belong together, and the key to it all is partnership. The growing belief in the commercial world is that good business depends on a healthy society.

In the eyes of Labor's True Believers, the challenge for the social sector is to acknowledge that it needs all the help and support it can muster from other sections of society, in order to change a culture of dependency into one of enterprise and initiative. It is axiomatic politically that individuals prosper in a strong and active community of others, where the meaning of citizenship demands not only individual rights, but also responsibility and obligation.

As an Australian I am disappointed that my own country is no longer part of the emerging Third Way consensus that is evident across Europe and the United States. Australia is languishing in a complacent comfort zone, unsure of its role in the global community. What appeared as a promising start during the Hawke-Keating years has fallen flat on its face under the present backward-looking conservative government, which continues to yearn for a lost past it can never recover. A warning to us all that there is nothing inevitable about progress. Race Mathews has remained a 'true believer'. This book is a testament to his continuing search for the Third Way in politics. It is full of optimism and hope. My wish is that it will be warmly received.

Author's Preface

THIS BOOK has been written in the belief that a neglected political philosophy called distributism is worth re-visiting as a contribution to debate about Third Way politics, stake-holder society and alternatives to the market and the state. Why distributism? Distributism — the idea that ownership should be widely distributed rather than concentrated in the hands of the state or rich minorities — offers remedies for many of the problems which perplex left-of-centre parties and governments. Important as are a kinder, gentler and better regulated global market and a 35-hour week, they are not in themselves the basis for a serious economic and social policy challenge to neo-liberalism, let alone the stuff of a mean-ingful and re-invigorated radical vision for the twenty-first century. Failing an adequate taking into account of distrib-utism, debates about 'Third Way' politics cannot be other than insufficiently comprehensive and thereby inconclusive.

Distributism in its modern, evolved form shows how citizenship and civil society can be reinvigorated, and ordinary people enabled to assume greater control over their lives. It offers a practical, workplace-based means of dispersing wealth as an alternative to re-distributing income through electorally unpalatable higher taxes. It draws on traditions and ideas as wide-ranging and diverse as democ-ratic socialist and social-democratic reformism, social Catholicism, mutualism, associative democracy and commu-nitarianism. It incorporates hands-on experience from the Antigonish Movement for economic development through adult education and co-operation in Atlantic Canada and the great complex of industrial, retail, financial, service and support co-operatives at Mondragon in the Basque region of Spain. Not least, it has no place for the anti-Semitism with which the extraneous prejudices of several of its originators were once mistakenly supposed to have tainted it.

My introduction to distributism — albeit at the time unawares — was through Mondragon. I became interested in Mondragon in the early 1980s through references to it by the British MP's Shirley Williams and Evan Luard. I visited there for the first time in 1985. As a member and chairman of a credit union — as I now know, a quintessentially distributist body — I was introduced a little later to the Antigonish Movement as having provided much of the inspiration for the explosive growth of the Australian credit union movement in the 1950s and 1960s.[1] Later again, in the course of research for a book about Australia's early Fabian socialists, distributism became familiar to me by name, in reports of the great debates in Britain in the early part of the century between the best known Fabian of the day, George Bernard Shaw and the best known distributist, Gilbert Chesterton.[2]

Distributism was among the more prominent topics on which Shaw and Chesterton disagreed. Re-tracing their exchanges led me to wonder if distributism, Antigonish and Mondragon might not in some way be connected with one another. The missing piece of the puzzle fell into place through an invitation to review two books about the great Catholic social doctrine encyclical letter *De Rerum Novarum* on the occasion of its centenary in 1991.[3] What subsequent research in Britain, Canada and Spain documented was successive phases in the development of modern distributism from its roots in mutualism, Christian socialism and the social Catholicism of *De Rerum Novarum* through Chesterton's British Distributism and the Antigonish Movement to Mondragon where it is now so spectacular a success.[4]

Discussion of distributism has a poignant quality for Australians. Maisie Ward reported in her biography of Chesterton in 1944 that 'In Australia, Distributism has given a fresh slant to both Labour and Catholic leadership ... Most important, however, of all the Australian developments has been the approval of the main Distributist ideal by the Australasian Hierarchy as the aim of Catholic Social Action'.[5] Distributism was in good standing in the Australian labour movement and the Labor Party well into the post-Second World War period. Reformers of all kinds including distributists rubbed along roughly in harmony with one another. There was a healthy — if at times robust — cross-fertilisation of viewpoints, and people could agree to differ in the interests of the movement's more pressing labourist priorities and electoral success.

Subsequently, in the 1950's, miscalculation or *hubris* by some predominantly Catholic bodies — notably the one-time Catholic Social Studies Movement, now known as the National Civic Council — resulted in a split between Catholic and largely non-Catholic elements within and around the party and the unions. The establishment of a mainly Catholic breakaway body — the Democratic Labor Party, which denied Labor office federally until 1972 — so much polarised opinion, sowed distrust and marginalised the influence of Catholic social thought and thinkers in mainstream labour politics that it is hard even today for social Catholicism to gain an objective hearing.[6] Distributism was a casualty of the rift. Anticipating a likely query: I am not a Catholic. My concerns are secular. What interests me about distributism and social Catholicism is their place in the history of ideas — and their promise of a better social order.

The danger for Britain is that Labour and the co-operative and mutualist movements could similarly lose touch with one another. While the Parliamentary Labour Party still has representatives from the Co-operative Party — the political arm of the co-operative movement — the attitude of the government is open to the interpretation that it has dismissed the sudden surge of conversions of mutualist bodies such as building societies and mutual assurance societies into conventional proprietary limited companies as being of no political concern. My worry is that, by the time New Labour gets round to fully appreciating the importance of the mutuals for its Third Way agenda, few of them may be left. Irrespective of whether in Britain, Australia or elsewhere, overlooking all that mutualism, social Catholicism and distributism have to offer is more by far than either the labour movement or the community more generally can afford.

To the greatest possible extent, protagonists in the book have been allowed to speak for themselves. Given a choice between quotation and paraphrase, quotation has been preferred. Surnames have also been preferred, other than where, as for example with members of the Chesterton family, given names are substituted to avoid confusion. Given that Gilbert Chesterton's sister-in-law — one of the few prominent women distributists — had the maiden name of Ada Jones, wrote under the pen-name of John Keith Prothero, was 'Keith' or 'Johnny' to her friends and published her book *The Chestertons* as Mrs C. Chesterton, it has seemed simplest to refer to her throughout as Ada Jones. Gilbert Chesterton and Shaw are sometimes referred to simply by the initials they made famous — "GKC" and "GBS".

Acknowledgements

I HAVE had more help in researching distributism than can adequately be acknowledged. My colleagues and friends at Monash University, Professor Owen Hughes of the Department of Management and Professor Hugh Emy of the Politics Department, have been unfailing sources of advice, information and encouragement. I have had generous support from Professor Bill Russell, while working for him at Monash as a Senior Research Fellow in the Public Sector Management Institute and the Graduate School of Government.

I am also deeply grateful to Professor Dan MacInnes of the Department of Sociology and Anthropology at the St Francis Xavier University in Antigonish and Father Greg MacLeod of the Tompkins Institute at the University College of Cape Breton, who looked after me during my stay in Nova Scotia in 1996; to my host in 1996 in the Archives of the English Chapter of the Order of Preachers at Blackfriars in Edinburgh, Father Bede Bailey; to Iñaki Idiazabal, Mikel Lezamiz, Itziar Bazanbide and all their associates at the Otalora Institute in Mondragon who made me welcome there in 1996 and again in 1997; and to my guide, interpreter, mentor and now friend in Mondragon, Fred Freundlich of Ownership Associates Inc, to whom my debt is incalculable.

I thank in particular the Archivist at the St Francis Xavier University, Kathleen MacKenzie, who opened her records to me under the exceptionally difficult circumstances of being in the throes of moving them to a new location; Amand Arsenault, who hosted me during a visit to the co-operatives on Prince Edward Island; and Sister Irene Doyle and Juan Larrañaga whose first-hand recollections respectively of the Antigonish Movement and Mondragon have been invaluable to me. Dr Peter Hunt, Dr Ian Britain, Professor John Barnes and Patricia Pugh stand out among the many other colleagues and friends — in Australian and abroad — who generously made available time for advice and comment, and guided me to key sources of information. Timely interventions by John Menadue and Father Michael Kelly kept up my spirits at a difficult stage. I am deeply grateful to Peter Thomson for his generous and inspiring Foreword, to my editors, Neil Thomas and Michael Wall, to my designer, Wendy Farley, and to my co-publishers, Tony Moore at Pluto Press and Russell Miller at Comerford and Miller.

As always, Michael Mamouney — and, more recently, Anna Hewitt — in the Library of the Victorian Parliament have been outstandingly helpful in obtaining reference material for me. I have also been fortunate in the willing assistance given by other libraries, including in particular, in Australia, the Monash University Library, the Melbourne University Library, the Newman College Library, the Joint Theological Library at Ormond College, the Catholic Central Library (now the Caroline Chisholm Library) in Melbourne and the State Library of New South Wales, and, overseas, the St Francis Xavier University Library and the University College of Cape Breton Library in Nova Scotia, the St Michael's College Library in Toronto and the Scottish National Library.

Special gratitude is due to the editor of *The Chesterton Review*, Father Ian Boyd, for permission to draw on the rich store of fascinating information which his journal provides, and for the on-going exchange of comment and analysis it encourages. I am grateful for permission for the use of extensive quotations from the work of Hilaire Belloc by the Trustee of the Belloc Estate, and from *Making Mondragon: The Growth and Dynamics of the Worker Co-operative Complex* by William Foote Whyte and Kathleen King Whyte by Cornell University Press. Credits for pictorial material are due to the Fabian Society, the Archives of the University of St Francis Xavier at Antigonish, the Beaton Institute Archives at the University College of Cape Breton, the National Film Board of Canada, the Otalora Institute and the editors of *The Chesterton Review* and *TU/Lankide*.

I am indebted finally to the authors and publishers of works cited in the Endnotes and listed in the Bibliography; to my mentors in politics, David Bennett and Gough Whitlam; and most of all to my wife, Iola Mathews, for all that her love, patience and support has meant to me.

PART I

BRITISH DISTRIBUTISM

Cardinal Henry Manning

1

Distributism: The Socialist Seedbed, the Catholic Harvest and the Public Benefit

Distributism

T HIS book is about a political philosophy called distributism. The basis of distributism is the belief that a just social order can only be achieved through a much more widespread distribution of property. Distributism favours a 'society of owners' where property belongs to the many rather than the few, and correspondingly opposes the concentration of property in the hands either of the rich, as under capitalism, or of the state, as advocated by some socialists. In particular, ownership of the means of production, distribution and exchange must be widespread.

Distributism emerged as one element of the widespread revulsion and agony of conscience over poverty in late-Victorian and Edwardian Britain. Its current importance is the greater because circumstances reminiscent of those which produced it are again evident. Distributism has assumed a new relevance and urgency in the light of the current substantial abdication of former government functions to the vagaries of globalisation, the free market and largely unfettered competition — and of the consequent further widening of the gap between the rich and the poor, the reappearance of great numbers of beggars and homeless people in cities like New York and London, the creation of a growing underclass whose members are effectively social outcasts and other adverse developments which in key respects vividly recall Britain in the 1880s.

The similarities between the 1880s in Britain — to which distributism was a response — and the 1990s cannot be too strongly emphasised. What is being witnessed currently is a managed reduction in the living standards of working people throughout the developed world. The relentless assault on wages, working conditions and job security — in conjunction with the crushing of the capacity of trade unions to protect the well-being of their members, and the dismantling of the welfare safety net built up during the twentieth century — is recreating the permanently dispossessed strata within society which late-Victorian Britain referred to as, respectively, the working poor and the *residuum*. Nor are large parts of the middle class any more immune to rampant insecurity today than in the Victorian and Edwardian eras.

'In the advanced industrial societies', writes the British scholar and former prominent MP David Marquand, 'one of the central themes of the golden age was "embourgeoisement": the spread to the working class of the job security, career ladders and lifestyles which had formerly been the prerogatives of the middle class'. Furthermore, he notes,

> Now the engines have gone into reverse ... The de-casualisation of labour, which a generation of trade union leaders saw as its life's work, has given way to re-casualisation — and in what used to be the middle class as well as the working class. Down-sizing, delayering, outsourcing and re-engineering haunt the suburbs as well as the inner cities, mocking the commitments and hollowing out the institutions which were once the lodestars of the salariat.

'Capitalism', Marquand concludes, 'is off the leash. Not surprisingly, it is behaving much as it did before its tamers put it on the leash during the extraordinary burst of institutional creativity which followed the Second World War'.[1]

What is no less troubling is the perceived absence of

credible alternatives. The failure of state socialism has left behind it a vacuum which nothing currently on offer seems likely to remedy. Astute and compelling as are analyses of the current situation from sources such as the communitarian and associative democracy movements, they have to date been handicapped by the lack of measures such as would comprise a meaningful program. There is no agreed body of policy — no clear model or blueprint for action — behind which those who share the communitarian and associative viewpoint can unite.

Broadly social-democratic reformism finds itself faced with a near-total dearth of useful new ideas — or is at least experiencing extreme difficulty in reconciling its abiding values with the currently dominant free market paradigm — and it could do worse than backtrack and re-evaluate other possible routes to its goals, from the rich storehouse of its history. One such route is via the idea of mutualism, which gave rise to the great friendly society, mutual assurance society, credit union and co-operative movements. Distributism in its current evolved form builds on and enriches mutualism, so as to hold out the promise of a new beginning. Where distributism points in practical terms is to a third way between the statist and market visions of society, which captures what is best from both of them.

The distributist emphasis — like that of communitarianism and associative democracy — is squarely on liberty, equality, democracy and sociability. Distributism counters the destructive onward march of ever greater concentrations of corporate power, loss of economic sovereignty of nations and the relegation to marginal status of major sections of the community. It is wary of statism, but insists that free market solutions are only reproducing the key social problem of poverty. It is squarely on the side of active citizenship, and embraces the ideal of civil society. It freely acknowledges the need to reconcile the moral case for greater democracy in the workplace with the requirements of productivity: to have productive organisations which are fair as well as efficient.

Consistent with these attributes, distributism looks less to the state than to initiative at the local and regional levels. Distributism is not something which can be handed to people or imposed from above. People have to set it in motion for themselves. It grows and spreads by example. Distributism is a big idea about small beginnings and what can come of them. It answers the need to build from below the just social order which can no longer be hoped for from above.

Influences

For all that distributism was a response to poverty, it was not a direct response. Rather it embodied an emergent synthesis between two more immediate reactions to poverty, namely those of British socialism as exemplified by the socialist revival of the 1880s, and the Catholic social teachings which Pope Leo XIII — acting in part at the instigation of the great British cardinal, Henry Manning — set out in in 1891, in his social doctrine encyclical letter *De Rerum Novarum* (known in English as *On the Condition of Labour*). In so doing, distributism married two differing but, at times, oddly complementary trajectories of thought, to produce a distinctive compromise in which the more useful elements of both are evident.

Distributism is in this sense the product of a seedbed of socialist agitation against poverty and a Catholic harvest from generations of debate on social doctrine within and around the Church. At a later stage in its development, distributism drew heavily on ideas and models of adult education as practised by the British Workers' Education Association and the Danish folk high schools, and of mutualist economic co-operation in the mould of the Rochdale consumer co-operatives and Raiffeisen credit unions. The personalist teachings of the prominent French Catholic philosophers, Jacques Maritain and Emmanuel Mounier, were widely seen as being supportive of distributism.

'A personalist civilisation', wrote Mounier, 'is one whose structure and spirit are directed towards the development as persons of all the individuals constituting it. They have as their ultimate end to enable every individual to live as a person, that is, to exercise a maximum of initiative, responsibility, and spiritual life'.[2] Evolved distributism is, in a sense, most usefully understood as the form in which socialism in its original mutualist, associative and communitarian form has been reborn, following its well-intentioned but ultimately disastrous flirtation with statism.

Manning, a giant of late-Victorian social activism whose

role has had insufficient acknowledgement, was the precursor of distributism. The example of social concern he set, and the emphasis on social reform in his translation and interpretation of *De Rerum Novarum* for English-speaking Catholics, played key roles in determining the nature of distributism. That he died before the word distributism was coined or its implications spelled out was a tragedy for the Catholic Church in Britain, as its commitment to social activism largely died with him; it was also a tragedy for the great-hearted ecumenical spirit which led him to reach out and make common cause with those who shared his social values and objectives irrespective of whether they might differ from him in other respects; and for the soon-to-be-created distributist movement which otherwise might have gained so greatly from his wisdom, stature and advocacy.

Most of all, it was a tragedy for the poor and the dispossessed to whom his life was dedicated. The doctrine of 'subsidiarity' which *De Rerum Novarum* contained — the doctrine that a higher body should not assume on behalf of a lower body functions which the lower body is able to perform for itself — was effectively Manning's key legacy to his church and his country. With the publication of *De Rerum Novarum* and the appearance of significant opposition within the socialist movement to state socialist orthodoxy in the first decade of the new century, the foundations for distributism were at last laid.

The distributist movement was instigated in Britain shortly after the turn of the century by the prominent Catholic writers Hilaire Belloc and Gilbert Chesterton, together with — a little later — Gilbert's younger brother, Cecil Chesterton. Like so many of their distributist associates, all three were former socialists — albeit differing from one another as to the content, depth and duration of their socialist convictions — whose schooling in and around the socialist movements of the day enabled them to think their way through to a clear understanding of what sort of social reform made sense to them. 'It is my experience', wrote Gilbert Chesterton, 'that the sort of man who does really become a Distributist is exactly the sort of man who has really been a Socialist ... Mr Belloc himself had been a Socialist; my brother had been a Socialist; I had been a Socialist'.[3]

Those of their contemporaries who remained socialists —

not least on the honourable grounds of their conviction that the suffering of the poor would be relieved more rapidly and with greater certainty through socialism than by any other means — in turn learned from the distributists, and key aspects of distributist thought were incorporated into new socialist philosophies such as guild socialism. The differences and tensions between the two camps, demonstrated in the ongoing debate on public platforms and in the weekly journals of the day, enriched both of them.

De Rerum Novarum to Mondragon

Distributism restated the doctrine of subsidiarity as the basis for workplace reform and a new social order. What followed was a protracted search for ways to put subsidiarity and distributism into effect. Successive stages in the search — the last a triumphant success — are exemplified, first, by British distributism; next, by the Antigonish Movement for community development through adult education and economic co-operation which was fostered by the Extension Department at the University of St Francis Xavier in Nova Scotia in Canada from the 1920s into the 1950s under the inspired leadership of two remarkable Catholic priests, Father 'Jimmy' Tompkins and Father Moses Coady; and, finally, by the 'evolved distributism' of the great complex of industrial, service and support co-operatives — now the Mondragon Co-operative Corporation (MCC) — which a further remarkable Catholic priest, Don José Maria Arizmendiarrieta, established in the 1940s and 1950s at Mondragon in the Basque region of Spain.

The leaders of the Antigonish Movement squarely acknowledged their indebtedness to British distributism. 'We of St Francis Xavier', Tompkins wrote in a draft sermon in 1938, 'have learned valuable lessons from the Distributist followers of Chesterton and Belloc'. He continued:

> The British Distributists told us that their idea is to preach the restoration of liberty by the distribution of property — restoring family and individual liberty in national life by a revival of agriculture, favouring small industries, attacking monopolies and trusts, opposing a servile press owned by the rich and denouncing the anonymous control of finance.[4]

Maisie Ward notes in her 1944 biography of Gilbert Chesterton that 'It was in the "Suburbs of England" that Distributism was first taken seriously and used as practical politics ... in Canada, the Antigonish Movement has shown a happy blending of theory and practice'.[5]

None of Arizmendiarrieta's surviving associates now recall having heard him mention Antigonish. However, so closely did his studies as a seminarian with a special interest in sociology, and subsequent sustained research while shaping the development of the Mondragon co-operatives, coincide with the peak of international interest in Antigonish in both lay and clerical circles — so closely did they coincide with the singling out of the work of Coady and Tomkins for explicit papal commendation — that it is hard to see how what was happening in Nova Scotia could have escaped his notice.

Anecdotal evidence suggestive of a link is available. When Tom Webb — currently a successor of Coady as Director of the Extension Department at the University of St Francis Xavier — visited Mondragon with a study group in the early 1980s, a fellow member of the group identified him to their hosts as having come from Antigonish. Webb was then singled out for a special welcome, and entertained at a dinner where reference was made to the importance of the Antigonish example for Mondragon, and to members of the Mondragon co-operatives having at some stage visited Antigonish.[6] Be the nature of the connection as it may, the credit for having at last made distributism a practical proposition belongs squarely to Arizmendiarrieta.

Whereas the British distributists largely restricted themselves to talking and writing about distributism, Tompkins and Coady in Canada were practical men who saw in co-operation on the traditional Rochdale model — the model of the great consumer co-operative and credit union movements — the means by which distributism could be given practical effect and their fellow citizens enabled to lift themselves out of poverty and so become as Coady constantly advocated 'masters of their own destiny'.[7]

If their analysis was fundamentally flawed — if their vision asked more of Rochdale than it could deliver, and the structures they based on Rochdale therefore ultimately failed or evolved along lines which fell short of their intentions — that in no way makes less admirable the selfless dedication to the advancement of the dispossessed which motivated them. Neither should it detract from the energy they devoted to their cause, nor from the short-to-medium term alleviation of suffering, the enhancement of human dignity and the restoration of hope which they accomplished.

The high regard in which they and the movement were held is evident in the fact that the Coady International Institute — established as a memorial to Coady following his death in 1959, as a means of taking the Antigonish program to developing countries — had as one of its first sponsors the then US senator, and future president, John F. Kennedy. Kennedy was a member of the Board of the Institute — albeit inactive — throughout his presidency, until his untimely death in 1963.[8]

The Antigonish Movement also enabled distributism to put behind it once and for all the crippling notoriety for anti-Semitism to which — as subsequent chapters will show — the extraneous prejudices of some British distributists had exposed it. Tompkins and Coady had no time for either racist or sectarian prejudice. Asked by a fellow priest what he should do, in circumstances where admitting negroes to the pews in his church had resulted in the white members of the congregation staying away, Tompkins replied: 'Take the Negro. Take the Negro. And let the white go — to hell. He's likely to go there anyway if he's gotten so choosy about his salvation. I tell you these people need to be jolted'.[9]

'There is no Catholic way of selling fish, no Methodist way, no Baptist way' was a saying which both Tompkins and Coady used frequently in condemning sectarian obstacles to the establishment of co-operatives.[10] The editor of Coady's writings and speeches, Alex Laidlaw — also a close personal friend, and Associate Director of the Extension Department from 1944 to 1956 — sees him as having 'ante-dated Vatican II by twenty-five years, especially as regards ecumenism'. 'Those who found his words troublesome to their comfortable way of life', Laidlaw continues, 'would have liked to dismiss him as a voice crying in the wilderness, but for us today, in a world shaken by disorder, violence and deepening conflict, his message and teaching have taken on new significance and fresh validity'.[11]

What remained, in terms of re-establishing the relevance of distributism, was for Arizmendiarrieta to perceive the fundamental flaws of the Rochdale model, and to reassert the core distributist truth that only work and property — as opposed, for example, to consumption or saving — were so central in the lives of ordinary people as to provide the foundations on which an enduring distributist social order could be built. Arizmendiarrieta endowed the structures and processes of the Mondragon co-operatives with so great a capacity to adapt to changing circumstances as for it to be said of them that 'we build the road as we travel'.[12]

If the road the co-operatives continue to build for themselves still has some way to go before arriving at a fully distributist social order, it has also already come a remarkable distance. Nor have the co-operatives been any less successful in purely commercial terms. The MCC has experienced exceptional rates of growth, and is now the ninth largest business group in Spain, with annual sales approaching $US6 billion. The co-operatives employ some 30,000 workers — and expect to take on more — in a region where unemployment is currently around 20 per cent.

The principal-agent relationship

Evolved distributism in the Mondragon mould owes its achievements largely to having overcome in part — and potentially in its entirety — what agency theorists call 'the basic agency dilemma'. Agency theory holds that how individuals and institutions behave socially and politically can be explained in terms of a series of 'contracts'. Where one party (the 'principal') commissions a second party (the 'agent') to act on the first party's behalf, an agency relationship — a 'contract' — is created. The substance of the contract — of the 'principal-agent relationship' — is the agreement by the agent to comply with the wishes of the principal, who, in turn, agrees to provide the agent with a specified reward.

Agents are seen as falling into the two broad categories: profit-seekers, who undertake to deliver a product for a price; and employees who are paid a wage in return for accepting instructions. In the case of the conventional profit-seeking, wage-paying firm, agency relationships of both types can be seen as coexisting within a layered structure of accountability:

Production workers are accountable to managers, and are

paid a wage in return for time on the job. Managers, in turn, are accountable to owners, and are paid a salary for directing and supervising production. Finally, the owners are accountable to customers, and collect a profit — the excess of revenue over costs — in exchange for organising the whole process.[13]

However, this still leaves a core problem — the 'basic agency dilemma'[14] — because individuals are, by nature, inclined to opportunism and the pursuit of their own self-interest. Divergences of interest, emerging inevitably between the principals and agents in an agency relationship, give rise to costs which defeat or detract from the purpose for which the relationship was created.

There is considerable scope for the expression of divergent interests, because principals and agents have only partial information about the real motives and interests of one another. Commonly mentioned examples of opportunistic behaviour on the part of agents include theft, collusion, misrepresentation, and underperformance as reflected by absenteeism and low productivity.[15] Principals in turn perpetrate comparable abuses by failing to deliver the letter or spirit of agreed rewards. 'The agency problem', in the view of the American scholar, John D. Donahue, 'is the difficulty, in all but the simplest relationships, of ensuring that the principal is faithfully served, and the agent is fairly compensated'.[16] A major study of the matter concludes:

> The problem of inducing an 'agent' to behave as if he were maximising the 'principal's' welfare is quite general. It exists in all organisations and in all co-operative efforts — at every level of management in firms, in universities, in mutual companies, in co-operatives, in governmental authorities and bureaux, in unions, and in relationships normally classified as agency relationships such as are common in the performing arts and the market for real estate.[17]

The remedy for divergences between the interests of principals and agents which theorists commonly favour is to further strengthen and refine the contract between them.

Agency theory constantly tries to find better ways in which contracts can be negotiated, written and monitored, so that the likelihood of injury to the interests of either party by the other is reduced. Contractual devices for securing compliance by agents with the wishes of principals include closer monitoring by principals of the behaviour of agents; principals requiring from agents a bond or guarantee of compensation in the event of contracts being breached; and the use by principals of incentives and sanctions so that their interests and those of their agents become more closely aligned. Such mechanisms are necessarily costly, in some cases to the point where it makes greater sense for principals to perform the required functions for themselves or abandon them.

Agents in turn may have a negative response to the imposition of tighter contractual conditions which makes them ineffectual or self-defeating. In either case, confidence is dampened, investment discouraged and opportunities for growth and employment lost. More broadly, agency costs are detrimental to the well-being of regions and nations in their pursuit of competitive advantage. Given these difficulties and costs, questions arise as to whether there are ways other than tightening compliance mechanisms by which the issue of divergent principal and agent interests — of the basic agency dilemma — can be addressed.

The genius of Arizmendiarrieta lay in rethinking co-operation on the Rochdale model so as to incorporate principles and structures which reduce — and perhaps will ultimately eliminate — the basic agency dilemma, both within and between the Mondragon co-operatives. From the perspective of creating a more rational — i.e. fair and efficient — productive system, what Mondragon is about is primarily the evolution — albeit as yet incomplete — of systems within which all principals are agents and agents principals.

Agency theory in this sense does not, as its proponents have hitherto insisted, lead logically to a conventionally privatised economy, which perpetuates the basic agency dilemma, but rather to co-operativisation on the Mondragon model which holds out the promise of a remedy. In short, since neither the public nor the private sector is free from the basic agency dilemma, the real need is for a further alternative — a distributist way — which more effectively deals with the deficiency.

Mutualism

Arizmendiarrieta found in the mutualist philosophy of the co-operative movement a vehicle closely attuned to his requirements. Co-operatives and other mutualist bodies are almost always formed as a means of enabling their members to acquire, through co-operation with one another, necessities such as would otherwise be difficult for them to afford. For example, the Rochdale Equitable Pioneers — the twenty-eight cotton weavers who founded a co-operative store in Toad Lane in Rochdale in 1844, and thereby launched the British consumer co-operative movement — were responding to a pressing social need for affordable access to such household requisites as food, fuel and clothing.

Credit co-operatives, now known generally as credit unions, were a response to the need for affordable carry-on loans for smallholder farmers, and later for affordable consumer finance. Friendly societies were initially a response to the need for funeral benefits, and, later, for unemployment benefits, sickness benefits and medical and hospital care. Access to affordable life assurance was offered by mutual life assurance societies, as was access to affordable home loans by building societies.

Processing and marketing co-operatives met a pressing social need on the part of farmers to capture value added to their produce beyond the farm gate. Worker co-operatives were a response to the need for labour to hire capital rather than capital labour, and so for workers to be the owners of their jobs and workplaces. Trade unions were originally mutualist bodies or co-operatives, formed by employees in response to the pressing social need to obtain a just price for their labour.

Co-operatives and other mutualist bodies can be seen in this respect as having the attributes of both businesses and social movements. As in other social movements, the typical lifecycle of a co-operative falls into three stages. There is, in the first instance, a utopian stage where the vision and commitment of the founders energise their followers and enable the co-operative to begin; secondly, a stage when the co-operative assumes a more formal and institutional character in order to more effectively go about achieving its objectives; and, finally, a stage — usually referred to as the 'system' stage — where bureaucracy takes over, and the survival and well-being of the organisation assumes precedence over whatever functional purpose it was originally intended to serve. Social movement theorists characterise the cycle in its entirety as comprising a 'generation-degeneration process'.[18]

Consistent with the social movement model, what the best known examples of mutualist bodies and co-operatives — the major credit unions, agricultural co-operatives, mutual life assurance societies, friendly societies and retail or consumer co-operatives such as in Britain — now have in common with one another is the blind alley or 'Rochdale cul-de-sac' they have come to occupy, as a consequence of having gravitated from the hands of their members to those of bureaucracies. In the absence of any meaningful measure of member involvement and participation, they have become for all practical purposes indistinguishable from their commercial counterparts.

Not least, they have wholly or in part forfeited their niche advantage over their competitors in terms of the principal-agent relationship. As will be seen in Chapter 8, recent experience suggests that the Rochdale cul-de-sac is not, as has been supposed, a stable — not to say stagnant — condition which can be counted on to continue indefinitely, but rather one of extreme fragility and precariousness. It invites either commercial failure as in the case of some major European consumer co-operatives — the one-time elite of the co-operative movement — or being taken over and looted either from without or within by predatory demutualisers.

However, the prospects for mutualism need not necessarily remain so grim. Thanks to Arizmendiarrieta, distributism in the Mondragon mould now holds out the promise of a mutualist renaissance. The co-operative movement has effectively been offered a reprieve from the extinction which currently threatens it, and has been handed a way to break out of the Rochdale cul-de-sac, reinvigorate its mutualist values and assume new significance within the wider context of evolved distributism. Were the original distributists alive today, the shape of evolved distributism as at Mondragon — the emergent synthesis between distributism and mutualism — might well surprise them, but it is unlikely that they would be displeased.

The approach

It is not possible to understand so notably idiosyncratic a philosophy as distributism without an understanding of the lives and times of the key distributists. The method adopted is in part group biography and in part social history. In as much as rounding out who the original distributists were — how what they stood for was arrived at, and the impact on their ideas and actions of what was in most cases their Catholic faith — has required dealing with aspects other than those most overtly related to their distributism, there have been notable benefits. This is nowhere more strikingly the case than with Belloc, who, as the founder of distributism, has a significance for the whole idea exceeded only, perhaps, by that of Arizmendiarrieta, who finally made it work.

For example, that Belloc had a French father, was inspired by Rousseau, steadfastly defended the French Revolution, revered Napoleon and served in the French artillery is only marginally less central to explaining the aggressive slant he imparted to distributism — and his rejection of parliament as a means of giving effect to distributism — than his Catholicism or his inheritance from successive generations of outspoken English Liberals on his mother's side of the family. Lines such as those from Belloc's evocative poem 'To My Regiment':

> Heard Ney shouting for the guns to unlimber
> And hold the Beresina bridge by night.

shed light less significantly on his romantic fascination with soldiering than on why his promotion of distributism was so excessively, incorrigibly and often counterproductively belligerent.

Lines as poignant as in Belloc's 'Ha'nacker Mill' are also relevant:

> Sally is gone that was so kindly
> Sally is gone from Ha'nacker Hill.
> And the Briar grows ever since then so blindly
> And ever since then the clapper is still,
> And the sweeps have fallen from Ha'nacker Mill.
> Ha'nacker Hill is in Desolation:
> Ruin a-top and a field unploughed.
> And Spirits that call on a fallen nation
> Spirits that loved her calling aloud:
> Spirits abroad in a windy cloud.

Spirits that call and no one answers;
Ha'nacker's down and England's done.
Wind and Thistle for pipe and dancers
And never a ploughman under the Sun.
Never a ploughman. Never a one.

Who can fail to detect here Belloc's intense patriotism and sorrow for the condition of England, or doubt the distinctively English flavour of much of what he wrote and had to say about distributism?

Who can doubt that British distributism was energised in the first instance largely by the passionate sense of history — the powerful historical imagination — evident in passages such as from Belloc's *The Cruise of the Nona*, where he describes the coming of the First World War in 1914? The passage, redolent as it is of the consciousness of the writer of his presence at a turning point in history, reads:

In this loneliness and content, as I sailed northward, I chanced to look after an hour's steering or so, eastward again towards the open sea — and then it was that there passed me the vision I shall remember for ever, or for so long as the longest life may last. Like ghosts, like things themselves made of mist, there passed between me and the newly risen sun a procession of great forms, all in line, hastening eastward. It was the Fleet recalled. The slight haze along the distant water had thickened, perhaps, imperceptibly; or perhaps the great speed of the men-of-war buried them too quickly in the distance. But, from whatever cause, this marvel was of short duration. It was seen for a moment, and in a moment it was gone.

'Then I knew that war would come', Belloc concluded, 'and my mind was changed'.[19]

Belloc's French origins and affiliations also go some way to explaining the bizarre flirtation with the European dictators, Mussolini and Franco, in which he and those closest to him engaged in the 1930s, to the enduring detriment of distributism. 'In all this', writes Dudley Barker in his 1973 biography of Gilbert Chesterton, 'Chesterton was pushed by Belloc, who was soon to be detecting Masonic Plots against the noble Italian, and who, during the civil war in Spain, could acclaim Franco as the saviour of us all'.[20]

Not least, the repeated disappointments which Belloc

experienced in his personal and professional life, and the profoundly pessimistic conclusions he drew from them, may in part account for the many instances in which he let down his fellow distributists by not honouring key undertakings such as to prepare a textbook on distributism, pouring cold water on their enthusiasms, being unavailable at moments when the movement was most in need of him and indulging his extraneous prejudices such as anti-Semitism at the movement's expense.

Any study of distributism necessarily entails a study of the psychology — and perhaps psychopathology — of its originator. A key assessment of Belloc's performance as a largely absentee vice-president of the Distributist League reads as follows: 'His failure to get anywhere with his views in the days when he was a Liberal Member of Parliament had perhaps led him to believe that nothing short of a catastrophe could change the course of history'. 'One astute participant in the inaugural meeting of the League', the account records, 'remembers Belloc's attitude as one of "Good luck for the future; but since I've failed, do you really suppose you can do better?".'[21]

What follows in Chapter 2 is an account of the roots of distributism in the poverty of late-Victorian and Edwardian Britain, and how the socialists of the day — predecessors of the distributists — responded to it. A key aspect is seen to be the revulsion of some socialists against what had, by the turn of the century, become a state socialist orthodoxy, and their renewed interest in worker ownership and self-management. The belief that workers should be the proprietors of their workplaces was common to guild socialism, distributism and — in the industrial sphere, and therefore mainly outside the compass of the present study — syndicalism.

Chapters 3 to 5 review the characters and careers of Manning, Belloc and Gilbert and Cecil Chesterton, and their contributions to the development of distributism. Distributism is seen here as having had its key precursor in Manning, its prophet in Belloc and its missionaries in Cecil and Gilbert Chesterton. Cecil Chesterton in particular assumes a larger significance than is usually ascribed to him: a St Paul of distributism to Gilbert's St Francis.

Chapters 6 to 10 have as their subjects British distributism, the Antigonish Movement and the Mondragon Co-operative

Corporation. What emerges is that the British distributists were undecided as to whether distributism should be a political ginger group or think tank on the Fabian Society model — which necessarily relied on parliament and the mainsteam political parties to give effect to its proposals — or instead a social movement implementing its thinking for itself on a grass-roots basis. It was also a constant source of complaint within the distributist movement that its leaders would not provide in a program or textbook a more precise description of what a distributist social order would look like, how it would function and what the difference would be for ordinary people.

In the event, the inability of the British distributists to choose between operating at a political or a social movement level meant that they did neither effectively, and British distributism had for all practical purposes withered on the vine prior to the outbreak of the Second World War in 1939. British distributism was a tragedy in the most literal and direct sense of men and women who, in regard to key practicalities, could not make up their minds.

The Antigonish Movement was, on the contrary, unambiguously a social movement which eschewed political affiliations. 'Trust the little fellow', was a phrase Tompkins used frequently to convey what a social movement was about. It also conveys the essence of subsidiarity. 'For your program', wrote Tompkins, 'you've got to get hold of the little fellow ... The little fellow, the little people together, is a giant; they make giants. You've got to give them ideas, then they'll blow the roof off'.[22]

Antigonish's contribution to distributism was to identify the role of adult education in lifting the consciousness of communities to the point where they are able to assume responsibility for their own development, and of co-operation as a means whereby the distributist objective of a well-judged distribution of property could be achieved.

It was left finally for the further social movement in Mondragon — referred to significantly among its adherents as 'the Mondragon Co-operative Experience' — to develop from the bottom up a completely new co-operative paradigm, which remains as dynamic now as at its inception forty and more years ago. Like Tompkins and Coady, Arizmendiarrieta engaged extensively in adult education and consciousness-raising. He also responded imaginatively to the 'Rochdale cul-de-sac' of declining member motivation and involvement and rising bureaucratisation, in ways which fully reflect the distributist emphasis on work and property.

Chapter 11 examines Mondragon in the light of agency theory and subsidiarity, and draws conclusions for areas of public policy such as competitive advantage, employment growth, local and regional economic development and social cohesion. A final question, which is implicit throughout the book, is whether, if poverty and conscience could once give rise to so great an upsurge of action as was experienced in Britain in the 1880s, may they not be able to do so again?

Is it perhaps the case that, in the evolved distributism of the MCC, we see reunited the broad streams of Catholic and socialist or social democratic reformism whose long estrangement has been to their mutual detriment? Is it perhaps possible that evolved distributism can go some way towards filling the aching gap at the heart of the cause of social reform which the comprehensive discrediting of state socialism — the fall from grace of the statutory corporation and the command economy — has left behind it?

THE WEBB OF DESTINY

Mr. Sidney Webb. "I AM WAVING THIS RED
FLAG, NOT PROVOCATIVELY, BUT TO
SIGNALISE WHAT I HAVE SO HAPPILY
CALLED THE 'INEVITABILITY OF
GRADUALNESS' WHICH MARKS OUR
ROLLER'S ADVANCE".

2

'Why Are the Many Poor?':
Conscience and the Rejection
of Poverty

Strands of the socialist response

DISTRIBUTISM owed its origin in the first instance to the idealism which fired the socialist revival of the 1880s. The sense of moral obligation and purpose of the founder distributists caused them initially to become socialists. It also caused them, a little later, to leave the mainstream socialist movement when its rejection of poverty, with which they passionately agreed, was overtaken, as they thought, by its increasingly statist and collectivist bias. The distributists in this respect closely resembled the guild socialists and the syndicalists. Distributism, guild socialism and syndicalism are best understood as associative and communitarian strands of the original socialist response to poverty which parted company, in similar circumstances and for similar reasons, with the statist and collectivist strands which became predominant within the labour movement and bodies such as the Fabian Society. Similar dissolvents — frustrations and feelings of urgency — within the mainstream socialist camp were responsible for all three of them. They experienced a common gestation process prior to going their separate ways. An examination of their subsequent development discloses many of the same attributes — notably regard for human dignity and the desire to see workers assume control of their working lives and retain the rewards of their labour — shaping guild socialism and syndicalism as shaped distributism. Like distributism, guild socialism and syndicalism had a powerful appeal for social-minded Catholics due to the elements of subsidiarity they incorporated.

Poverty

The moral origins which socialism shares with distributism are plain. England is said by some to have rediscovered poverty in the 1880s.[1] The claim is misconceived. What was rediscovered was a sense of the moral untenability of insufficiency in the presence of excess. What the selection by the newly formed Fabian Society, in 1884, of the topic *Why Are the Many Poor?* for the inaugural Fabian pamphlet, signalled was an interest, less in whether the incidence of poverty was higher or lower than had previously been the case, than in whether it was tolerable in moral terms for large sections of the population to be without adequate access to the necessities of life. If not, how should the situation be remedied?

The groundbreaking research into the incidence of poverty by Charles and Mary Booth in London and Seebohm Rowntree in York in the 1880s and 1890s — and of pioneering statisticians such as Robert Giffen who established that the purchasing power of the working class had already undergone major improvement in real terms and was continuing to do so — was secondary, in this sense, to moral revulsion and agony of conscience over the objective living conditions of the poor, and the division of England into what the future Tory Party prime minister, Benjamin Disraeli, characterised memorably in his novel *Sybil* in 1845 as 'the two nations'. Disraeli wrote that England was:

> Two nations between whom there is no intercourse and no
> sympathy; who are as ignorant of each other's habits, thoughts,
> and feelings, as if they were dwellers in different zones or
> inhabitants of different planets; who are formed by differ-
> ent breeding, are fed by different food, are ordered by
> different manners, and are not governed by the same laws.[2]

What is striking to the modern eye is the contrast here with
attitudes in the late twentieth century, when the middle class
has so largely turned its back on the poor, welfare measures
are being systematically reduced, and poverty is once again
widely held to be the fault of its victims.

A widely read and much-discussed penny pamphlet by a
congregationalist clergyman in 1883, *The Bitter Cry of Outcast
London: An Inquiry into the Conditions of the ABJECT POOR*, reads:

> While we have been building our churches and solacing
> ourselves with our religion and dreaming that the millen-
> nium was coming, the poor have been growing poorer, the
> wretched more miserable, and the immoral more corrupt;
> the gulf has been daily widening which separates the lowest
> classes of the community from our churches and chapels,
> and from decency and civilisation. THIS TERRIBLE
> FLOOD OF SIN AND MISERY IS GAINING UPON US.[3]

More than a third of all Londoners were living in families
huddled six to a room, and more than one in eight dying in
the workhouse.[4] 'The wages paid for unskilled labour in
York', reported Rowntree, 'are insufficient to provide food,
shelter, and clothing adequate to maintain a family of
moderate size in a state of bare physical efficiency'.[5]

That poverty could not be ignored was due in part to the
fact that the poor and the well-to-do were often around the
corner from one another.[6] The point was made forcibly in an
article on the Royal Borough of Kensington which Cecil
Chesterton contributed to the London weekly *Outlook* in
1903. Cecil contrasted the rich and aristocratic character of
much of Kensington with areas within its boundaries where
'its population consists of laundresses, flower girls, a sprin-
kling of criminals, and of the less successful members of Mrs
Warren's profession'. 'There they live', the account continues,
'herded together in narrow rooms, filthy, overcrowded,
hungry, naked, demoralised, their children dying like flies'.[7]

For all this, the discovery by the Booths that around one in every three of the population of London was either 'very poor' or 'poor' was a shock, not least to its authors. Charles Booth freely owned up to having at the outset inadequately grasped the enormity of the problem:

> For myself it was so. In 1888 I made an estimate based on the facts as to East London, and the comparative density of population in other parts, on the theory that density would probably coincide with the degree of poverty. The result was to show a probable 25 per cent of poor for all London, or nearly 6 per cent less than we now get.[8]

Booth's candour was the more impressive because his research had been undertaken to refute previous investigations, including one by the Marxist Social-Democratic Federation, which he denounced as having 'grossly overestimated the case'.

'He was surprised to discover', writes the social historian, Raymond Williams, 'that, if anything, the Social-Democratic Federation had erred in under-estimating the extent of London poverty.'[9] The moral gravity of the revelations by Booth and Rowntree is summarised starkly by Samuel Hynes in *The Edwardian Turn of Mind*: 'One third of the nation, it appeared, was being starved by the other two-thirds'.[10]

Further striking evidence was also forthcoming from other quarters, notably as a result of compulsory school attendance and concerns about the nation's military preparedness. In the 1870s, the height of public school boys aged eleven to twelve was on average five inches greater than of boys from industrial schools. Public schoolboys at all stages of their adolescence were three inches taller than boys from working-class families.[11]

Statistics compiled by the newly formed school medical service in 1908 revealed that:

> Out of 1000 girls in a country area, some 600 would have hair infested with nits. Out of 1000 children 700-800 would have decayed teeth, 150-200 diseases of the nose and throat, 100-130 with malnutrition, 26-80 with diseases of the heart and circulation and 10-30 with diseases of the lung.

> Out of every 1000 children attending elementary schools, between 700 and 970 were 'dirty', including at one extreme 100 who were 'very dirty' and at the other extreme 270 who were no more than 'somewhat dirty'.[12]

The high cost of the nation's neglect of its children was made further evident with the recruiting of volunteers for the Boer War around the turn of the century, and the introduction of universal medical screening for military service in 1917. Two out of every three of the 12,000 volunteers for service against the Boers examined in Manchester had to be rejected as unfit, and fewer than one in ten was classified as fully fit.[13]

Ten per cent of the young men examined for compulsory service under the conspicuously more relaxed standards of 1917 were totally unfit for service, 41.5 per cent had 'marked disabilities' and 22 per cent had 'partial disabilities'. In all, only marginally more than a third of the potential conscripts were in sufficiently sound physical condition to be acceptable.[14] The figures strikingly confirm the enduring validity of Disraeli's 'two nations' view of England.

The 'rediscovery of poverty', which was more accurately a new awareness of the indefensibility of want in the midst of plenty, coincided with the freeing up for social reform of energies previously absorbed by religion. 'The passion for religion', writes the American scholar, Gertrude Himmelfarb, 'was transmuted into the compassion for humanity'.[15] A much-quoted passage from the diary of the young Beatrice Potter — the future Beatrice Webb — in 1884 reads: 'Social questions are the vital questions of today. They take the place of religion'.[16]

Beatrice and her future husband, Sidney Webb, were to stand out among the most influential social thinkers and Fabian socialists of their generation. From small beginnings, the new awakening of conscience rapidly assumed major proportions. 'In a massive surge of social consciousness', writes Himmelfarb, 'respectable middle-class people pronounced themselves socialists, and socialist organisations vied for membership and recognition with each other and with a multitude of other causes and societies — land reform leagues, charitable associations, settlement houses, model building projects, children's homes, missions to the poor'.[17]

What emerged was in effect a dual response to poverty. On the one hand, bodies such as the Charity Organisation Society tried to help out of poverty those of the poor who were perceived as also being able and willing to help themselves. That 'the poor are always with us' was in the view of the charitable bodies axiomatic. Debate within their ranks was largely restricted to which of the poor should rightly be assisted and by what means.[18]

The political reformers, on the other hand, wanted action to alleviate or eradicate poverty across the board. Where they differed among themselves was over whether doing so should be accomplished through collectivist measures taken within the framework of the established social order, as was the view of the New Liberals — luminaries of the stamp of the political philosopher T.H. Green and the rising star and future grave-digger of the Liberal Party, David Lloyd George — or whether, as in the view of the socialists, a totally new social order was required.[19]

Socialist bodies

What then was the nature of the socialist movement — of this crucible of conscience — in which so many future distrib-utists such as Cecil Chesterton underwent their formative political experiences? How did the effect of those experi-ences come to be so negative as to chiefly teach the future distributists what it was about socialism they were against? Can other dissident elements within the movement be identi-fied, and, if so, to what extent were their discontents the same as those of the future distributists?

What the various schools of socialist thought had in common with one another, where they differed, and how their thinking evolved over time, was reflected in the remark-able proliferation of new socialist-minded and explicitly socialist bodies which occurred in and immediately after the last quarter of the nineteenth century. To name only the more prominent, the Anglican Guild of St Matthew was formed in 1877, as were the Progressive Association and the Democratic Federation (later the Social-Democratic Federation) in 1881, the Land Nationalisation Society in 1882, the Land Reform Union (later the English Land Rest-oration League) in 1883, the Fellowship of the New Life, the Fabian Society and the Socialist League in 1884, the Christian Socialist Society in 1886, the Christian Social Union in 1889, the Independent Labour Party in 1893, the Christian Socialist League in 1894 and the Church Socialist League in 1906.

The proliferation of socialist journals was no less remark-able. Harry Champion — a general's son who was educated at Marlborough and saw active service as a Royal Artillery officer in Afghanistan, prior to becoming a leader of the land reform and single tax movement and perhaps the most outstanding socialist agitator and organiser of the 1880s — was an editor successively of *The Christian Socialist, Today, Common Sense* and *The Labour Elector*.[20] Other notable socialist editors included the Reverend Stewart Headlam of *The Church Reformer*, H.M. Hyndman of *Justice*, William Morris and Belfort Bax of *Commonweal*, Charlotte Wilson of *Freedom*, Annie Besant of *Our Corner*, Thomas Bolam of *The Practical Socialist* (which preceded the exceptionally long-lived *Fabian News*), Robert Blatchford of *The Clarion* and A.R. Orage and Holbrook Jackson of *The New Age*.

The socialist ferment had disparate intellectual origins. The Guild of St Matthew was the heir to the producer co-operativism of the Society for Promoting Working Men's Associations which the founder generation of Christian socialists — John Ludlow and the Reverend Frederick Maurice foremost among them — had launched in mid-century. Other society members included Thomas Hughes, who is best known as the author of *Tom Brown's Schooldays* but was also a member of parliament, and his fellow writer the Reverend Charles Kingsley, author of *The Water Babies*. Others again were the future General Secretary of the Central Board of the Co-operative Movement, Edward Vansittart Neale, and Lord Goderich (later, as Lord Ripon, a notable Viceroy of India) who linked the Christian socialists with Disraeli's 'Young England' movement for social reform in the early 1840s.

Ludlow in particular was deeply impressed by the pioneering advocacy of producer co-operatives by French socialists such as Louis Blanc and Joseph Buchez, and the social catholicism of Félicité de Lamennais. The Society for Promoting Working Men's Associations had as its objective the seeding of small 'Working Associations' — worker co-operatives — which would in their turn become the basis for a new and explicitly Christian social order. The founder and longtime Warden of the Guild of St Matthew, the Reverend Stewart Headlam, proved to be — in the words of Kingsley's biographer, Brenda Colloms — 'a fine recruit, receptive to the outlook of the old-time Christian Socialists and full of energy'.[21]

The guild and Headlam were also extensively influenced by the single tax ideas of the American writer Henry George.

George's book *Progress and Poverty* and his lecture tours in the early 1880s were later credited by many leading socialists with having introduced them to socialism. Prominent among them was the future leading Fabian, Bernard Shaw, then by his own account 'a young man not much past twenty-five ... full of Darwin and Tyndall, of Shelley and De Quincey, of Michelangelo and Beethoven and never in my life having studied social questions'.[22] He acknowledges how in 1882:

> I went one night, quite casually, into a hall in London; and there I heard a man deliver a speech which changed the whole current of my life. That man was an American, Henry George ... He struck me dumb, and shunted me from barren agnostic controversy to economics.[23]

Shaw's account of the aftermath of the meeting reads:

> The result of my hearing that speech and buying ... at the meeting a copy of *Progress and Poverty* for sixpence ... was that I plunged into a course of economic study and at a very early stage of it became a socialist. When I was swept into the great Socialist revival of 1883, I found that five-sixths of those who were swept in with me had been converted by Henry George. This fact would have been far more widely acknowledged had it not been that it was not possible for us to stop where Henry George stopped. If we outgrew *Progress and Poverty* in many respects so did he himself too.[24]

'To George', recalls Edward Pease, the long-serving secretary of the Fabian Society, 'belongs the extraordinary merit of recognising the right way to social salvation ... the great conception he contributed to the thought of the 'eighties was that poverty was an evil preventable by State action'.[25]

What nascent socialists such as Champion went on to when it was not possible for them 'to stop where Henry George stopped' was, at the start, mostly the Democratic Federation. What was, at the federation's inception, a moderate platform, designed to appeal to Georgists and other radical Liberals, gave way, with the renaming of the organisation as the Social-Democratic Federation in 1883, to a full-blooded advocacy of Marxist 'scientific socialism'. By Champion's account, 'On Whit Monday, 1883, a memorable meeting was held in an underground room at Palace Chambers, Westminster ... Before we left the room we were the Social-Democratic Federation and I was the hon. sec.'[26]

The SDF was linked inseparably in the public mind with the paradoxically bourgeois appearance and insurrectionary utterances of its founder, Hyndman. This frock-coated, high-hatted, cricket-playing, Eton-educated, Cambridge-trained stockbroker, journalist and one-time independent candidate for parliament — whose book, *England for All*, is widely credited with having introduced Marxism to English readers — argued in January 1881 that 'There must be a great social re-organisation to secure for all the same happiness and enjoyment of life that now belongs to the few'.[27]

In the Marxist view of the SDF, working people were poor because the added value they created through their labour was then taken away from them by their employers. In this way, an insufficiency of demand was brought about in the economy, resulting in unemployment and further impoverishment. The competition between workers and employers for the surplus value which the workers created was of so fundamental a character as to properly be referred to as a war between them, or class war. It was inevitable that the workers would at some point take a stand against the loss of the value which properly belonged to them and was the means of their livelihoods. The coercive powers of the state, as exemplified by the police and the armed forces, might in so potentially rebellious a confrontation be used against them.

The members of the SDF differed among themselves as to whether, as Hyndman and others at times advocated, insurrectionary action should be actively encouraged with a view to bringing about the inevitable confrontation with the ruling class at the earliest possible opportunity, or whether, as in the view of the federation's most distinguished recruit, William Morris, the possibility of a change in the social order from capitalism to socialism then being achieved depended upon a widespread demand for, and understanding of, socialism having previously been created.

In the view of Morris and those of similar mind, the proper business of the SDF, and of socialist bodies generally, was to painstakingly nurture among working people, through protracted education and social and industrial agitation, the mass socialist consciousness and competence which a revolutionary but peaceful transition to socialism would require. 'Education towards Revolution' wrote Morris, 'seems to me to express in three words what our policy should be'.[28]

Morris further believed that, to the extent that the socialists allowed their energies to be diverted to parliament as the
erratic Hyndman and some other SDF members also at times
argued, or engaged in gradualist reforms, there was a likelihood that they would arouse false hopes and so unnecessarily
put off the moment when a just social order might otherwise
be achieved. There was another reason for rejecting gradualist measures, in that employers and the ruling class might
under pressure grant even quite substantial concessions and
improvements, but such measures could always be withdrawn
when the workers again found themselves in the weaker
bargaining position. A falling-out between Hyndman and
Morris, in 1884, caused Morris and a group of close associates
to hive off and establish the Socialist League. In the process,
the SDF was weakened, while by the mid-1890s Morris was
dead and the league had ceased to exist.

Meanwhile, in 1883, Champion and the founder of the
Progressive Association, John C. Foulger, had become
partners in the Modern Press printery. Champion steered the
Progressive Association in the direction of social reform. In
this way, the association became the direct forerunner of the
Fabian Society, and Foulger, in the view of Shaw, 'the
genuine, original Fabian'.[29] When a further association
member, Percival Chubb, convened a series of meetings in
Pease's home in 1883 with a view to forming a further organisation directed to moral advancement and spiritual brother-
hood, Champion attended along with his SDF associates,
R.P.B. Frost and J.L. Joynes, and again insisted that social
reform should be given priority.[30]

In place of the single new body Chubb had envisaged, two
bodies were now created — the Fellowship of the New Life
and the Fabian Society.[31] Shaw's most recent biographer,
Michael Holroyd, sees the fellowship as having attracted the
aspiring saints, and the society 'the world-betterers whose
religion became socialism'.[32] Shaw summarises the respective
characters of the two groups as having been 'the one to sit
among the dandelions, the other to organise the docks'.[33]
The saints were the poorer stayers, and by 1898 the fellowship
was extinct. Many of the most able members of the SDF —
including, for example, Pease, Frederick Keddell, Sydney
Olivier, Hubert Bland and his wife, Edith Nesbit — defected

to the Fabians in the months following the establishment of the society, so that the federation's losses at the hands of Morris and the Socialist League were exacerbated.

Shaw noted in regard to the SDF in 1884 that 'But for Frost and Champion, who, though nominally Hyndmanites, practically boss the whole Federation between them by sticking together and working, the whole body would have gone to pieces long ago'.[34] Falling out with Hyndman, as had Morris before him, Champion now became estranged from — and ultimately, in 1888, was expelled by — the SDF. Two of his closest associates — the future leading militant union leader and syndicalist, Tom Mann, and John Burns, who was to serve as a minister in the 1906 Liberal government — parted company with the SDF at the same time.

As in the case of Morris, the issue was in part Hyndman's windy and erratic insurrectionist advocacy and overall inconsistency. Champion wrote in 1887 that 'No Social Democrat in England advocates a resort to physical force revolution, so long as we enjoy even our present somewhat limited right of free discussion, meeting and combination, and so long as our imperfectly representative form of government is not rendered less representative'.[35]

Champion's energies — in conjunction with those of Mann, Burns and Keir Hardie, who was to be Labour's first leader in parliament — now focused increasingly on the electoral and industrial agitation which in part gave rise to the Independent Labour Party and ultimately to the Labour Party. Champion was quicker than most to recognise the key significance of the Trades Union Congress's Labour Electoral Committee and its successor body, the Labour Electoral Association, which for a time employed him as its metropolitan organiser. He linked the eight-hour day campaign to the need for a labour party through the columns of his paper *The Labour Elector* and vigorously backed the campaign to put workingmen into parliament which Hardie dramatised to such telling effect with his candidature for the Mid-Lanark by-election in 1888.[36] 'Champion', writes the prominent labour movement historian, Henry Pelling, 'should now be remembered as one of the most important of the party's pioneers'.[37]

By contrast, Hyndman and the SDF for their part largely remained aloof from the trade union movement and the nascent Labour Party which Champion so far-sightedly embraced, and to which the future of British socialism was now so overwhelmingly to be entrusted. The consequence was that, even before the turn of the century, the SDF and the Marxism it espoused had effectively been marginalised. While the organisation lingered on, it was a shadow of its former self and failed to live up to the high hopes of its founders. It remained for the Communist Party of Great Britain to inherit — and ultimately betray — the mantle of the SDF and such of its surviving members as stuck to their Marxist faith.

The Fabian Society

The major beneficiary of the failure of the Socialist League and the SDF was the Fabian Society. The Fabians were second to none in their abhorrence of poverty. The society's first manifesto, which was drafted by Shaw in 1884, reads in part that 'We would rather face a civil war than such another century of suffering as the present one has been'.[66] By the middle 1890s, majority opinion within the society as reflected by the 'Old Gang' or 'Great Fabians' as the core of its membership has variously been known[39] — luminaries of the enduring stature of Shaw, the Webbs, Graham Wallas, who was a leading political scientist of the day, and the Colonial Office civil servant and future governor of Jamaica, Sydney Olivier — had arrived at less draconian conclusions.

A settled view had been reached that what distinguished true socialism from false was public ownership.[40] Recalling his brief and tumultuous career as a Fabian, Cecil Chesteron writes that 'If you were a Fabian, you were supposed to believe that land and industrial capital should be controlled by the political officers of the State. That was the dogma which, unless a man well and truly believed, he could not be a Fabian'.[41] It had further been determined that the means for achieving socialism should be the nationalisation of industries and services throught acts of parliament. The aims of the Fabian Society were accordingly socialist, but its focus was statist and its methods evolutionary and reformist.

Sidney Webb summarised the Fabian approach in succinct and memorable terms as 'the inevitability of gradualness'.[42]

The name Fabian was derived from the Roman general, Quintus Fabius Maximus Cunctator, whose delaying tactics and guerilla warfare were said to have turned back Hannibal's invasion of Italy in the third century BC. The society's motto reads: 'For the right moment you must wait, as Fabius did patiently, when warring against Hannibal, though many censured his delays, but when the time comes you must strike hard, as Fabius did, or your waiting be in vain and fruitless'.[43] The Fabian emblem is a tortoise with its right paw raised, over the inscription 'When I strike, I strike hard'.[44]

The strength of the Fabians stemmed from their insistence on painstaking research and reasoned argument. Beatrice Webb saw clearly that social reform could not be brought about by 'shouting'. 'What is needed', Beatrice wrote, 'is hard thinking'.[45] 'Above all', writes the English historian Ben Pimlott, 'the Fabians believed in the power of ideas'.[46] The society adopted the tradition of social investigation which Charles and Mary Booth had pioneered with their *The Life and Labour of the People in London*. It was axiomatic for the Fabians that careful examination of social problems would provide the basis for their solutions. The solutions, in turn, could be counted on to be along socialist lines.

In the view of the Webbs, it was from the actual facts and coldly impassive arguments that socialism drew its irresistible energy. A list of key Fabian achievements drawn up by Margaret Cole — chairman of the Fabian Society 1955-56 and president 1962-80 — includes 'having insisted on laying a foundation of facts for all assertions'.[47] Fittingly, it was Sidney Webb who most eloquently summarised what was finest about the Fabian outlook and approach, in a passage which reads 'I believed that research and new discoveries would prove some, at any rate, of my views of policy to be right, but that, if they proved the contrary, I should count it all the more gain to have prevented error, and should cheerfully abandon my own policy'.[48]

Once facts had been accumulated and ideas and policies developed, the society had the further task of publicising and disseminating them. The Fabian *Basis* — a statement of objectives adopted in 1887 — in part commits the society to further its objectives 'by the general dissemination of knowledge as to the relation between the individual and society in its economic, ethical and political aspects'.[49] *Fabian Essays in*

Socialism — the society's first book — sold 46,000 copies prior to the First World War, and is still in print.

Shaw's preface to the 1931 edition describes the collection as 'inextinguishable'.[50] The establishment of the London School of Economics in 1895 and the launching of *The New Statesman* — a weekly journal of fact and discussion — in 1912 were further Fabian initiatives, instigated by the Webbs in order to gain converts for socialism. A diary entry by Beatrice Webb in 1898 reads: 'No young man or woman who is anxious to study or to work in public affairs can fail to come under our influence'.[51]

In the absence of a Labour Party — which was not formed until 1900 — the Fabians used their facts and arguments to induce the Liberal Party and the Tories to adopt socialist ideas without recognising their socialist implications. The tactic was known to the society as 'permeation'. As Shaw recalled in his *The Fabian Society: Its Early History*: 'We permeated the party organisations and pulled all the wires we could lay our hands on with our utmost adroitness and energy'.[52] G.D.H. Cole, a long-serving member of the executive committee of the Fabian Society and its chairman 1939-46 and president 1952-59, saw the Fabians as having managed in this spirit 'to express an essentially Socialist philosophy in terms of immediate proposals which made a strong appeal to many reformers who were by no means Socialists'.[53]

Permeation gained the society a number of notable successes, such as the adoption of Fabian policies by the Liberal-dominated Progressive Party in the London County Council in the 1890s, and the enactment by the then Tory government of Arthur Balfour in 1902 and 1903 of Education Acts which were recognised widely as 'very nearly the dream of Fabian "permeators" come to life — proposals drafted by intelligent and hard-working Fabians, conveyed to puzzled or sympathetic administrators and carried into effect by a Conservative Government'.[54] Well before the turn of the century, the Fabian Society had acquired both within Britain and internationally a reputation for offering a philosophy, a process and a capacity for getting results. Overseas Fabian societies were formed, most notably in Australia.[55]

How the Fabian Society worked in practice is illustrated by its enduring campaign against poverty. As has been seen, the commitment of the original Fabians to overcoming poverty was manifest in the choice of the title for the first Fabian tract: *Why are the Many Poor?*. Tract Five, entitled *Facts for Socialists*, followed shortly, devoted in part to a statistical comparison of the conditions of the 'two nations' within British society. More Fabian publications — and more Fabian energy — have been devoted to poverty than to any other topic.

The outcome of the society's concern was in part the proposals for a 'National Minimum' which Beatrice and Sidney Webb put forward in 1897 in their book *Industrial Democracy*. The appointment of Beatrice Webb to the Royal Commission on the Poor Law by Balfour in 1905 was a further Fabian milestone, enabling Beatrice to produce a *Minority Report* which is seen by Margaret Cole in her *The Story of Fabian Socialism* as 'one of the greatest State papers of the century'. Margaret Cole concludes: 'All that is implied in the later phrase "Social Security", including some things not yet put into effect, is to be found in essence in the *Minority Report* of fifty years ago'.[56]

Following the rejection of the *Minority Report* by the Liberal government in 1909, the Fabians launched a National Committee for the Breakup of the Poor Law — later the National Committee for the Prevention of Destitution — which rapidly attracted over 16,000 members. The *Minority Report* and the activities of the National Committee failed in their objective of securing an immediate implementation of Beatrice Webb's recommendations, but contributed massively to a climate of opinion in which change was inevitable.

Forty years later, the Poor Law was finally abolished — and the modern welfare state finally put in place — by Clement Attlee's predominantly Fabian 1945 Labour government, on the basis of the wartime *Beveridge Report*. Beveridge, a Liberal, described his work as having 'stemmed from what all of us have imbibed from the Webbs'.[57] Subsequent Fabian experts such as Richard Titmuss, Brian Abel-Smith, Peter Townsend and David Donnison have written widely about ways of further strengthening the welfare state and harnessing it more closely to the core Fabian value of a more equal society.

The First World War gave rise to an historic friendship between Sidney Webb and the secretary of the Labour Party, Arthur Henderson. Webb and Henderson were brought together in the War Emergency Workers' National Committee, which Henderson chaired. Webb was the driving force behind the committee, and did most of its creative work. Joint action by Webb and Henderson gave the Labour Party a new constitution, which Margaret Cole describes as 'a very "Fabian" compromise' between the party's socialist and trade unionist adherents.

Webb and Henderson were also the co-authors of a new party program — *Labour and the New Social Order* (1918) — which represented in Margaret Cole's view 'as nearly as possible the purest milk of the Fabian word'.[58] The upshot was an enduring partnership between the Fabian Society and the Labour Party which outlived the vicissitudes of economic slump, party schism and war to emerge triumphantly as the pre-eminent intellectual influence in the postwar government.

An amendment to the Fabian Society rules in 1939 — known widely as the society's 'self-denying ordinance' — reads:

> No resolution of a political character, expressing an opinion or calling for action, other than in relation to the running of the Society itself, shall be put forward in the name of the Society. Delegates to conferences of the Labour Party, or to any other conference, shall be appointed by the Executive Committee without any mandatory instructions … All publications sponsored by the Society should bear a clear indication that they do not commit the Society, but only those responsible for preparing them'.[59]

The changes marked the culmination of a process by which the society had ceased increasingly to be a body advocating specific policies as had been the case at its inception, and instead devoted itself to researching and publicising ideas within a broad framework of democratic socialism and parliamentary democracy. In so doing, Fabianism was reinvented as being primarily about the method and process for social reform, and the society reaffirmed its identity as the original political think-tank.

Guild socialism

None of this meant that the society's state socialist objectives or gradualist approach were in any sense regarded by their authors at the time of their adoption as other than regrettable expedients, or that they were uncontested by minority elements within the society. Shaw's contribution to the society's best-selling *Fabian Essays in Socialism* in 1889 reads in part 'Let me, in conclusion, disavow all admiration for this inevitable, but slow, reluctant, cowardly path to justice'.[60]

In the early years of the new century, the writer H.G. Wells was responsible for a notable — albeit ultimately unsuccessful — campaign to have the society transform itself into an overtly socialist political party, and contest parliamentary elections against other parties, including the Labour Party. Most significantly, questions were voiced increasingly by dissidents within the society as to whether earlier associative forms of socialism, such as those of Ludlow, Morris and the founder of the co-operative movement, Robert Owen, might not have more to offer than the conclusions of the 'Old Gang' allowed.

'Six years ago', Cecil Chesterton wrote in the distributist weekly *The New Witness* in 1914, 'practically all the intelligent youth of England were theoretically Collectivists':

> One met men who called themselves 'Young Liberals' or 'Tory Democrats'; but they all hastened to assure one that they accepted Collectivist theory, with whatever qualifications, as fundamentally sound. But, if you search out the same kind of young men now, you will find that, whatever they are, hardly any of them are Collectivists ... The other day I visited the Oxford Fabian Society. It was long since I had been to a Fabian meeting, and I fell into the error of assuming that the young Fabians were still Collectivists.

'I soon found', Cecil concluded, 'that hardly any of them were anything of the sort'.[61]

The alternative which many came to favour was guild socialism. The originators of guild socialism, A.R. Orage and A.J. Penty, were younger Fabians who met around the turn of the century in Leeds, where Orage was a primary teacher and Penty 'a shaggy-looking architect with a fearful stammer'.[62] They and Holbrook Jackson, a lace merchant by trade and another of the society's younger members, then formed the widely admired Leeds Arts Club.

'The local bourgeoisie', writes Orage's biographer, Philip Mairet, 'were flabbergasted when the shocking views of such as Nietzsche, Ibsen and Shaw were acclaimed in their midst by this heterodox seminary, and advocated with a mixture of aestheticism, moral earnestness and moral flippancy':

> There were gala nights, too, when a star like Shaw himself would appear, or G.K. Chesterton, or Edward Carpenter, and set the town talking for weeks. In addition to all this revolutionary brilliance, some of which at first discouraged the respectable from giving their support, the club began to do solid educational work which compelled their recognition. Its exhibitions of craft work, of paintings and drawings, were of distinguished excellence ... There was also a Fabian section of the club, led by Holbrook Jackson, which dispensed sound teaching in modern sociology.[63]

By 1906, the three friends had moved to London, where Orage and Jackson worked as journalists.

Penty, whose seminal book *The Restoration of the Gild [sic] System*[64] appeared in 1906, was associated with Orage later the same year in the establishment of the Junior Art Workers' Guild and the Gilds Restoration League. A disciple of John Ruskin and William Morris, he ultimately parted company with the Fabian Society on the grounds of what he saw as its philistine disregard for aesthetic considerations, excessive materialism and lack of intellectual rigour. The break is said to have occurred when Penty learned that the society's executive had assessed the architects competing for the right to design the London School of Economics building on the number of square feet provided by their respective designs, and awarded the work to the proposal with the most floor space.

The Restoration of the Gild System argued — as had previously Morris and Ruskin — that there had been a decline in the spiritual well-being of the community, stemming from the replacement of individual craftmanship by the use of machines and the division of labour. In Penty's view, ordinary producers needed to have their status raised in both industry and the overall community, and the power of their representatives made equal to that of other economic interests. These aims could be achieved by guilds developed from the existing trade unions. The guilds would include among their members both employers and employees; take responsibility for the quality of the goods produced by their members; and have monopolies of their respective trades. There would be a two-chamber parliament in which members would be elected to the lower house on a territorial basis and to the upper house by the guilds. Penty's ideas were marred for many by a medievalist bias and distaste for machinery and the factory system.

The aim of the Gilds Restoration League — as Orage wrote to Wells in 1906 — was:

> ... to bring about a union between the economic aims of the Trades Unionists and the aesthetic aims of the craftsman. Hitherto, the collectivist proposals have been designed solely to make economic poverty impossible; it is necessary to design them not only to make economic but also aesthetic poverty impossible. This, of course, would involve a considerable modification of the usual collectivist formulas. As a member of the Fabian Society, I should have been glad to see the Society take up the present propaganda; but I am afraid the major part of the Fabians is too rigidly bound to the collectivist formulas to make such a hope practicable.[65]

Frustrated as Jackson and Orage had become with what they and their associates saw as the entrenched philistinism and bureaucratic preoccupations of majority opinion within the Fabian Society — and querying whether 'the Fabian Society has not ceased to be the medium of free discussion, whether in fact, it has not become so dogmatic as to make its future as an intelligent organ of discussion and inquiry very doubtful'[66] — they shortly established the Fabian Arts Group as a forum for the exploration of more adventurous ideas and opinion and a platform for the guild socialist thinking which was rapidly becoming their major preoccupation.

While the objective of the Fabian Arts Group was nominally to involve the Fabian Society in the development of a distinctively socialist attitude to art and philosophy, the group is seen widely as also having been characterised by 'vague efforts to deprive Fabianism of its webbed feet'.[67] 'Jackson and Orage', notes the Australian historian Ian Britain, 'clearly saw themselves as missionaries of light attempting to save Fabianism from the power of greyness'.[68] A further major platform for Fabian dissent and the dissemination of guild socialism was created in 1907, when Orage and Jackson acquired the ailing weekly journal *The New Age* with financial backing from — among others — Shaw. Jackson was obliged to pull out a year later, leaving Orage in full control.

In Shaw's view, Orage was the most brilliant editor England had had in a century.[69] T.S. Eliot sees him as having been 'the finest critical intelligence of our day'.[70] 'Under his editorship', writes the American scholar Jay P. Corrin, '*The New Age* quickly became one of the premier cultural and political journals of the first two decades of the twentieth century'.[71] Belloc describes it as 'for many years the only newspaper in England at once intelligent and uncorrupt'.[72] Although the circulation of the weekly — subtitled as it now was 'An Independent Socialist Review of Politics, Literature and Art' — was never extensive, it attracted writers from a broad range of opinions, and was soon the major vehicle for the exchange of ideas between more orthodox socialists of the Fabian and SDF stamp and those who were exploring alternatives such as the guild socialist model. Orage's informal Monday afternoon editorial meetings at the ABC restaurant in Chancery Lane were a key forum in which the guild socialists sharpened up their arguments on one another. The leading historians of Fabian socialism, Norman and Jeanne Mackenzie, describe the meetings as 'a running seminar for those who wanted new worlds for old'.[73]

The key contributors to the debate on guild socialism in the pages of Orage's weekly included the writer S.G. Hobson. Hobson was yet another Fabian dissident, who had stood for parliament for East Bristol in 1895 and for Rochdale in 1906. He left the society in 1910, after trying unsuccessfully to persuade it to disaffiliate from the Labour Party in order to work towards 'a definite and avowedly socialist party'. His articles — originally featured in *The New Age* in 1912 — were reissued in book form in 1914 under the title *National Guilds: An Inquiry into the Wage System and the Way Out*. Hobson was able to free up guild socialism from the nostalgic medievalism with which Penty had, to largely counterproductive effect, invested it.

Orage and Hobson now argued that the goal of the labour movement should be to get rid of wages.[74] To this end, the trade unions of the day should be reorganised into national guilds. There would be a national guild for each occupation or industry, controlled exclusively by their respective workforces. The state would own the industries, and the workers would be responsible for their management. The wage system would be abolished in favour of workers sharing among themselves the value their labour created, and the guilds would assume responsibility for welfare services in place of the state.

The guilds collectively would also be responsible for industrial planning and social objectives such as achieving a more equitable distribution of wealth. The functions of government should be to regulate the guilds, enact legislation in such areas as might not be covered by the guilds and look after foreign affairs. 'Guild Socialism', writes the historian S.T. Glass, 'was an attempt to steer a mid-course between syndicalism, which made a too-inclusive claim for producers' self-government, and orthodox socialism, which in effect ignored it'.[75]

Other key contributions came from G.D.H. Cole and Maurice Reckitt, who also were Fabians — 'the one more so', as Mairet puts it, 'and the other less'.[76] Cole and Reckitt were largely responsible for carrying on the fight for guild socialism within the society. The Fabian Research Department, which Cole led, effectively became the rallying-point and nerve centre for those of the society's members who favoured the guild system.

'We admit the claim of collectivism to be one interpretation of socialism', Cole and Reckitt wrote, 'but we demand an open platform, a clean severance from Liberalism and liberty to fight within Fabianism for the necessary change of Fabian orientation'.[77] External to the society — but largely on the initiative and through the efforts of Cole and his fellow dissident Fabians — a national guilds manifesto, the 'Storrington Document', was produced in 1915, in the course of a week-long discussion at the White Horse Inn in Storrington in Sussex. A National Guilds League was then established.

In the event, the high hopes of the National Guilds League were disappointed. What appeared, in the years immediately before and during the First World War, to be a tide favourable to guild socialism ebbed rapidly in the postwar period. By the middle 1920s, the guildsmen, as the league's members and supporters had become widely known, were in disarray. It remained for desperation born of the Great Depression of the 1930s to complete the debacle, by confirming in the view of the labour movement that only through parliamentary socialism, on the statutory corporation and command economy model favoured by the Fabian 'Old Gang', could a future free from want and insecurity be assured. By the time Attlee — a one-time executive member of the Fabian Society and chairman of the New Fabian Research Bureau — led the Labour Party and the Fabians to their electoral triumph in 1945, guild socialism was all but forgotten.

*Cecil
Chesterton*

3

Precursors and Converts: Henry Manning and Cecil Chesterton

Manning and De Rerum Novarum

THE unfolding of the development of guild socialism was closely paralleled by that of distributism. How this occurred — how both distributism and guild socialism became differentiated from state socialism, why each developed as it did and how much in key respects each owed to the other — is exemplified in the personal odysseys of those to whom distributism owes its inception. These were, in the first instance, Manning in his role as the precursor of distributism, and Cecil Chesterton, who exemplifies the restless, impatient younger Fabians who ultimately rejected both state socialism and guild socialism in favour of distributism.

The Catholic contribution to the development of distributism — the Catholic harvest from generations of debate on social issues within and beyond the Church — is evident in the life and career of Manning. Manning's record is eloquent testimony to the capacity of the Church to take a stand in defence of the poor, the needy and the oppressed, and to think creatively about remedies for their condition.

Manning was born to wealthy parents in 1808, raised in the Anglican Church and educated at Harrow and Oxford. His close friends at Oxford included the future Prime Minister, W.E. Gladstone. Manning's father — a prominent sugar merchant and one-time governor of the Bank of England and member of parliament — failed in business in 1831, while Manning was still at the university. Manning, reports the writer, Paul Johnson, 'had the horrifying experience of watching his father handing over his gold watch, the symbolic last possession of the bankrupt'.[1]

His father's difficulties obliged him to consider briefly giving up becoming an Anglican clergyman as he had originally intended, in favour of a career in politics.[2] Contemporaries at Oxford saw Manning as having the makings of a Prime Minister, and Gladstone of an Archbishop of Canterbury. In the event, faith prevailed over politics. At the time of his conversion to Catholicism around 1850, Manning was the Anglican Archdeacon of Chichester and a man marked out for preferment to the highest offices of the Established Church.[3]

As a Catholic, Manning was an ultramontane conservative in religious matters — serving as he did as the majority whip for the adoption of papal infallibility at the First Vatican Council in 1870 — but a political radical.[4] He was introduced to poverty at first hand among the agricultural labourers in the rural parish of Lavington in West Sussex, where he became a curate after his ordination in the Anglican ministry in 1832. 'The father who works', he wrote in 1847 in regard to the diets of the local poor, 'has a pound of pork in the week, it may be. The wives and children live on vegetables and bread, they *keep a perpetual Lent* ... We need no famines afar off to work on our charity'.[5]

The experience was repeated in the setting of London following his appointment to the see of Westminister in 1865 by Pope Pius IX. Manning told an audience in the Mechanics Institute in Leeds in 1880 that 'The inequalities of our social state, and the chasms which separate classes, the abrupt and harsh contrasts of soft and suffering lots, unless they be addressed by humility and charity, sympathy and self-denial, are dangerous to society and our spiritual welfare. In London, all these inequalities and evils are before us'.[6]

Manning's conclusions drew on those of both contemporaries within the Church and generations of Catholic social thinkers before them. The times were conducive to ferment. Like socialism, social Catholicism gave birth to descendants which differed radically from one another. Reformers of the stamp of de Lamennais (1782-1854), Frédéric Ozanam (1813-1853), René de la Tour du Pin (1834-1925) and Albert de Mun (1841-1914), in France, Wilhelm von Kettler (1811-1877) in Germany and Guiseppe Toniolo (1845-1918) in Italy suggested ways of grappling with poverty as conspicuously divergent as the mixture of 'romantic conservatism with Protestant social reformism' advocated by the Prussian Karl von Vogelsang (1818-1890) and the close approximation of Christian democracy in its modern industrial and parliamentary forms advocated in France by Léon Harmel (1829-1915).

'Instead of State socialism', writes the Australian redemptorist scholar, Father Bruce Duncan, 'von Vogelsang called for the establishing of a "social kingdom" as an integrating element for the reorganisation of society into corporations or modernised trade guilds, working together as co-operatives, but under the paternalistic control of the owners'.[7] The undervaluing of democracy in von Vogelsang's thought recalls a piece of graffiti seen on a wall in Paris during the student uprising in 1968. It read 'Socialism without liberty is the barracks'.[8] Duncan sees von Vogelsang as representing the dark side of social Catholicism. 'This stream of thinking', he writes, 'was greatly to influence the Christian Social Party of Austria (1888-1907) in an authoritarian and anti-democratic direction, and anticipate the thinking for the ill-fated "corporative" state of Dolfuss and Schusnigg in Austria in the 1930s, which prepared the ground for the Nazi take-over'.[9]

On a more positive and democratic note, Harmel, an industrialist, set up worker-directed mutualist welfare bodies and councils of workers to advise the managers of his factories. Most of all, Archbishop von Ketteler of Mainz in Germany was an outspoken advocate of trade unions, producers' co-operatives and other mutualist bodies. 'The task of religion, the task of Catholic societies in the immediate future', he argued as early as 1848, 'has to do with social conditions'.[10] The Swiss sociologist and Catholic activist Kaspar Descurtins credits von Ketteler with 'the undying honour of having met the manifesto of the Communists with a program of Christian social form that stands unsurpassed to this day'.[11] Von Ketteler was a key source for the doctrine of subsidiarity that Leo XIII incorporated in *De Rerum Novarum* and Pius XI further elaborated in *Quadragesimo Anno*. Leo XIII gratefully acknowledged von Ketteler's contribution, in a handsome reference to him as 'my great predecessor'.[12]

The Union of Fribourg — a group of adherents of social Catholicism from different countries meeting at Fribourg in Switzerland between 1885 and 1891 — also prepared statements of social principles which were drawn on in the drafting of *De Rerum Novarum*. 'The Church', the Council reported, 'should recall the too-forgotten rules of her doctrine on the nature of property, the use of goods, and the respect due to the most precious of all goods, human life in the person of the poor'.[13] Nor was the Catholic social thought of the day lacking in Manning's sense of urgency over the predicament of working people. 'Labour', Cardinal Gaspar Mermillod warned Leo XIII in 1889, 'is treated as a mere commodity, the existence of the workers is at the mercy of the free play of material forces and the workers are reduced to a state that recalls pagan slavery'.[14]

Manning's outrage, grief and compassion over the poverty of great numbers of his fellow citizens and co-religionists — and his determination to make a difference — equalled those of even the most dedicated socialists. His work as a member of the Royal Commission on the housing of the working class in 1884 made him, in the view of the chairman, Sir Charles Dilke, the commission's 'greatest revolutionist'.[15]

An eloquent, but far from exhaustive, tribute to Manning's record as a social reformer by Cardinal Newman's principal biographer, Sheridan Gilley, reads:

> Well in advance of any Anglican bishop, he stepped forward to bless the Nonconformist, Joseph Arch and his Agricultural Workers' Union. He publicly defended 'The Dignity and Rights of Labour'. To the scandal of the respectable, including some of his own priests, he endorsed the journalist W.T. Stead's campaign against the horrors of the white slave trade in young girls, christened in Apocalyptic fashion 'the maiden tribute of modern Babylon'; and, when Stead was gaoled, he sent him his blessing. He moved the Mansion House resolution against the pogroms against Russian Jews, and extolled General Booth of the Salvation Army. He combined with Cardinal

Gibbons of Baltimore to save the Knights of Labour from ecclesiastical censure. He wrote witheringly of English cruelty to children. He invited the land reformer, Henry George, and the trades union leaders, Tom Mann and Ben Tillett, into the sacred precincts of Archbishop's House. He resolved the London Dock Strike of 1889. With the reservation that he did not wish to lose the Irish Catholic members from the House of Commons, he approved Home Rule for Ireland. He demanded a just price for goods and a just wage for labour.[16]

'For more than fifty years I have lived among the people', Manning was to declare in the closing stages of his life; 'I have seen and heard and known their wants, sufferings, hardships and the defeat of their petitions and hopes, and my whole soul is with them'.[17]

The dock strike episode in particular exemplified Manning's close links with some socialists and union leaders, and the high regard in which he was held by them. In 1887 Manning had called in Harry Champion — then in the forefront of public agitation against unemployment — to discuss ways to help the unemployed and alleviate poverty. The two men had continued to see another at intervals, and a friendship had arisen. On the occasion of the dock strike in 1889, their roles were reversed, with the invitation directed by Champion to Manning.

The London dockworkers had gone on strike under the leadership of Ben Tillett for an increase in their wages from 5d to 6d an hour. Champion, Mann and Burns had so much become involved with the strikers as for Champion by his own account to have 'written all the manifestoes and controlled their policy'.[18] With the dispute deadlocked and threatening to escalate, it was suggested to Champion that Manning might be prepared to act as mediator.

As Champion later recalled, 'I went to see him about it. I found him immensely interested, and the result of our interview was that he took the matter up with his usual energy'.[19] Manning was able to broker a settlement between the employers and the strike leaders which a meeting of the rank and file of the strikers subsequently repudiated. Faced with a further deterioration which might well have resulted in widespread violence, Manning then arranged to address a further mass meeting. 'His eloquence', Champion was to recall later, 'carried the day; and when that meeting broke up, the strike was over'.[20]

The gratitude and admiration of the workers and their allies for the settlement was expressed in an address to Manning which reads in part:

> When we remember how your Eminence, unasked and unsolicited, under the weight of four score years and two, came forward to mediate between masters and men; when we remember your prudent and wise counsels not to let any heat of passion or unreasonable view of the situation beguile us or lead us away from a fair point of duty to our employers and ourselves; and when in fine we recall your venerable figure in our midst for over four hours in Wade Street School, listening to our complaints and giving us advice in our doubts and difficulties, we seem to see a father in the midst of a loving and well-loved family, rather than the ordinary mediator or benefactor in the thick of a trade dispute.[21]

'I shall ever remember him as the finest example of genuine devotion to the downtrodden', wrote Mann. 'He was never too busy to be consulted or too occupied with Church affairs to admit of his giving detailed attention to any group of men whom kindly influence could help, and he was equally keen to understand any plan of ours to improve the lot of these men'.[22]

Manning's career as a social reformer and friend of the working class climaxed with Pope Leo XIII's great social encyclical letter *De Rerum Novarum* in 1891. *'De Rerum Novarum'*, writes Reckitt, 'is the charter of Social Catholicism, and stands to that movement in the same relation as the Communist Manifesto of Marx and Engels does to revolutionary socialism'.[23] By the account of Cardinal Hinsley — a successor of Manning as Archbishop of Westminster, and therefore well-placed to know — 'Pope Leo XIII declared that one of his most famous encyclicals on the social question, *Rerum Novarum, On the Condition of Labour*, was really Manning's'.[24]

Authorities differ as to whether Manning's contribution was simply to instigate the encyclical by sheer force of example or also to involve himself actively in its preparation.[25] What is beyond doubt is that the encyclical was effectively the bestowal by the Pope of his official blessing on such key elements of Manning's vision as approval of trades unions, affirmation of the right to property and condemnation of employers who exploited their workers.

More particularly, from the distributist viewpoint, the encyclical also included — albeit in an incompletely developed form — the doctrine of subsidiarity which Pope Pius XI subsequently elaborated in his encyclical letter *Quadragesimo Anno* (known in English as *On Social Reconstruction*) in 1931. *Quadragesimo Anno* reads in regard to subsidiarity:

> Just as it is wrong to withdraw from the individual and commit to the community at large what private enterprise and industry can accomplish, so, too, it is an injustice, a grave evil and a disturbance of right order for a larger and higher organisation to arrogate to itself functions which can be performed efficiently by smaller and lower bodies. This is a fundamental principle of social philosophy, unshaken and unchangeable, and it retains its full truth today. Of its very nature, the true aim of all social activity should be to help individual members of the social body, but never destroy or absorb them.[26]

It was from subsidiarity that the distributist idea was shortly to be developed.

Manning, along with Archbishop Walsh of Dublin, was responsible for translating *De Rerum Novarum* into English. It was also his responsibility to ensure that the encyclical was fully understood and accepted by British Catholics. The operation was undertaken with his customary vigour and disregard for opposition or obstacles. A commentary on the encyclical which he contributed to the *Dublin Review* in July 1891 singled out, in regard to poverty and exploitation, the declaration by the encyclical that:

> By degrees, it has come to pass that working men have been given over, isolated and defenceless, to the callousness of employers and the greed of unrestrained competition. The evil has been increased by rapacious usury, which though more than once condemned by the Church, is nevertheless, under a different form, but with the same guilt, still practised by avaricious and grasping men; and to this must be added the custom of working by contract; and the concentration of so many branches of trade in the hands of a few individuals, so that a very few rich men may have been able to lay upon the masses a yoke little better than slavery itself.

'No Pontiff', the commentary noted, 'has ever had such an opportunity to speak, for never until now has the world of labour been so consciously united, so dependent upon the will of the rich, so exposed to the fluctuations of adversity and to the vicissitudes of trade'.

In industrial terms, the commentary echoed the encyclical's criticism of the interest groups which labelled as 'socialists' those who tried to protect working people from what purported to be 'free contracts', when their real aim was to isolate the workers from one another and so make them dependent upon their employers for what were effectively starvation wages. By contrast, the commentary pointed out, the encyclical supported the right to a minimum wage which was sufficient to maintain a man and his home.

Where wages or conditions were not just, workers had a right to strike. 'A man has a right and an absolute liberty to work for such wages as he thinks just; to refuse to work for less', wrote Manning. 'Men have both right and liberty to unite with others of the same trade or craft, and to demand a just wage for their labour. If this just wage is refused, he has both right and liberty to refuse to work — that is, to strike. Leo XIII fully recognises this liberty. So long as the cause is just, the right to strike is undeniable'.

Turning to socialism, Manning's commentary reiterated the encyclical's condemnation of 'what is called Socialism' while emphasising that its application had limits. The socialism which *De Rerum Novarum* rejected was not 'nominal Socialism' as the word was widely understood in Britain, but 'the original socialism' which nationalised land and, perhaps, made the workers dependent for their livelihoods on the state. The distinction was important, not least for Manning's own purposes.

Clearly what the encyclical said was wrong with socialism in no sense applied to socialism as Ludlow and his fellow Christian socialists would have understood it, or as it continued to be understood by many within bodies such as the Guild of St Matthew and the Christian Social Union, as well as among the dissident Fabians. For Manning to have countenanced the banning of socialism on an indiscriminate basis would have been for him to obstruct the movement of the social order in the associative and communitarian direction he so outspokenly favoured.

'For a century', the commentary concluded, 'the Civil Powers in almost all the Christian world have been separating themselves from the Church, claiming, and glorifying in their separation ... And now of a sudden they find that the millions of the world sympathise with the Church, which has compassion on the multitude rather than with the State or the plutocracy which has weighed so heavily upon them'.[27] It was a fitting note on which to draw to a close a career which had been given over so largely to the service of the dispossessed.

That Manning's concern was understood and appreciated was evident following his death the following year. The crowds on the successive days of the lying in state and the funeral — 'the most striking, certainly the most spontaneous, demonstration of mass emotion in the capital during the late Victorian period'[28] — numbered more than one hundred thousand. The funeral procession was more than four miles long. Manning's influence extended beyond the grave. Its part in transforming even some dedicated state socialists into distributists is evident in the life and career of Cecil Chesterton.

Cecil Chesterton and the defection to distributism

Cecil Chesterton's older brother, Gilbert, once wrote: 'I remember the days when a vast Fabian population was growing up under the name of the Fabian nursery; in which little toddling Socialists were trained to toddle in the straight, but narrow, way of Socialism. As a fact, many of them toddled away in totally different directions; and not a few turned up in the Distributist Nursery, demanding to have their dolls back and the control of their own domestic dolls' houses'.[29]

As has been seen, Cecil was a case in point. He was the quintessential product of the socialist seedbed from which distributism emerged. Other notable examples include Maurice Reckitt, W.R. Titterton, who was an assistant editor to Orage at *The New Age* and later for the distributist weeklies *The New Witness* and *G.K.'s Weekly*, and Sir Henry Slesser, who was the Solicitor-General in the first Labour government in 1924 and a judge in the Royal Court of Appeals from 1929 until 1940.

Others again were the London County Council social worker turned printer Hilary Pepler, and the sculptor and printer Eric Gill. Pepler and Gill founded the distributist community at Ditchling. The originators of guild socialism, Orage and Penty, in the end came to see themselves as distributists, albeit with idiosyncratic outlooks in which key elements from both distributism and guild socialism were combined.[30] Cecil's specialty was aggression. He was the warrior priest of the distributist movement, perpetually carrying the fight into the camp of its adversaries, and laying about him through its periodicals with a deadly turn of phrase.

The First World War cut short his life and promise as it did those of so many of his generation and so much of what had been most hopeful about Britain in the prewar period. He was deeply missed. There is a moving moment in Hugh Hudson's film *Chariots of Fire* when the Master of Caius College at Cambridge in the 1920s speaks to newly arrived students who are dining for the first time under the college honour board. 'I take the War List and I run down it', the Master begins, 'name after name which I cannot read, and which we who are older than you cannot hear, without emotion'. Cecil meant something like that for distributism and his fellow distributists. Had he lived longer he might have succeeded Belloc as their philosopher-king. Instead he became the first distributist martyr. Deprived of Cecil, distributism had to wait forty and more years for Arizmendiarrieta and Mondragon to make it work.

Cecil was born in 1879, seven years after Gilbert. Their father, known affectionately among his relatives as 'Mr Ed', was a partner in the real estate firm of Chesterton and Sons, who retired early to devote himself to his hobbies. 'Always apprehensive of ill-health', it has been said 'Edward decided to hand over the conduct of the firm to his brother Sydney, and arranged for a prolonged and agreeable saunter through life'.[31] His wife, Marie Louise — 'the mother who gave her sons their brains and quenchless love of liberty'[32] — was the more practical parent. The relationship between Cecil and Gilbert was, in the words their fellow distributist, Titterton, one of 'two brothers, who loved reason and honest thought before they loved God, and loved each other then and until death did them part as few brothers have loved'.[33]

'There were two giants growing up in that home', writes Titterton, 'For in his own way Cecil was as great a man as his brother'.[34] Others thought even more highly of Cecil. Father Ferdinand Valentine reports in his biography of his great fellow Dominican, Father Vincent McNabb, that Father John O'Connor — the original for Father Brown in Gilbert's detective stories — believed Cecil was potentially a greater man than Gilbert and had a clearer understanding of current affairs and a clearer grasp of underlying principles. The account continues that this was also McNabb's view. 'Father Vincent', Valentine concludes, 'considered Gilbert Chesterton's mind woolly compared with that of his brother Cecil'.[35]

Cecil's close personal friend, Arthur Ransome — a foreign correspondent who 'flitted into the publishing world in the intervals of roaming far-off lands for the *Manchester Guardian*'[36] — recalls Cecil as a man 'whose kindly, gnarled face I can see now lit by the match he was holding to his pipe, sitting on the edge of my bed in the dusk, letting his pipe go out and lighting it again to go out once more, but never interrupting his tremendous spate of talk'. Ransome also has an engaging account of visiting Cecil and his family unexpectedly in 1908 (Gilbert had by then long since left home) and finding them at some meal in their dining-room, 'each behind a rampart of books, with food growing cold beside them'.

'He told me', writes Ransome, 'that all their meals were like that, and that often, engrossed in their reading, they would forget to eat at all until startled by the arrival of their next meal with the other still waiting on the table'.[37] The family had traditionally been Liberals and Unitarians. Gilbert and Cecil opted for an altogether more robust approach to life than their parents, with a new faith and new political affiliations.

Like his brother and Belloc, Cecil was appalled by the predicament of the poor. He became a socialist at the age of sixteen, when a school friend lent him Robert Blatchford's great socialist tract *Merrie England*. What he understood by socialism was the assumption by the state of all the means of production, distribution and exchange. He emphasised his point regularly, by echoing 'with a rational relish' the declaration by the Tory Prime Minister of the day, Arthur Balfour: 'That is socialism, and nothing else is socialism'.[38] Leaving school in 1898, Cecil trained as a surveyor in the family business, before becoming a journalist in London in 1900.

His forays into investigative journalism made him a controversial figure. Gilbert ascribes to Cecil 'a living and most menacing sort of intolerance; a hatred of the real corruptions and hypocrisies of modern politics and an extraordinary idea of telling the truth'.[39] To Desmond MacCarthy, a leading literary critic of the day, Cecil was 'the most pugnacious journalist since Cobbett'.[40] The downside was that Cecil's professional judgment — what he chose to investigate and his interpretation of it — was flawed by an obsessive anti-Semitism which Gilbert and Belloc in varying degrees also exhibited. Assessing the extent of their anti-Semitism is complicated by their association with seriously depraved racists such as F. Hugh O'Donnell, whose breathtakingly anti-Semitic outbursts featured prominently in the distributist weekly, *The New Witness*.[41] O'Donnell — previously an Irish MP under Parnell with an unsavoury reputation for disloyalty to his leader — would not have been out of place in the notorious Julius Streicher's Jew-baiting Nazi journal *Der Sturmer*.[42]

It is unclear how decent human beings could have allowed themselves to have anything to do with O'Donnell, much less constantly given him space in a periodical which was trying to be taken seriously, and allowed him to chair the National League for Clean Government — the future Distributist League in embryo — which they established in 1913. As will be seen in the next chapter, Belloc is widely regarded as having introduced Gilbert and Cecil to anti-Semitism. Cecil outdid his example. Belloc's most recent biographer, A.N. Wilson, writes that 'In Cecil Chesterton, Belloc found his hostility to the Jews mirrored, distorted and magnified to an almost grotesque degree. Cecil was spittingly, uncontrollably anti-Semitic'.[43]

Gilbert Chesterton was the luckier brother, in that he lived long enough to be shocked into a change of heart by Hitler. 'I am quite ready to believe now', he wrote shortly before his death in 1936, 'that Belloc and I will die defending the last Jew in Europe'.[44] Belloc and the Chestertons are poorly served by those of their admirers who persist in denying or downplaying their anti-Semitism. What matters is less that their vilification of the Jews was greatly to their discredit than whether their more positive attributes atone for it.[45]

In 1901 Cecil became a strongly Anglo-Catholic member of the Church of England. He also joined the Fabian Society and the socialist-leaning Christian Social Union, which the Reverend Charles Gore and the Reverend Henry Scott Holland had established in 1889. Many of the members of the CSU were also members of the Fabian Society. Clergymen at this stage made up the second largest occupational category — after journalists — within the society's ranks.[46] Cecil's Fabian mentors included two of the more turbulent Anglo-Catholic priests of the day, Conrad Noel and Charles Marson,[47] together with Shaw and the society's treasurer, Hubert Bland. Bland — 'a flamboyant personage with a black-ribboned monacle and a liking for sexual adventure'[48] — was a former Tory democrat and a Catholic. Noel and Bland in particular left indelible impressions on Cecil.

Gilbert Chesterton credits Noel with having introduced him and Cecil to what were initially their Anglo-Catholic affiliations, and so set them on the road to the Catholicism which finally became their faith. Cecil's biographer, Father Brocard Sewell, writes that 'As a young man, before he met Belloc, it was Bland more than anyone else who influenced Cecil's thought. Cecil's reverence — the word is hardly too strong — for virility and for what he called "the profession of arms" was expressed in terms that seem almost like an echo of Hubert Bland'.[49]

Long after Cecil had ceased to be a Fabian, he retained warm memories of the society and his former associates. 'My personal recollections of my connection with the society', he recalled in 1916, 'are wholly grateful, and I trust that I shall never, whatever becomes of my speculative opinions, forget the debt which my nonage owes to the generous encouragement of two men in particular — Hubert Bland and Bernard Shaw'.[50]

Cecil and Bland — along with Headlam, Gilbert Chesterton and the socialist writer Edgar Jephson — also formed the Anti-Puritan League. The league was a response to 'the kill-joy movement that tried so hard to suppress the social life of the people and their legitimate enjoyments'.[51] What this meant in practice was agitating against attempts by the London County Council to 'smell out alleged indecencies' in music halls, and regulations which prohibited singing or playing pianos in public houses without a licence, or barred poorer families from bringing their children with them into public houses when the rich could do so freely at restaurants and other 'more expensive but equally alcoholic premises'.[52] The inaugural meeting was held at Headlam's house in Upper Bedford Place. Cecil became the secretary.

An account of the League has been given by Cecil's then future wife, Ada Jones. Ada was a prominent journalist, fifteen years Cecil's senior, and a significant contributor to the distributist cause in her own right, not least through her work for its weeklies. She writes that the league caught on quickly:

> 'Meetings were held and sympathisers rolled up. The Rev. Stewart Headlam, hero of innumerable lost causes, joined hands and roped in the members of his Church and Stage Guild, founded in the hope, he always said, that every chorus girl would convert at least one curate'.[53]

Gilbert Chesterton recalls the league as having issued pamphlets and held 'certain convivial evenings at which there was much delightful talk and exchange of opinions'. It suffered as a propagandist body from the very first, he believed, 'owing to its adopting too provocative a title'.[54]

Cecil and Headlam fell out over the future of the Guild of St Matthew, which Cecil also joined. The dispute centred on how closely the guild should relate to other socialist bodies. 'You may be very clever', Headlam would retort to the urgings of his truculent critic for a more ecumenical approach, 'but you are wrong'.[55] Overall, there can have been few groups on the left of the political spectrum in whose affairs Cecil did not at some stage take part. Like Champion a decade and more before him, he was an inveterate joiner and founder of organisations. He revelled in the ferment of ideas in the innumerable London debating clubs and other intellectual forums of the day, and at Well House in Kent, where Bland and his author wife, Edith Nesbit — 'a raffish Rossetti, with a long full throat and dark hair, smoothly parted ... large hearted, amazingly unconventional, but with sudden reversions to ultra-respectable standards'[56] — held court among a brilliant circle of political and literary celebrities.

In 1904 Cecil was elected to the executive committee of the Fabian Society, and rapidly acquired the reputation of being among its hardest-working members. He served on the society's committees on electricity and transit, the committee on feeding school children and the literature sub-committee, was a member of the Fabian delegation to the International Socialist Congress in Amsterdam in 1904 and, jointly with Bland, drafted the Fabian manifesto for the 1906 general election.

Bland, Shaw and Cecil were appointed by the society as its official spokesmen. However, even so sound a record, and the energetic support of members of the 'Old Gang' such as Bland and Shaw, were insufficient to secure Cecil's re-election at the society's Annual General Meeting in 1907, in circumstances where, as his biographer sees it, 'He continued to speak his mind bluntly, careless of the feelings of members who were pacifists, feminists, vegetarians, and other things he disapproved of'.[56]

'Shaw', as Cecil has recalled the episode, 'risked his own popularity and influence in an attempt, which proved fruit-less, to prevent my being turned off the Executive by the lady members of the society who were at the moment suffering from daimonic possession engendered by the Suffragette agitation'.[58] The final straw may well have been in regard to the effort by Wells to rejuvenate — as he saw it — the Fabian Society, by having it become a socialist political party. Cecil initially sided with Wells, but then defected to the 'Old Gang', thereby alienating numbers of his former supporters in both camps. Following his defeat, his energies were redirected for a time to the Christian Social Union, and the more outspo-kenly socialist Church Socialist League, which had been formed in 1906, largely by disaffected CSU members and Fabians, many of whom were interesting themselves increas-ingly in associative and communitarian forms of socialism such as had been favoured by Ludlow and his founder Christian socialist associates.

For all his difficulties with the Fabians, Cecil so far showed no inclination to deviate from his state socialist convictions, much less embrace distributism. That he remained a state socialist even after he finally resigned from the Fabian Society in 1909 is evident from an article which he contributed to *The Church Socialist Quarterly* in April 1912. Cecil wrote:

> On the main principles on which Socialism rests, the conviction that the sufferings of the great mass of the people are due to the fact that they are defrauded of the true reward of their labour, the conviction that this arises from the appropriation of the means of production by a small class, and the conviction that the remedy is to be found in the transfer of property in such means to the common-wealth, I have no marked change of conviction to record.

'What I believed fifteen or sixteen years ago', the article concluded, 'I believe today'.[59]

Even so, he was not immune to persuasion. His work as a journalist on weeklies such as Orage's *The New Age* involved him in the great debates about socialism and other major issues of the day, where, for example, he and Shaw put the case for socialism against the distributist views of his brother, Gilbert, and Belloc. Opposing what they were saying obliged him to understand it. Their differences over socialism aside, Belloc had long since taken the place of Bland as the mentor who most influenced him. It was by Belloc that Cecil and Gilbert were introduced to the Catholic social doctrines of *De Rerum Novarum*, with the result that, in Titterton's words, 'As soon as it was explained to the Chestertons they knew that they believed in it'.[60]

Gilbert suggests that Cecil's change of heart also came about in part because he was hostile to bureaucracy:

> All the primary forms of private property were to be given to the Government; and it occurred to him, as a natural precaution, to give a glance at the Government. He gave some attention to the actual types and methods of the governing and official class, into whose power trams and trades and shops and houses were already passing, amid loud Fabian cheers for the progress of Socialism.[61]

The upshot was that Cecil shortly came to see the distributists as having the stronger arguments, and to question the socialist convictions of which he had previously been so staunch an adherent.

Precisely how and when the break with his past became final is unclear, since he continued to describe himself as a socialist even after his reception into the Catholic Church by Father Sebastian Bowden at the Brompton Oratory on 7 June 1912.[62] However, further stages in the evolution of his thinking were marked by the reviews of Belloc's great distributist treatise *The Servile State* and Hyndman's *Further Reminiscences* which appeared over his name in *The Eye-Witness* and *The New Witness* later that year.

A significant passage from his review of *The Servile State* in October reads:

> Socialists are getting more and more sharply divided into two camps, and the interesting thing is that neither camp

is disposed to talk much about that public ownership which is after all the essence of the Socialist creed ... Those Socialists whose motive is the noble one of pity for the poor will advocate every proposal which tends to secure for them some measure of sufficiency and security without asking whether its ultimate tendency is not to divide the nation legally into persons responsible to the State and persons for whom they are responsible, ie. into masters and slaves; while, finally, *those few Socialists who foresee and abhor such a conclusion (as I do) grow more and more unwilling — particularly if they know as much about the politicians as I do — to involve the authority of the State, well knowing in what direction, as things stand, the drive of the State is likely to be.*[63]

Reviewing Hyndman's book in December, Cecil wrote in regard to the veteran SDF leader, 'I feel towards Mr Hyndman as one might imagine a Catholic who has involuntarily lost the faith feels towards one who has kept it. I envy him the splendid certitudes of which I can no longer be certain'.

None of this, Cecil continued, meant that he had rejected the need for revolutionary change, or was in any way more accepting of capitalism:

I feel as strongly as ever that the present social system is detestable and intolerable. I hold as strongly as ever that the iniquitous distribution of wealth would fully justify today Confiscation and Civil War. But am I now prepared — for that after all is the crux of the matter — to entrust the control of all the means of production permanently to the political officers of the State?

'I fear' he concluded, 'that I could not assent without considerable qualification'.[64] The turning point was now behind him. Cecil from then on squarely aligned himself with the distributists, with whom he had so often previously debated or otherwise found himself at odds.

Cecil's career and influence as a writer were also now at their zenith. He was the assistant editor of the distributist weekly, *The Eye-Witness,* which he and Belloc established in 1911, and he soon succeeded Belloc as editor and proprietor. The paper then became *The New Witness.* Cecil's books sold well and were widely discussed. They included *Gladstonian Ghosts* (1905), *G.K. Chesterton: A Criticism* (1908), *Party and People: A Criticism of the Recent Elections and Their Consequences*

(1910), *The Story of Nell Gwyn* (1911), *The Party System* (co-authored with Belloc in 1911) and *A History of America* (1919). *A History of America* was completed in the trenches at Ypres, where Cecil was a private with the East Surreys regiment in the First World War.

His death from nephritis in a military hospital in France in 1918 — in Gilbert's words, from 'the effects of exposure in the last fierce fighting that broke the Prussian power over Christendom'[65] — robbed distributism of one of its most promising thinkers and advocates. An eloquent testimony to the gap Cecil left behind him in this respect is provided by Ada Jones. She wrote:

> Neither G.K. nor Belloc seem to have made any effort to have produced a textbook formulating their belief, and in its absence, Distributism remains a creed without a dogma, evoking sympathy but lacking support. Had Cecil lived, the dogma of the theory would have been thrashed out. He was too keen a rationalist to tolerate loose thinking. But without his help Distributism has remained a roseate hope lacking shape or form, and quite without first principles.[66]

The distributists were likewise denied the links with the labour movement — and the consequent avenues for giving practical expression to their ideas — which Cecil's down-to-earth outlook and determination to enter parliament and reform it from within might in due course have led him to forge.[67]

Cecil was the decisive distributist, who, had he lived, might well have rescued British distributism from its characteristic state of indecision and vacillation and made it into an unambiguously political entity. Alternatively, the profound reservations about parliament and the party system, which he shared with fellow distributists such as Belloc, might have caused him to conclude that it was as a social movement that distributism would have the better chance of success. What he is unlikely to have tolerated is the interminable, demoralising and debilitating inability of the distributists to arrive at a decision one way or the other. Ada had finally married Cecil after a sixteen-year courtship, shortly before his departure for the Front. 'I always think of him as the most courageous man I have ever known', she was to conclude. 'He never showed, nor do I think he felt, the least tinge of apprehension as to what might be coming to him'.[68]

Hilaire Belloc

4

The Originator: Hilaire Belloc and the Idea of Distributism

THE originator of the distributism which Manning foreshadowed and Cecil embraced was Hilaire Belloc. 'We were the converts', writes Gilbert Chesterton, 'but you were the missionary'.[1] Belloc's book *The Servile State* (1912) — the key text of the distributist movement — was a devastating critique, both of capitalism and of the likely consequences of trying to replace capitalism with socialism in the state socialist mould. It also restated the papal doctrine of subsidiarity as the basis for the distributist social order which Belloc called the Distributive State. Belloc, along with Gilbert and Cecil Chesterton, was the public face of distributism.

That his involvement should have been so central was not in all respects to the advantage of the distributist cause. Belloc was a gifted historian, political theoretician, polemicist, novelist and poet whose contributions enriched and enlivened public debate on major issues for more than half a century. His Catholicism was deeply felt and militant. His fellow historian, A.L. Rowse, credits him with having been 'a man of genius'.[2] However, he was also at times conspicuously careless with facts, overbearing, offensive and intolerant. His anti-Semitism in particular cost distributism support in quarters in which it might otherwise have had a more attentive hearing. In the 1930s the admiration he and his associates expressed for Mussolini, and their championing of Franco in the Spanish Civil War, divided the distributist movement and brought distributism into a disrepute from which, half a century and more later, it has only recently begun to recover.

Belloc was born in France in 1870 to a French father, Louis Belloc, and an English mother, Elizabeth ('Bessie') Rayner Parkes. Bessie Parkes was a grand-daughter of the founder of modern chemistry and leading radical of his day, Joseph Priestley, and daughter of a further prominent Liberal, Joseph Parkes. She was herself a woman of passionate radical and feminist convictions who rejected her family's Unitarian affiliations in 1864 and became a Catholic. A chalet which she rented in France in the village of La Celle Saint Cloud in 1867 belonged to the talented writer Louise Swanton Belloc, a fellow Catholic, who had recently been widowed by the death of her husband, the portrait painter Hilaire Belloc.

The Bellocs were staunch republicans. Louise's father and eight of her mother's brothers had been soldiers in Napoleon's armies. One brother, Baron Chasseriau, died in the charge of the French cavalry at Waterloo. Louis, Louise's son, was in poor health, and unable to practise his profession as a solicitor. He and Bessie were shortly married. The first of their two children, Marie, was born in La Celle Saint Cloud in 1868.[3] Their son, Hilaire, followed on 27 July 1870. That the birth coincided with a notably noisy thunderstorm was perhaps a portent of his later character.

Growing Up

Louis Belloc died in 1872, leaving Bessie to divide the upbringing of the children between France and Britain. Belloc was a much loved and indulged child. Recalling the circumstances of his birth, Bessie called him 'Old Thunder' when he screamed or had tantrums.[4] By Wilson's account, she and his nurse, Sarah Mew, 'had much to answer for, when they taught the strutting, posturing little boy that he was most charming when most aggressive'.[5] Belloc attended Cardinal Newman's Oratory school in Birmingham, where he excelled in English and mathematics. Leaving school at the age of seventeen —

to enter university, he believed — he had to come to terms suddenly with the fact that much of Bessie's capital had been lost through failed investments of which he had been unaware.

Belloc was no longer, as he had confidently believed, the heir to a comfortable fortune. Even for him to proceed to the university as had been intended was, for the time, beyond the family's means. An extended period of uncertainty about his future followed. He was briefly a French naval cadet at the Collège Stanislas in Paris; took up and abandoned careers as a land agent and an architect; was among Manning's more frequent visitors and attentive listeners at Archbishop's House — the 'great gloomy barracks' which had once been a club for the Brigade of Guards[6] — in the closing months of the great cardinal's life; launched the first of many periodicals with which he was to be associated, *The Paternoster Review*, and completed the year of military service for which he was liable as a French citizen, with the 10th Battery of the 8th Regiment of Artillery at Toul. Meanwhile, he had fallen in love with an Irish-American visitor from California, Elodie Hogan, and, in 1891, followed her home with an offer of marriage which, for the time being, was refused. The episode exemplified Belloc's already formidable willpower and determination. He is said to have arrived in the United States with no money, and crossed the continent to California on foot.

Back in Britain, the meetings with Manning which Belloc's American travels had interrupted were resumed until Manning's death in 1892. It is likely to have been in talking with Manning that the core ideas which were to culminate in distributism first suggested themselves to Belloc. The period when he was Manning's protege was also that of Manning's involvement in the preparation, translation into English, publication and explanation of *De Rerum Novarum*. Manning's enthusiasm for the project — his sense of the encyclical as being the culmination of his lifelong efforts on behalf of the dispossessed — could hardly have passed by the young man who was so avidly hanging on his every word.

What also may not have escaped Belloc's sharply observant eye was that Manning's great heart and fertile political imagination were not in all respects matched by a comparable intellectual consistency. As the American historian, Dermot Quinn, points out, this was so much the case as for there to be in effect not one Manning but two:

One argued for economic 'rights', for supply and demand, for the division of labour, for factories and machines, for an incessantly active State. The other argued that the market was no god, that materialism offered no balm, that the state was not master but servant. From time to time, the two would bump into one another, perhaps even tip a hat in greeting. It must be reported, however, that neither Manning recognised the other.[7]

It may well have been Belloc's conclusion that he had inherited from Manning the task of finally reconciling the disparate threads of Manning's thinking and example, and bringing them together in the overall integrated social vision, which was to be achieved to such triumphant effect with the publication of *The Servile State* in 1912.

In 1893, Belloc — fired imaginatively as he now was with both the Parkes family's radical liberalism and Manning's social Catholicism — was at last able to enter Balliol College at Oxford. His academic prowess secured him a Brackenbury scholarship in history at the end of the first year of his studies and first class honours in history at his final examinations. Outside the classroom, he was librarian and later president of the Oxford Union in whose debates so many British leaders have first mastered the cut and thrust of public controversy. Contemporaries saw him as 'one of the most remarkable speakers the Union has ever known'.[8] He was also a major contributor to the revival of liberalism at Oxford in the middle 1890s, championing the liberal cause in union debates against conservative critics such as the no less eloquent future leading Tory F.E. Smith.

Smith — who was later to become the first Earl of Birkenhead and a conspicuously reform-minded Lord Chancellor of England — is perhaps best remembered for his aphorism 'The world continues to offer glittering prizes for those who have stout hearts and sharp swords'.[9] About this, if little else, he and Belloc may well have been in agreement. Belloc's success in student politics at Oxford had within it the seeds of future difficulties for distributism. He had mastered the Union. To what mastery in the wider spheres of national politics might he not now ascend, as had so many presidents of the Union before him? That the glittering prizes then failed to materialise astonished and embittered him. As will be seen, Belloc was seldom at his best when disappointed.

Nor was he averse to blaming conspiracies for his misfortunes. Neither attribute was ideally suited to paving the way for a new social order.

A Republican Club which Belloc and some associates formed at Oxford in 1895 — 'one of the smallest, the shortest-lived and most famous Oxford Societies'[10] — fostered serious discussion of liberal philosophy and policies. The editors of the seminal *Essays in Liberalism by Six Oxford Men*, which appeared in 1897, wrote in their preface that:

> Mr Belloc has been the leading spirit. We cannot refrain from gratefully expressing our admiration for his kindling eloquence, his Liberal enthusiasm, and his practical idealism. Much that he has not written is indirectly derived from him, inspired by a companionship which we have all found a liberal education.[11]

That Belloc left behind so indelible an impression in the minds of his fellow students reflected in part that — at twenty-three — he was older than most of them, had seen more of the world and created a strikingly exotic impression with his French accent, soft hat and large dark cloak.

It also reflected the extent to which his key beliefs were already entrenched. 'In the course of his life, inevitably, some of his views shifted', notes Wilson; 'But it is striking how few of them did'.[12] One passionate conviction in which — true to the Manning legacy — he never wavered was his detestation of the waste and injustice of poverty and his determination that it should be overcome. As he was to recall years later from an election platform, 'When I went back to a University, I went back plunged through and through with this conception — that the first duty of a man who has travelled, who has read, who has met men, is to change the social condition of England so that the rich of England shall be made less rich and the poor shall be made less poor'.[13]

Liberalism

The Oxford student newspaper, *Isis*, complained that liberalism as defined by Belloc in his contribution to *Essays In Liberalism* did not correspond to the views of 'any recognised section of the Liberal Party'.[14] The observation is unlikely to have surprised or troubled Belloc. His politics were nothing if not idiosyncratic, drawing as they did on all his richly varied antecedents and affiliations. As the grandson of Joseph Parkes and an heir to generations of family involvement in the liberal cause, Belloc looked back with satisfaction on the achievements of radicals before him — to 'the men who made the Reform Bill, who repealed the Corn Laws, who demanded a juster basis for the suffrage and a better distribution of seats, who abolished some of the grosser privileges, and who crowned the effort of the century with the recognition of claims of self-government in the secondary nationalities of the empire'.[15]

He was also, on the French side of the family, an heir to the democratic, republican and egalitarian ideals of Rousseau's *Du Contrat Social* and the French Revolution. Most of all, his Catholicism required that his political convictions should be in harmony with his faith. The social order he and his fellow members of the Republican Club wanted was one where independence and freedom could be exercised to the full, personal capabilities as fully as possible developed and entrepreneurial energies unleashed. In as much as both capitalism and the collectivism of some socialists and some liberals were incompatible with the dignity, autonomy and self-sufficiency of the individual citizen, Belloc rejected them. He was only briefly a socialist, and never a member of the socialist bodies to which so many of his distributist associates belonged. What he for the most part saw Britain as needing was not capitalism or socialism, but a liberalism where society's right to require observance of its laws stemmed from — and was conditional on — the participation of its citizens in developing them. What liberalism had to be about was liberty.

The basis for such a liberalism — the 'only possible foundation of self-government' — would then be 'the citizen independent of personal control, and conscious also of a moral force restraining him from its abuse'. As Belloc wrote:

> He was to be answerable, but answerable not to individual men so much as to the general condition of the nation around him. He was an individual possessor and producer of wealth. He was to exercise that faculty of self-restraint which is, even in the narrow field of mere economic science, the basis of accumulation and of all sufficient material happiness. He was, again, to be so self-respecting

a member of a society which depended upon his consent, that he might be counted upon not to give his vote upon a general issue for purposes lower than the common good.[16]

In all this, Belloc was influenced deeply not only by his inherited radicalism but by his reading of *Du Contrat Social*. Like Rousseau, he believed passionately in popular sovereignty as expressed through the 'general will' of the community. 'Men nowhere do or can deny that the community acting as it thinks right is ultimately sovereign', he declared; 'there is no alternative to so plain a truth'.[17]

Sovereignty by the whole community required in his view that 'the executive was to become openly and by definition its servant; the vague thesis of equality, upon which jurisprudence reposed, was brought with exactitude and vigour into every detail and made a test of every law; the limits of individual liberty were to be enlarged till they met for boundary the general liberty of all'.[18] While he so far remained committed to parliament as the means for bringing about the reforms that Britain needed so desperately, he also believed like Rousseau that an authentic democracy was possible only in communities which were small and largely self-sufficient. Representative bodies such as parliaments ceased to be democratic — and became subject to the corrupting influence of the rich and privileged — to the extent that they were distanced from their electors.

Larger communities might be better served by a strong leader through whom the general will could be expressed. Here again the seeds of future difficulties for distributism are apparent. The scepticism about parliament which Belloc learned from Rousseau was not calculated to make him more patient with the frustrations which are inextricably associated with the early stages of life as an MP. His view that parliament was intrinsically an undemocratic — and even an anti-democratic — body may well have helped him to rationalise cutting short his parliamentary career and so depriving himself of the platform from which distributism might otherwise have been argued for so effectively. The decision had significant implications for the key issue as to whether distributism was to develop as a political or a social movement — and for the difficulty the distributists had in choosing between them. The bias towards strong leaders which Belloc also acquired from Rousseau may well have made him the more susceptible to Mussolini and Franco, with calamitous consequences for distributism.

Catholicism

Belloc's democratic and egalitarian sentiments were further fortified by his Catholic faith. Catholicism had brought him to Manning. What Manning had taught him now set him on the road by which he would ultimately arrive at distributism. His book, *The French Revolution*, argued eloquently that 'There is not and cannot be any necessary or fundamental reason why conflict should have arisen between a European democracy and the Catholic Church'.[19] His vision of Catholicism was universalist but also profoundly Eurocentric.

'The Faith is Europe', he declared in a much-quoted passage, 'and Europe is the Faith'.[20] Belloc saw the Church he loved as being descended in uninterrupted continuity from the Roman Empire in whose traditions and achievements his classical education at the Oratory school had so deeply steeped him. The Empire had created within its borders a consciousness of common Roman identity, which transcended ties such as those of geography, ethnicity and religion.

Belloc noted in his *Europe and the Faith* that 'From the Euphrates to the Scottish Highlands, from the North Sea to the Sahara and the Middle Nile, all was one state ... Men lived as citizens of one state which they took for granted and which they even regarded as eternal'.[21] He believed passionately that — far from the coming of the Church having undermined and ultimately brought down the Empire as many had supposed — the Church had enabled the Empire to endure in circumstances where it would otherwise have vanished.

'The Faith is that which Rome accepted in her maturity', he declared, 'nor was the Faith the cause of her decline, but rather the conservator of all that could be conserved'.[22] Fortified by its adherence to a common faith, Europe had again in the Dark Ages turned back the invading barbarian and Islamic armies — the 'universal attack of the Mohammaden, the Hun, the Scandanavian'[23] — which might otherwise have obliterated its culture and identity.

Thanks largely to the Church, a just and stable social

order had emerged in the Middle Ages, when widespread distribution of property enabled the peasant proprietors, self-employed craftsmen and small traders of the day to enjoy freedom and independence, subject only to their obligations to religion and the community. 'In the Middle Ages', wrote Belloc, 'the Catholic notes not hypotheses but facts':

> He sees the Parliaments arising not from some imaginary 'teutonic' root — a figment of the academies — but from the very real and present great monastic orders, in Spain, in Britain, in Gaul — never outside the old limits of Christendom. He sees the Gothic architecture spring high, spontaneous and autochthonic, first in the territory of Paris and thence spread outwards in a ring to the Scottish highlands and to the Rhine. He sees the new universities, a product of the soul of Europe awakened; he sees the marvellous new civilisation of the Middle Ages rising as a transformation of the old Roman society wholly from within, and motivated by the Faith.[24]

Belloc's profound pride in the achievements of the Church was matched by a no less profound sense of loss and failure. He believed that the fracturing of the unity of Christendom by the Reformation had enabled predatory and secretive financiers to enrich themselves at the expense of the common people.

He noted in regard to the Reformation that: 'Through it, there arose in England first, later through the more active Protestant nations, and later still in various degrees throughout the rest of Christendom, a system under which a few possessed the land and the machinery of production and the many were gradually dispossessed'.[25] Belloc's benign view of the Middle Ages is sometimes seen as meaning that he advocated returning to them. The supposition misrepresents him. Belloc was under no illusions as to the the desirability — much less the possibility — of recreating the institutions of a long-gone era. What was important to him — what mattered from the viewpoint of distributism — was that there should be new institutions which gave effect in the present to the distributist values of the past.

The French Revolution

'Belloc', in Corrin's view, 'saw Protestantism as the progenitor of all evil'.[26] What he believed could also be seen — what his vision of social Catholicism most vividly conveyed to him — was the need for the intimations of an authentic distributist social order which he ascribed to the Middle Ages, to now, in his own era, finally be brought to fruition. That replacing capitalism with distributism might have to be achieved by violent means in no way deterred Belloc. Catholicism was for him not a passive but a militant faith. So evil did he see capitalism as having become that its overthrow was mandatory. Unlike the overwhelming majority of his contemporaries and co-religionists, it was from France and the French Revolution — and also from Napoleon — that he now derived inspiration, encouragement and example.

Pre-revolutionary France exemplified for Belloc the predicament to which the Reformation had reduced the greater part of Europe. The simplicity which he saw as being the key prerequisite for human happiness — of a social order where 'the king ruled, the knight fought, the peasant dug in his own ground, and the priest believed'[27] — had largely been destroyed. What had taken its place was a situation where 'as the eighteenth century falls further and further into decay, all is gone':

> Those who move in comfort above the souls which they have beneath them for a pavement, the rich and the privileged, have even ceased to enjoy their political and theological amusements; they are concerned only with maintaining their ease, and to do this they conjure with the name of the people's memories. They build ramparts of sacred tombs, and defend themselves with the bones of the Middle Ages, with the relics of the saint and knight.

The revolution had begun 'when suddenly the spirit of the Middle Ages, the spirit of enthusiasm and of faith, the Crusade, came out of the tomb and routed them'.[28] The principles the Revolution then embraced — 'Equality within the State and the government of the State by its general will'[29] — were those of *Du Contrat Social*. 'The apostolic quality of Rousseau', Belloc concluded, 'had touched the mind of France'.[30]

Opinion in Britain and among Belloc's fellow Catholics was generally hostile to the French Revolution. Its leaders were remembered widely as the authors of the Terror, executioners of their king and persecutors of the Church. Belloc disagreed. By Corrin's account, 'To Belloc, the French Revolution was essentially a violent return to conditions necessary for the health of any community'.[31] The revolution was in his view the inevitable response of a nation provoked beyond endurance by intolerable living conditions and an oppressive and incompetent government.[32] There was no quarrel between the theory of the revolution and that of the Church, but only between 'the Revolution in action and the authorities of Catholicism'.[33]

The leaders his countrymen condemned as blood-soaked ruffians were for him mostly men of outstanding integrity, motivated by principles he wholeheartedly supported. Robespierre — a man 'wholly maligned by history' — was a case in point. Belloc's opinion of Robespierre improved as his reservations about parliamentary democracy multiplied. It may well be that he detected in Robespierre elements of his own character and outlook. 'Robespierre', he wrote, 'was sincerely attached to the conception of an ideal democracy; he was incorruptible in the pursuit of it'. The conventional wisdom was astray, in that 'Robespierre was not the chief influence in the Committee of Public Safety; that he did not use it, that he even grew disgusted with it and that, in general, he was never the man who ruled France'.[34]

Accounts of the revolution such as those of the historian Michelet fired Belloc's imagination with the profoundly moral character of the issues, the towering stature of the protagonists and the triumph and tragedy of the struggle. 'What possessed him as an idea in Rousseau', notes Belloc's original and principal biographer, Robert Speaight, 'possessed him as a narrative in Michelet':

> Dogma became passion in the men who strove, so desperately and imperfectly, to realise the democratic dream. The reasoning of Rousseau had its own cold beauty, but it required for complement the enthusiasm of St Just's 'The words we have spoken shall never be lost on earth', and the defiance of Danton's 'Assailed by the Kings of the earth, we hurl at them the head of a King'. Belloc warmed to the task of re-interpreting these men to a public who had written them off as rogues.[35]

Thanks to the devotion of its leaders to its principles — to 'the formula of the Revolutionary Creed' in *Du Contrat Social* — the revolution had survived. The Committee of Public Safety — with Carnot rather than Robespierre foremost among its leaders — had crushed the opponents of the revolution within France, while the new armies required to defend the country against invasion were created, and a new commander to rally them was found in Napoleon Bonaparte.

As with Robespierre, Belloc may well have detected elements of himself in Napoleon. Might it not be his destiny to succeed where Napoleon had failed in endowing Europe with a new social order — a social order based in this instance on the distributist principles which, at Manning's instigation, he was now actively exploring? Belloc's view of history and his distributism were inextricably intertwined. What he saw as being the essence of distributism was, in the first instance, the legitimacy it derived from his Catholic faith; secondly, its continuity with a Catholic past; thirdly, its relevance to the problems arising from the exclusion of Catholicism from the contemporary social order in England; and, finally, the French experience as grounds for hope that a better future — a distributist future — might yet be achieved.

Anti-Semitism

That the French connection had its darker side — that there were negatives as well as pluses for distributism in the inspiration Belloc derived from his roots in French history, culture and institutions — is evident from what Speaight sees as Belloc's 'strident, exotic anti-Semitism'.[37] His distrust and dislike of the Jews originated in part with his exposure to the prejudices of the French naval cadets with whom he served briefly at the Collège Stanislas in Paris, and his fellow artillerymen at Toul.

It was fanned by the violently anti-Semitic rhetoric of prominent right-wing French nationalists such as Paul Déroulède — a neighbour of the Belloc family in Le Celle Saint Cloud — whose *Ligue des Patriotes* Belloc had joined when he was fifteen. Another source was Charles Maurras — publisher of the notorious anti-Semitic journal *Action Française* — who was Belloc's mentor in French politics. 'Belloc', in Wilson's view, 'knew perfectly well' that his baser nature was dominated by a crude streak of anti-Semitism, the legitimacy of which a better part of him rejected.[38]

John McCarthy writes in his political biography of Belloc that Belloc's anti-Semitism was 'undisguised, particularly as manifest in his novels and occasionally in his poetry'.[39] His close friend and fellow author, Maurice Baring, recalls him at supper parties at Oxford discoursing on the Jewish Peril 'with indescribable gusto and vehemence'.[40] At Oxford also he was 'incredulous' that a close friend was in love with a 'Jewess'.[41] When a Jew — Captain Alfred Dreyfus — was falsely tried and convicted for treason by the French Army, Belloc gained notoriety as 'the only man in England who did not side with Dreyfus'.[42] When Dreyfus was exonerated and his main accuser committed suicide, Belloc refused to admit that he had been wrong. The most that he would concede was that he had 'no settled opinion about the matter'.[43]

Belloc's vilification of individual Jews and groups of Jews — of the 'curly-headed men' of the tasteless verse in which he mocked the Rothschild family — was incessant, obsessive and oblivious to its own enormity and offensiveness.[44] His book *The Jews* — 'my admirable Yid book', as he called it — purported to refute the charge that he was anti-Semitic while further justifying it.[45] Unsurprisingly other than to the author, a Jew who read the proofs at the request of the publisher reported that the book was 'unjust' and that Jews would refuse to read or sell it.[46] 'Israel', Belloc argued in *The Jews*, 'is a nation apart, is not, and cannot be, of us, and shall not be confounded with ourselves'.[47] It was necessary, he continued, that 'the Jew' should be clearly identified by means such as distinctive dress, prohibited from anglicising his name and segregated in every possible way from other sections of the community.

The instigation of these measures — of what Speaight calls 'a kind of mitigated apartheid'[48] — should for preference be by 'the Jew' himself. Should 'the Jew' refuse any such 'bargain' — should he 'dig his heels in and insist, as many another privileged class has insisted before him, that he will continue to enjoy all that he has ever enjoyed, that he will continue his demand for dual allegiance, that he will insist on the very fullest recognition as a Jew, and at the same time on what is fatal to such recognition, the fullest recognition as a member of our own community' — then the community would be compelled to legislate in spite of him.[49] That in later life Belloc denounced the persecution of the Jews by Hitler was to his credit. However, it in no way expunged or made less disgraceful his many contributions to the pervasive climate of anti-Semitism from which Hitler was so conspicuous a beneficiary.

It is likely that no other factor so greatly damaged British distributism as its association in the public mind with anti-Semitism. That the identification of distributism with anti-Semitism should have become so widespread and entrenched was due more by far to Belloc than to any other of his fellow distributists. It was with Belloc that the infection of anti-Semitism originated, and through him that it was spread to numbers of his associates, including most of those who were seen as representing distributism in the public arena.

A sterile debate is sometimes pursued as to which of the original distributists — Belloc, Gilbert and Cecil Chesterton and those closest to them — were more and which less anti-Semitic. To argue along these lines is to miss the point that all of them were caught up in a common hothouse culture of anti-Semitism in which even fantasies as grotesque and malevolent as those of O'Donnell could be taken seriously, given currency and permitted to mutually reinforce one another.

That the vehemence of the anti-Semitic utterances of those concerned might vary from one to another was less important than the fact that they shared a world view which fundamentally denied Jews their humanity. When in due course, in the run up to the Second World War, the issue arose of whether — and if so to what extent — the distributists were sympathetic to fascism, their position was made the more vulnerable and difficult by reason of the reputation for anti-Semitism which — as will be seen in the discussion of the distributist weeklies in Chaper 6 — numbers of them had so long and recklessly courted.

Property

In the case of England, Belloc's vision of citizenship — of 'the responsible propertied voter'[50] — led him finally to two major conclusions. He believed in the first instance that, far from the radical project of extending the franchise having been completed with the inclusion of the middle class, there was an obligation on the part of the radicals to make 'further attempts to admit much wider portions of the nation to the benefits of a representation which they had made, so far as districts were concerned, equitable and just'.[51] Secondly, the key attribute required of those newly franchised — 'that their economic and political independence was not indeed irresponsible'[52] — would need to be underpinned by a much wider distribution of property. Belloc asserted:

> 'The conditions which industrial development have brought about in England are the very antithesis of those which Liberalism devises in the State: capital held in large masses and in few hands; men working in large gangs under conditions where discipline, pushed to the point of servitude, is almost as necessary as in an armed force; voters whose most immediate interests are economic rather than political; citizens who own, for the greater part, not even their roofs'.[53]

While the specific reforms his contribution to *Essays in Liberalism* advocated were mainly directed to making more widespread the ownership of land rather than of industry, the principle in each case was the same — the restoration of a social order where 'all the institutions of the state repose upon an underlying conception of secure and well-divided private property which can never be questioned, and which colours all men's minds'. 'And that doctrine', Belloc pointed out, 'like every other sane doctrine, though applicable only to temporal conditions, has the firm support of the Church'.[54]

Belloc's analysis in *Essays in Liberalism* foreshadowed the distributist philosophy which he would describe a decade and more later in *The Servile State*. What was integral to the whole notion of distributism was stakeholder democracy. It was only through the experience of stakeholding — through the actual ownership of property for which direct responsibility was incurred — that members of a community could be motivated to inform themselves about and become actively involved in its affairs.

It was by this direct, hands-on approach — through consciousness-raising in the most practical terms rather than by education in abstractions — that the new distributist social order could be achieved. Belloc's emphasis on stakeholding and stakeholder participation (like the distrust of parliament he learned from Rousseau) thereby predisposed him towards the view that distributism should be a social rather than a political movement. The pity was that — as will be seen — when the time came for him to influence his fellow distributists in that direction, his energies had been so much sapped by grief and disappointment as to prevent him from doing so effectively.

L o n d o n

Following his outstanding results in his final examinations, Belloc was confident that he would be offered a fellowship at an Oxford college and stay on at the university as an historian. He looked forward to marrying and establishing a family in the comfort and security a fellow's income would provide. Once again, as over the fortune he had once counted on inheriting, he was disappointed. The positions for which he applied were denied to him because of what he saw as bias against his Catholic faith.

The experience soured and embittered him. 'Oxford', he later wrote, 'is for me a shrine, a memory, a tomb, and a poignant possessing grief. All would have been well if they would have received me'.[55] Even the consolation of believing himself to have been a victim of bigotry was compromised when a co-religionist, F.F. Urquhart, was awarded a fellowship in 1898. A more likely explanation is that the Dons felt they had good reason to question the wisdom of taking in a man whose prejudices and intemperate manner of expressing himself might make his company uncongenial.[56]

It was to his talents as a writer and a public speaker that Belloc now turned, in re-establishing on a wider stage the prominence he had enjoyed at Oxford, and supporting Elodie, who had become his wife. Following a lecture tour in the United States in 1897, he and Elodie and their baby son, Louis, moved to a new home in London. His by-line began to appear regularly in the *Liberal Daily News* and also on occasion in its Tory competitor the *Daily Mail.*

The books for which he is now best remembered — works of the stature of *Danton, Robespierre, Paris, The Path to Rome and Esto Perpetua* — were also appearing. While the proceeds helped the family to make ends meet, they were no substitute for the salaried position as a writer which continued to elude him. 'First Oxford wouldn't give me work' he complained to a friend in 1906, 'and now after all these efforts London won't'.[57] When events seemed to take a turn for the better with his appointment as literary editor of the *Morning Post* later that year, the relief was short-lived.

The magnitude of the difficulties Belloc habitually created for himself, through his general irascibility and insensitivity to the feelings even of those on whose goodwill he most depended, is apparent from a letter the managing editor of the *Morning Post*, Fabian Ware, addressed to him in 1909. Ware wrote: 'I owe you an apology for the way I shouted at you this afternoon; but please don't, on your rare and unexpected visits to the office (about which I shall say more on another occasion), stand at my door and wag a finger at me when I am engaged on private and difficult business'.[58] In the course of a dispute about his conditions of employment in 1910, Belloc imprudently offered Ware his resignation. The offer was accepted.[59]

Belloc had held a steady job for the last time. It was on his freelance writing and lecturing that he from then on depended for a frequently precarious livelihood. With rare exceptions, such as his memorable *The Cruise of the Nona*, the subjects and quality of his books were determined less by choice than by the need for new titles to be turned out as frequently as possible, at the highest prices his publishers could be induced to pay. The major casualty was his reputation as a serious literary figure.

'Had he written just fifteen books instead of ten times that number', a literary critic comments, 'his achievement would be easier to discern'.[60] The loss to posterity was considerable. Belloc was a writer of major stature, who had it in his grasp to be greater still. The best of his poetry — much if it still unpublished or not available in its final form — hints at the heights to which he might have risen had he had fewer distractions.[61] The prose at times reads like poetry. Belloc is overdue to be rediscovered. The mystery is why it has taken so long.

Among the journals for which Belloc wrote following his arrival in London in 1897 was a liberal weekly, *The Speaker*. Established in 1886, in response to the crisis in the Liberal Party over Home Rule, *The Speaker* was being revitalised by a group of young Liberals. The group included some of Belloc's former associates from Oxford. *The Speaker* became a focus for Liberal opposition to the Boer War. In the eyes of

Belloc and the 'Little Englanders' who thought like him —
otherwise known as Liberal Nationalists — the war was being
fought in order to protect the international speculators and
investors who had financial interests in the mines of the
Transvaal. The Boers had had no honourable alternative
other than to defend themselves.

More broadly, the Liberal Nationalists opposed those
within the Liberal Party — luminaries of the stamp of
Asquith, Haldane and Grey — who saw themselves as imperi-
alists. *The Speaker* also reflected the disquiet of some Liberals
over leanings within the party towards the collectivist
solutions to social problems advocated by, among others, T.H.
Green. Meanwhile, Belloc had decided on a political career,
and was establishing the political contacts within the radical
wing of the Liberal Party — Lloyd George prominent among
them — whose support enabled him to secure adoption as
the Liberal candidate for the South Salford constituency in
Manchester. He was elected to the House of Commons in the
great Liberal landslide of 1906. A telegram he sent to his
friends on the occasion reads 'This is a great day for the
British Empire, but a bad one for the little Bellocs'.[62]

Parliament

Belloc was now regarded widely as a coming man, for whom
a notable future could be expected. No less importantly, he
was regarded as a man who was now in a position to pursue
the implementation of the distributist thinking of which he
had so long been the most outspoken advocate. There was a
considerable build-up of expectations, not least by Belloc of
himself. 'I am already predicting', a Catholic priest of his
acquaintance wrote to him, 'that if the Liberals remain in
office for five years, and are again returned to power, you will
hold Cabinet rank in the second administration'.[63] In the
event, Belloc was to have no more success as an MP than at
Oxford or the *Morning Post*. In parliament, his initial enthusi-
astic support for the Liberal government was dampened by
the exigencies and compromises of parliamentary life. The
government may similarly have had dampened such enthusiasm as it may have entertained for his increasingly maverick
and wayward presence within its ranks.

Belloc's support for the key 1906 Education Bill was qualified by his belief that it failed to provide equal treatment for the instruction of Catholic children in their faith. 'The House', he stated, 'may tyrannically insist on their having less, but English Catholics cannot be content with less for their Catholic children than Catholic schools with Catholic teachers teaching the Catholic religion and impressing the children all the time'.[64] The no less important 1908 Licensing Bill incurred his criticism on the grounds that it was motivated by 'the principle that fermented liquor was a bad thing for the individual or for the state and in some way to be legislated against' rather than, as in his view should properly have been the case, the desire to resume control of the liquor industry and tackle the monopoly of tied or brewery-controlled public houses.[65]

Belloc escaped a showdown between his reservations about the legislation and his party loyalties when the government became tired of the incessant debates and amendments and allowed the bills to lapse. In the sphere of imperial policy and foreign affairs, he was let off less lightly. His handling of the topic exposed him to charges of — to put it no higher — inconsistency.

Belloc opposed imperialism on principle, and was condemnatory of the abuses in which it involved Britain. His maiden speech was critical of the government for failing to halt the flow of Chinese labourers to the goldfields in the Transvaal, which in opposition the Liberals had denounced and undertaken to remedy. Later he attacked the government's acquiescence to sentences of imprisonment and flogging and execution imposed on villagers in Egypt by a special tribunal following a riot in the Nile Delta village of Denshawai; the enforcement in India of regulations prohibiting public meetings and providing for the deportation without trial of agitators; and delay in the granting of Home Rule for Ireland.

He then reversed himself by opposing calls from the Congo Reform Association for action by Britain to restrain the more than usually brutal exploitation of native labour in the Congo Free State by its Catholic ruler, King Leopold II of Belgium. In the face of widespread support for the association's call in Liberal circles, Belloc argued that no action should be taken. 'Such cruelties', he claimed, 'were inevitable whenever Europeans came into contact with primitive races "under our modern system of production".'[66]

Far from the Congo posing moral or humanitarian issues as claimed by the association — or the association's being genuinely disinterested or motivated other than by commercial concerns — the situation was one where Belloc believed:

> It is a square fight between two financial interests, the interests of old Leopold and the interests of those few merchants in this country who want to break down Leopold's monopoly and deal in rubber and gin with the enfranchised natives ... It is the opinion of experts that we shall be able to break down the barrier and pour cheap spirits from our ships into the Congo upon such a scale as will dwarf even the five million gallons we unload upon our own West African negroes.

Moreover, British power had so much declined as for Britain to no longer be confident of imposing its moral judgments on other nations. To attempt to do so where the outcome was uncertain would be inviting humiliation.[67]

Belloc's perhaps over-elaborate explanations largely fell on deaf ears. Having convicted himself in the eyes of the government and many of his colleagues of being unpredictable and unreliable, he was now seen to apply double standards: to have less stringent requirements for his fellow Catholics than for adherents of other faiths. The episode again exemplifies Belloc's capacity for snatching defeat from the jaws of victory. Had he focused more on his legitimate reservations as to the limits of British power, and less on denigrating the motives of Leopold's critics, he might have been judged less harshly.

Belloc's immediate differences with the government and his parliamentary colleagues were less important than his growing tendency to blame conspiracies for his personal frustrations and disappointments and the major political and social problems of the day. Wilson writes that in personal terms:

> Financiers were the bogey-men who had deprived his mother of her holdings on the Stock Market. 'Dons' were the men who had deprived his wife and children of a regular income, a cheap, substantial house and an orderly domestic life. Both categories of persons were to receive the most scathing Bellocian abuse for the next half-century.[68]

In the wider sphere, Belloc's long-standing distrust of the

'money power' was now much more pronounced. He was convinced that England and Europe more generally were being manipulated from behind the scenes by 'a united plutocracy, a homogeneous mass of the rich, commercial and territorial, into whose hands practically all power, political as well as economic, has now passed'.[69]

By the time parliament was dissolved for the general election of January 1910, the coming man of four years earlier was taken much less seriously. When a further general election was called in December 1910, he declined to recontest his seat. Belloc now had nothing but contempt for the body to which he had so recently belonged. 'I am relieved', he observed in a parting shot, 'to be quit of the dirtiest company it has ever been my misfortune to keep'.[70]

Nor did he allow to escape unscathed the party leaders whose patronage he had previously courted. Lloyd George, he wrote, was 'the most odious type of man imaginable, a sham workman, loud-mouthed reformer on the make'.[71] Wilson believes that Belloc may have turned against Lloyd George in part because he was jealous of him. 'Can one doubt', he queries, 'that Belloc imagined, if the "Radicals" looked for a leader after 1906, they should have found it in the grandson of Joseph Parkes?'[72]

While the falling-out had its uses for distributism, in that it enabled Belloc to focus the more closely on the thinking which shortly was given expression in *The Servile State*, there were also major adverse consequences. So great was Belloc's bitterness towards his former associates and the parliament more generally, as to rule out any dispassionate consideration on how distributism might now most usefully be furthered. Former friends and potential distributist sympathisers such as the Liberal MP Charles Masterman — a one-time committed socialist and Anglo-Catholic social activist, who became a minister in Asquith's government — were needlessly alienated, and, in the case of Masterman, subjected to a systematic and unscrupulous harassment which ultimately cost him his political career.

That the needy and dispossessed whose interests distributism was intended to champion were in any way helped by excluding Masterman from parliament was, to say the least, not self-evident. Belloc and those who were most sympathetic to his predicament were laying about them so venomously as to court a comprehensive isolation of distributism from mainstream politics. How deep their rejection of parliament ran — and how little regard they had for its implications in terms of bringing about the new distributist social order on which their hopes increasingly centred — became apparent with the appearance of a further book, *The Party System*, which he and Cecil Chesterton wrote in 1911. *The Party System* marked a turning point, at which the future of the British distributism was in effect mortgaged to narrowly anti-parliament sentiments, with consequent contradictions from which the movement was never able to free itself.

The party system

Belloc and Cecil took as their subject what was wrong with parliament and how it should be put right. The first half of the book is thought to have been Cecil's work, and the second to have been by Belloc.[73] Belloc was writing from his first-hand experience as an MP. Cecil had addressed himself to the topic earlier on, in 1910, in a book of his own: *Party and People: A Criticism of the Recent Elections and their Consequences.*

If in the eyes of the two friends the plutocracy was the author of much of what troubled Britain, the parliament and the parties were only marginally less culpable. Belloc and Cecil saw the parliament as being manipulated from within in the same conspiratorial manner as the plutocracy manipulated the affairs of the nation more generally. In the first instance, what purported to be the rivalry between the front benches of the respective parties was in reality a fraud, directed at concealing from the public the mutual understanding of the two sides that each was entitled to its turn of 'office and emolument'.[74]

The Party System argued that what occurred in practice was that 'unreal issues, defined neither by the people nor by the Parliament, but by the politicians' were raised from time to time in order to give 'a semblance of reality to their empty competition'.[75] There was now no difference of economic interest or political principle between the front benches such as would distinguish them from one another in any meaningful sense along party lines. What Belloc and Cecil saw as this 'one close oligarchical corporation' — as 'a political committee for which no official name exists (for it works in secret), but which may be roughly called "The Front Benches"'[76] — selected its members for itself, without reference to the will of either parliament or the people.[77] The matter was put in a nutshell by Gilbert Chesterton in his memoirs. 'There were not two real parties ruling alternately', the memoirs read, 'but one real group, "the Front Benches", ruling all the time ... Parliament had come to mean only a secret government by the rich'.[78]

Belloc and Cecil were concerned finally by what *The Party System* saw as the corruption of parliament by 'secret funds'. These included funds raised for the Front Benches by their respective party organisations through 'the sale of peerages, baronetcies, knighthoods and other honours in return for subscriptions'.[79] They also included the proceeds of 'a much more serious traffic in policies'. 'Many rich men', *The Party System* noted, 'subscribe secretly to Party Funds in order to get a "pull" or a measure of control over the machine which governs the country — sometimes to promote some private fad of their own, but more often simply to promote their commercial interests'.[80] Cecil Rhodes, for example, had contributed 'sums running into tens of thousands' to the Liberal Party funds in return for an undertaking that a Liberal government would maintain British rule in Egypt and favour a Cape to Cairo railway.[81]

'That is the party system as it exists today', *The Party System* concluded, 'and by it the House of Commons has been rendered null, and the people impotent and without a voice'.[82] The downside of all this was that it stored up future dilemmas for distributism in determining whether to be a political or a social movement. Was the option of a social movement to be adopted purely as a consequence of rejecting parliament and the party system? And, if so, how effective — how whole-hearted and accordingly how energised — was the social movement model likely to be if adopted more for negative than for positive reasons? If on the other hand the political movement model was preferred, could it — given the hostility of the founder distributist to parliament and the party system — be other than half-hearted and ineffectual? In these circumstances, it is not surprising that the distributists vacillated so greatly over which path to take.

The servile state

It was from the ruin of Belloc's prospects for a brilliant parliamentary career and his loss of faith in the party system and its leaders that his greatest accomplishment now emerged, with the publication of *The Servile State* in 1912. That the impact of the book was immediate and extensive has been widely recognised. 'I cannot overestimate the impact of this book on my mind', writes Reckitt, 'and in this I was but symptomatic of thousands of others'.[83] Belloc's contribution to *Essays in Liberalism* in 1897 had given eloquent expression to his concerns over the servitude to which he believed capitalism — 'the evil plant' as he came to term it[84] — had reduced its workers, and the even greater servitude which would result from a reform of the social order along socialist lines.

Fifteen years later, these concerns had undergone a significant change of emphasis. Belloc now no longer believed that there was any likelihood of the socialists achieving their objectives. Nor did he believe that capitalism in its current form could survive what he saw as its inherent instability. What he now argued and profoundly feared was that the attempt by socialists to create an ideal socialist society — 'the Socialist ideal, in conflict with and yet informing the body of Capitalism'[85] — would instead have the totally different and perverse outcome of a society where 'those who do not own the means of production shall be legally compelled to work for those who do, and shall receive in exchange a security of livelihood'.[86]

As Gilbert Chesterton was once again to summarise succinctly: 'The compromise will take the form of saying "We must feed the poor; we won't rob the rich; so we will have the rich to feed the poor, handing them over to be the permanent servants of a master-class, to be maintained whether they are working or no, and in return for that complete maintenance giving a complete obedience".'[87] It was capitalism in this new form — and not, as is so often mistakenly supposed, socialism — that Belloc called 'the Servile State'.

Belloc argued in the opening chapters of *The Servile State* that, for the greater part of European history, the basis of the social order — the 'one fundamental institution whereupon the whole of society reposes' — had been slavery.[88] The coming of Christianity had set in motion a protracted evolutionary change, so that, by the Middle Ages, slavery had given way to what was largely 'a society of owners'. Belloc also called it 'the Distributive State' and 'the Proprietary State'. The new order had as its basis 'the three forms under which labour was exercised'. They were 'the serf, secure in his position, and burdened only with regular dues, which were but a fraction of his produce; the freeholder, a man independent save for money dues, which were more of a tax than a rent; the Guild, in which well-divided capital worked co-operatively for craft production, for transport and for commerce'.[89] This was not to say that a completely free distributive state had been reached, but rather that it was in the process of formation.

The Reformation had then arrested the further development of the distributive state — of 'this excellent state of affairs which we had reached after many centuries of Christian development, and in which the old institution of slavery had been finally eliminated from Christendom'[90] — and brought about its replacement by capitalism:

> For a society in which the determinant mass of families were owners of capital and land; for one in which production was regulated by self-governing corporations of small owners; and for one in which the misery and insecurity of a proletariat was unknown, there came to be substituted the dreadful moral anarchy against which all moral effort is now turned, and which goes by the name of *Capitalism*.[91]

Capitalism was in Belloc's view 'a society in which the ownership of the means of production is confined to a body of free citizens not large enough to make Property a general character of that society, while the rest are dispossessed of the means of production, and are therefore proletarian'.[92] 'The essential of Capitalism', Belloc later added, 'is a refusal to the many of Property *in significant amounts*'.[93]

The arrival of the Industrial Revolution in a capitalist society rather than in a society of owners — 'upon a people which had already largely lost its economic freedom' — caused the industrial system to assume a capitalist form rather than the co-operative form which in Belloc's view would otherwise have eventuated. The origins of this misfortune were in England:

> It was in England that the Industrial System arose. It was in England that all its traditions and habits were formed; and

because the England in which it arose was already a Capitalist England, modern Industrialism, wherever you see it at work today, having spread from England, has proceeded upon the Capitalist model.[94]

Even so, capitalism was inherently unstable, 'because its social realities were in conflict with all existing or possible systems of law, and because its effects in denying sufficiency and security were intolerable to men'. An alternative was required: 'to wit, the establishment of some stable form of society whose law and social practice should correspond, and whose economic results, by providing sufficiency and security, should be tolerable to human nature'.[95]

Belloc believed that there was a choice in theory between three options: a socialist or collectivist society; a distributive state or 'society of owners'; and the servile state. The choice was in practice more restricted, as there was no likelihood that the socialist objective — 'the placing of the means of production in the hands of the political officers of the community, to be held in trust for the advantage of all'[96] — would be achieved. In as much as the means of production might to a limited extent be taken out of the hands of their present owners, the owners would be fully compensated for their losses and their position relative to the great majority of the community who had little or no property would remain as privileged as before. Belloc maintained that:

> When Municipal and State enterprise accompanied by Municipal and State Regulation is based upon loans instead of Confiscation, nay, loans devised to avoid Confiscation, it is the negation of Socialism ... Attempts to mask the character of such operations by the machinery of sinking funds and the rest are logically worthless. You cannot 'buy out' Capitalism.[97]

What was more likely to occur — and was in fact already occurring — was that the socialists would settle for the achievement of a security and sufficiency of income for working people consonant with the means of production remaining the property of their present owners.

In return, the many would be required by law to work for the benefit of the few — to observe contracts 'which one man was free to take or leave, but which the other man was not free to take or leave, because the second had for his alternative starvation'.[98] Therefore the workers would forfeit the surplus value created by their labour. The conditions workers experienced under such a system — how the system 'would administer, would pay wages, would promote, would pension off, would fine'[99] — would not seem to them to differ significantly from those to which they were already accustomed.

Nor was the loss of freedom it entailed likely to be unacceptable to them:

> The great mass of wage-owners upon whom our society now reposes understands as a present good all that will increase even to some small amount their present revenue and all that may guarantee them against those perils of insecurity to which they are perpetually subject. They understand and welcome a good of this kind, and they are perfectly willing to pay for that good the corresponding price of control and enregimentation, exercised in gradually increasing degree by those who are their paymasters.[100]

'The pursuit of this ideal Collectivist State which is bred of Capitalism', the argument continued, 'leads men acting upon a Capitalist society not towards the Collectivist State nor anything like it, but to that third utterly different thing — the Servile State'.[101]

> The future of industrial society, and in particular of English society, left to its own direction, is a future in which subsistence and security shall be guaranteed for the Proletariat in a status really, though not nominally, servile. At the same time, the Owners will be guaranteed in their profits, the whole machinery of production in the smoothness of its working, and that stability which has been lost under the Capitalist phase of society will be found once more.

'The internal strains which have threatened society during its Capitalist phase will be relaxed and eliminated', Belloc concluded, 'and the community will settle down upon the Servile basis which was its foundation before the advent of the Christian faith, from which that faith slowly weaned it, and to which in the decay of faith it naturally returns'.[102]

The distributive state

The Servile State was an eloquent plea by Belloc for the establishment of a distributive state — of a society of owners such as would arrest and reverse the impending return of the servile relationships of the past. When it came to saying precisely how so great a change could be brought about, Belloc was less forthcoming. The omission was one for which distributism was to pay a heavy price. As Belloc acknowledged freely in his *An Essay on the Restoration of Property* in 1936:

> I propose no general scheme for restoring freedom and property. All reform depends upon some clear doctrine postulated and developed. No reform (it would seem) can hope to prosper which does not advance a programme covering all the field. I have not attempted to do so.[103]

His uncharacteristic reticence reflected in the first instance an increasing pessimism as to whether the desire for property had not been eradicated so completely as to make reinstating it impossible.

Belloc argued in *The Servile State* that a generation had grown up which was 'definitely and hopelessly proletarian':

> The present instinct, use and meaning of property is lost to it: and this has two very powerful effects, each strongly inclining our modern wage-earners to ignore the old barrier which lay between a condition of servitude and a condition of freedom. The first effect is this: that property is no longer what they seek, no longer what they think is obtainable for themselves. The second effect is that they regard the possessors of property as a class apart whom they always must ultimately obey, often envy, and sometimes hate; whose moral right to so singular a position most of them would hesitate to concede, and many of whom now strongly deny, but whose position they, at any rate, accept as a known and permanent social fact, the origins of which they have forgotten, and the foundations of which they believe to be immemorial.[104]

His conclusion in his *An Essay on the Restoration of Property* was that 'The evil has gone so far that, though the preaching of a new doctrine is invaluable, the creation of a new and effective immediate machinery is impossible'.

'The restoration of Property', Belloc continued, 'must essentially be the product of a new mood, not a new scheme.

It must grow from seed planted in the breast. It is too late to reinfuse it by design, and our effort must everywhere be particular, local, and, in its origins at least, small'.[105] In Belloc's view, all that was possible for the present was to take such piecemeal and ameliorative action as might impede developments conducive to servility, and 'sow fresh seed, from whence the institution of property shall begin to re-arise'.[106]

The measures involved would aim at strengthening the position of family businesses such as those of small farmers, shopkeepers and craftsmen, and distributing property rights in larger enterprises among the greatest possible number of shareholders, including in particular their employees. There would be guilds — 'chartered and established by positive law' — through which the various categories of small businesses could protect their hard-won economic freedom.[107] Credit co-operatives and co-operative banks would provide an alternative source of credit to that of the conventional banks. What more all-embracing action might be required — how his 'new mood' might be created and his 'fresh seed' brought to flower — were matters Belloc now felt he could in good conscience leave to others.

Decline

Belloc's reticence about how the distributive state should be brought about was perhaps also due in part to a deepening personal unhappiness. His hopes and ambitions had by 1912 largely turned to ashes.[108] The comfortable income which he expected to inherit had failed to eventuate, and — relative to his friends and associates — he was chronically short of money. His greatness — perhaps genius — as a writer was compromised increasingly by the need to turn out what he regarded as pot-boilers for ready cash. Little of his wider promise as a young man had been fulfilled. Oxford, Fleet Street and now the parliament had successively rejected him. His love of liberty, his passionate individualism and his advocacy of a wider distribution of property were out of tune with times in which society was turning decisively to collectivist remedies for its festering social and economic difficulties.

Profoundly disillusioned as he had become with parliament and the party system — seeing as McCarthy puts it 'imperialist, protectionist and collectivist departures from the radical ideal as largely motivated by the opportunity for private gain and the yellow press and the disciplined political parties as the instruments used to advance such ends'[109] — it failed to occur to him that what he condemned might be in reality no more than the inevitable adaptation by the system and its leaders to new challenges and a radically altered economic and political environment. His alternative vision of Europe — in Wilson's words of 'a unified culture drawing its strength from Imperial antiquity which would purify and supplant the monied interests of both "democrats" and parliamentarians on the one hand and of international financiers' on the other[110] — largely fell on deaf ears.

Major personal misfortunes were to follow. Belloc's wife, Elodie, died before her time in 1914. His oldest son, Louis, was a casualty of the First World War in 1918, and another son, Peter, of the Second World War in 1941. Most of the friends who were closest to him — the brilliant constellation which included Maurice Baring, George Wyndham, Raymond Asquith, Lord Lucas, Philip Kershaw, John Phillimore and Cecil and Gilbert Chesterton — similarly predeceased him. Bereaved, disappointed and politically isolated — a prophet increasingly unheard — Belloc was reduced finally to applauding despots of the stamp of Mussolini and Franco.[111] Corrin notes that 'As late as 1939, Belloc could argue that Mussolini's fascists had saved Italy and the heart of Western civilisation from Communism and that Mussolini, in the process, had created "for the first time within living memory a guild system".'[112]

'The champion of democratic liberties in 1910', writes Speaight, 'became the champion of whoever, in any corner of Europe, decreed or threatened the death of parliamentary institutions'.[113] In the United States, Belloc identified himself publicly with the notorious Father Charles Coughlin, whose high profile as the rabidly anti-Semitic and pro-fascist 'Radio Priest' — and as a thorn in the side of the New Deal and the Roosevelt administration — was a major source of scandal and embarrassment, not least to his bishops and other fellow Catholics.[114] Meanwhile, the task of carrying forward the distributist cause had long since largely been taken over by Belloc's associates and other contemporaries. The shoulders which assumed the greater proportion of the burden were those of Gilbert Chesterton.

Gilbert Chesterton

5

The Missionary, the Doctrine and the Debates

The Chesterbelloc

GILBERT Chesterton and Belloc were introduced over a bottle of Moulin-a-Vent burgundy at the Mont Blanc Restaurant in Soho in 1900. The credit for bringing them together is claimed variously by Gilbert's lifelong friend E.C. Bentley, his future brother-in-law Lucian Oldershaw and his fellow writer F.W. Eccles. The story has Belloc complimenting Gilbert on his writing in the street outside the restaurant. 'You write very well, Chesterton' is said to have been his opening remark. Inside, the two men were immediately drawn to one another.

Such was the character of the conversation — Belloc 'talked into the night and left behind in it a glowing track of good things'[1] — that, as Gilbert has recalled, 'I was already conscious of a curious sympathy with him ... And when, on that night and many subsequent nights, we came to talking about the war, I found that the subconscious sympathy had something of real significance':

> Something of the same mystery united our minds; we were both Pro-Boers who hated Pro-Boers. Perhaps it would be truer to say that we hated a certain number of unimagina-

tive, unhistorical anti-militarists who were too pedantic to call themselves Pro-Boers. Perhaps it would be truer to say it was they who hated us. But anyhow that was the first link in the alliance ... It was from that dingy little Soho cafe, as from a cave of witchcraft, that there emerged the quadruped, the twinformed monster Mr Shaw has named the Chesterbelloc.[2]

The war in South Africa was only the first of the many causes in which Belloc and Gilbert were to be allied with one another. Belloc became in Gilbert's eyes 'the man who has made the greatest fight for good things of all the men of my time ... What he brought into our dream was this Roman appetite for reality and for reason in action, and when he came into the door there entered with him the smell of danger'.[3]

'Hilaire Belloc', writes Titterton, 'was to crystallise G.K.C.'s religious beliefs and give to Chesterton's fighting faith in the common man ... the shield of an economic doctrine and a social philosophy'.[4] The consequences for distributism were far-reaching. Gilbert was among the pre-eminent literary figures of his day. He was also an outstanding working journalist, who by choice gave priority to raising what he saw as the key issues of the day, in language which was readily accessible to the nascent mass newspaper-reading public.

Meanwhile, the case for Gilbert's Christian faith was set out in a series of more considered works which began with *Heretics* (1905) and *Orthodoxy* (1908) and culminated in *St Thomas Aquinas* (1933). The leading Thomist scholar, Etienne Gilson, describes *St Thomas Aquinas* as 'without possible comparison the best book ever written about St Thomas'.[5] Gilbert's views on where the social order had gone wrong and how to remedy its errors were given forceful expression in *What's Wrong with the World* (1910) and *The Outline of Sanity* (1926). The novels which began making their appearance — popular favourites and enduring best-sellers of the stature of *The Napoleon of Notting Hill* (1904), *The Man Who Was Thursday* (1908), *The Ball and the Cross* (1910), *Manalive* (1912), *The Flying Inn* (1914) and the much-loved Father Brown detective stories — had an underlying serious-ness of purpose and raised significant questions in ways which were readily accessible to their readers.

His appearances on public platforms attracted substantial audiences, as did also, towards the end of his life, his broadcasts for the BBC. For all his great popularity, his attitude to himself had an endearing quality of self-deprecation. Disqualified on medical grounds from military service in the First World War, he found himself on one occasion asked by a young woman handing out white feathers in Fleet Street why he was not out at the Front. 'My dear madam', the conspicuously overweight Gilbert replied, 'if you will step round this way a little, you will see that I am'.[6]

'While there here are no jokes against small property', wrote Gilbert, 'there are jokes against me. They range from the ancient but admirable story that my old-world chivalry prompted me to give up my seat to three ladies to the more recent and realistic anecdote, which tells how my neighbours remonstrated with a noisy local factory, pleading that "Mr Chesterton can't write", and received the serene reply "Yes. We are aware of that".[7] Summing up his output as a writer, Gilbert concluded that 'my real judgement of my own work is that I have spoilt a number of good ideas in my time'.[8] A more outstanding recruit for the distributist cause is hard to imagine, nor could Belloc have hoped for an associate whose qualities more precisely complemented his own.

If Belloc was the philosopher king of distributism and Cecil the warrior priest, Gilbert was its St Francis. His role was to win over by force of reason and advocacy — in particular, by the use of the parables and paradoxes in which he so conspicuously revelled and excelled — converts for the new gospel of distributism. While as trenchant in argument as either Cecil or Belloc, he largely eschewed their acrimony. The qualities which motivated his distributism were conscience and compassion.

'His continual criticism of the society in whch he lived', writes the historian Margaret Canovan, 'resolves itself into one fundamental point: the incompatability of riches and poverty with the fundamental equality of man'.[9] He honoured and was honoured by many such as Shaw, to whose beliefs he saw distributism as being most robustly opposed. His characteristic good humour, warmth and humanity — reminiscent as they were in so may respects of the work of Charles Dickens, which he so greatly admired — repeatedly kept alive distributism when its demise seemed imminent. So closely was distributism identified with Gilbert that it is often mistakenly supposed to have died with him.

Gilbert's politics

Like Cecil and so many of their contemporaries, Gilbert initially described himself as a socialist. As with these close associates and friends, his motive was outrage and pity over the abject destitution of great numbers of his fellow citizens, and the indifference to the predicament of the poor on the part of so many of those who were more fortunate. 'I called myself a Socialist', he was to write in his memoirs, 'because the only alternative to being a Socialist was not being a Socialist. And not being a Socialist was a perfectly ghastly thing. It meant being a small-headed and sneering snob, who grumbled at the rates and the working-classes; or some hoary horrible old Darwinian who said that the weakest must go to the wall'.[10]

Where Gilbert differed from Cecil and most of his fellow Fabians was over his understanding of socialism. Unlike Cecil, Gilbert was never — or, at the most, only very briefly — a state socialist. The socialism he favoured was more akin to that of Ludlow and the founder Christian socialists. 'The points in which Christian and Socialistic collectivism are at one are simple and fundamental', he wrote shortly before the turn of the century. 'That the main trend of Jesus' character', he continued, 'was compassion for human ills, that he denounced not merely covetousness but riches again and again, and with almost impatient emphasis, and that he insisted on his followers throwing up personal aims and sharing funds and fortune entirely, these are plain matters of evidence presented again and again, and, in fact, of common admission'.[11]

The distinction between state socialism — 'modern socialism', as he rather saw it — and Christianity was explored in a note written about the time when he was being introduced to his future wife, Frances Blogg, in 1896. It reads:

> The modern socialist is saying 'What will society do?' while his prototype, as we read said 'What shall I do?'. Properly considered, this latter sentence contains the whole essence of the earlier Communism. The modern socialist regards his theory of regeneration as a duty which society owes to him, the early Christian regarded it as a duty he owed to society; the modern socialist is busy framing schemes for its fulfilment, the early Christian was busy considering whether he would himself fulfil it there and then; the ideal

of modern socialism is an elaborate Utopia to which he hopes the world may be tending, the ideal of the early Christian was an actual nucleus 'living the new life' to whom he might join himself if he liked.

While Gilbert later on in the same passage takes to task William Morris's *News from Nowhere* for failing to say how 'the give-and-take cameraderie' of its ideal state would be brought about, his sympathy with Morris is plain.[12] Morris's core belief that 'Education towards Revolution seems to me to express in three words what our policy should be' — that making socialists must necessarily precede the making of the socialist social order — was one which Gilbert could readily identify with and applaud.[13]

That Gilbert's debt to Morris was in no sense unique is evident from other leading distributists such as Titterton. The affinities and continuities between Morris's associative and communitarian socialism and distributism — 'What Socialism meant to us when Morris was still alive, when Hyndman was in full vigour, when Blatchford was starting *The Clarion*, and when 'England Arise' was sung at every Socialist meeting'[14] — were given eloquent expression by Titterton in his contributions to *G.K.'s Weekly*.

'William Morris', wrote Titterton, 'was our representative man, and he today would call himself a Distributist and write for *G.K.'s Weekly*':[15]

> In our Socialist State there were to be no inspectors! ... We were to be a nation of craftsmen and husbandmen (I am afraid the emphasis was on craftsmen) each living his own life in his own house or workshop, or on his own farm. It was, in all essentials, such a state as the Distributist desires. Somehow not only capitalism, but commercialism with its monstrous machinery would have disappeared. That was our ideal: Morris' *News from Nowhere* secured, not a beautiful dream, but a reasonable perspective, and, for most of us, Bellamy's *Looking Backwards* was a horrible nightmare. We wanted freedom, fellowship, and the chance of doing fine work.[17]

'It was *News from Nowhere* we wanted and sang about', Titterton concluded. 'It was a fine time that, and the vision which possessed us might at last have captured England, too. If we had not met Sidney Webb!'[17]

However, by the turn of the century, communitarian and associative socialism had so much been abandoned in favour of state socialism by the Fabian socialist mainstream as for Gilbert to feel that the word 'socialist' no longer properly conveyed his position. 'He had begun feeling after a more Christian arrangement of society than Socialism offered', writes Ward, 'and particularly after an arrangement better suited to the nature of man'.[18] It was in this sense of rejecting state socialism that Gilbert now decided to cease being what he termed 'a reluctant socialist', and instead to describe himself, like his family before him, as a Liberal.[19]

That the overt exchange of affiliations was probably a less drastic break than has generally been supposed requires some explanation. 'Liberalism', as Sheridan Gilley rightly emphasises, 'is now so identified with laissez-faire Capitalism that it is difficult to re-capture its affinities in the Edwardian era with the Socialism which shared both its rejection of tradition and authority and its hopefulness about the future.[20]

In adopting as Gilbert now did a position much more closely aligned with that of the Liberal Nationalists with whom he was working on *The Speaker*, he was in no way renouncing his former associative and communitarian beliefs. What Liberal Nationalism gave him as well was more congenial company and a doctrine which in key respects anticipated the distributism to which his life was later so largely to be devoted. The opposition of the Liberal Nationalists to the Boer War and imperialism apart, they favoured the classic Radical Liberal platform of the 1880s: more widespread ownership of land, mutualist as opposed to collectivist institutions, free trade, Home Rule for Ireland, Disestablishment of the Church and free public education — to which Gilbert also adhered.

Nor, in turning his back on the state socialism of Cecil and the Fabian mainstream, had Gilbert in any sense rejected the permeation and propaganda tactics on which the Fabians had so far relied to achieve social reform. On the contrary, while the Liberal Nationalists were small in number, Gilbert saw them as having a prophetic role within and beyond the Liberal Party. 'It is while we are in the desert', he wrote, 'that we must have the vision: we being a minority, must all be philosophers: we must think for both parties in the state'.[21] His undiminished faith in permeation and propaganda likewise prompted Gilbert to work vigorously for the Christian Social Union — the socialist-minded body which he and Cecil joined in 1901 at the instigation of Conrad Noel — and also for the much more outspokenly socialist Church Socialist League to which Noel and Cecil gravitated in 1906, and of whose London Branch Gilbert was subsequently a member. The League's platform reads:

> The Church Socialist League consists of Church people who accept the principles of socialism. viz.: The political, economic and social emancipation of the whole people, men and women, by the establishment of a democratic commonwealth in which the community shall own the land and capital collectively and use them for the good of all.

The League's principles were:

1 The Church has a mission to the whole of human life, social and individual, material and spiritual.

2 The Church can best fulfil its social mission by acting in its corporate capacity.

3 To this end the members of the League accept the principles of socialism.

4 Socialism is a fixed principle according to which the community should own the land and capital collectively and use them co-operatively for the good of all.[22]

As has been seen, while Cecil was still at this stage a state socialist, and would therefore have read the reference to 'the community' as being synonymous with the state, Gilbert's views were closer to those of their fellow members for whom the significance of 'community' was associative and communitarian.

The diversity of opinion within the league has been recalled by George Lansbury, the Labour MP who was to lead the Labour Party between 1933 and 1935. Lansbury writes in regard to the inaugural meeting of the league in London:

> I also helped form the Church Socialist League. We were a small and very mixed band of adventurers, who some years ago, gathered in Egerton Swann's rooms at Paddington. We were all rebels against the Capitalist system: this was the one and only thing we agreed about. Some of us, like G.K. Chesterton, were strong individualists. Others were fanatical Guild Socialists, others Syndicalists.

'The Countess of Warwick, Lewis Donaldson, Conrad Noel, T.C. Gobat, J. West, Percy Widdrington and others were Parliamentarians', Lansbury concludes, 'but very few had any faith in the Labour Party'.[23]

Gilbert spoke widely from CSU and CSL platforms and was a contributor to the CSL's journal, *The Church Socialist Quarterly* (previously *The Optimist*), until it ceased publication in 1911. The Patriots Club, which he, Noel, Oldershaw and Masterman founded in 1902, likewise had permeative and propagandist objectives, with a special emphasis on directing attention to poverty.[24] When, in 1909, Beatrice Webb and the Fabians formed their National Committee for the Breakup of the Poor Law — a quintessentially permeative and propagandist body — Gilbert was among the distinguished company of literary figures, economists, clergymen, trade unionists and Liberal, Labour and Tory MPs who sponsored it.

Gilbert's actions and affiliations — as opposed to his often hardline anti-socialist rhetoric[25] — contradict the view that he was hostile to socialism in its broad sense, rather than to the state socialism in the Fabian mould over which he and Cecil had been arguing virtually since their schooldays. Like Manning before him, Gilbert was capable of distinguishing very clearly between 'what is called socialism', as *De Rerum Novarum* had condemned it, and the largely mutualist 'nominal socialism' as it was still widely understood in Britain. Where Gilbert differed from Manning and *De Rerum Novarum* was in his pragmatic view that confusion should be minimised by reserving the word 'socialist' for state socialism, and having a new name for the vision of an alternative associative and communitarian social order towards which Belloc in particular was now working his way. That name was 'distributism'.

If, for the time being, Lansbury and his associates had lost their faith in the Labour Party, Gilbert was no less disillusioned with the Liberals. Like Cecil and Belloc, he had worked hard for the Liberal Party and its candidates at the 1906 elections, and had supposed his hopes for social reform to be on the point of fulfilment with the return of a Liberal government which had the largest working majority of any government since 1832. The Liberals now had 377 seats in the House of Commons, as opposed to 157 for the Tories, 53 for the Labour Party and 83 for the Irish Nationalists. The new Liberal MPs included both Belloc and Masterman, as well as Gilbert's other fellow writers, Leo Chiozza Money, who was yet another prominent Fabian, and P.W. Wilson. 'Radicalism and socialism alike', writes the historian, Sir Robert Ensor, 'were radiant with sudden hopes of a new heaven and a new earth'.[26]

In the event — failing as it did to reconcile the competing demands of higher living standards and higher outlays for armaments with the reduced means consequent on Britain's declining share of world trade, frustrated at every turn by the entrenched, bloody-minded and irresponsible Tory majority in the House of Lords, and deeply factionalised within itself — the government accomplished few of the things the reformers expected of it.[27] The effect in the long term was such that 1906 is now seen as having been the victory from which the Liberal Party has never recovered.

More immediately, Belloc and both the Chesterton brothers largely lost confidence in parliament. Other Liberals such as Masterman came to see government less as a crusade than as a career. 'I have not lost my faith in the least', Gilbert wrote in 1908; 'my faith in fundamentals is exactly what it was. What I have lost is my old childlike faith in practical politics ... As much as I ever did, more than I ever did, I believe in Liberalism. But there was a rosy time of innocence when I believed in Liberals'.[28]

That the disillusionment Gilbert and his associates experienced was in no sense unique is evident from the great upsurge of syndicalist sentiment and industrial militancy which extended without significant respite — other than during the war — from around 1910 until its culmination in the General Strike of 1926. Cheated as artisan and lower middle-class households now saw themselves to have been of reform through parliament, and with their purchasing power eroded increasingly by the then current combination of stagnant wages and rising prices, they turned increasingly to direct action as the only practical means of obtaining redress for their grievances.

The repeated refusal by the House of Lords to pass Lloyd George's 1909 Budget led trade unionist circles to query widely: 'If the peers may sabotage the Constitution for their own purposes, why may not we?'[29] A similar willingness to resort to direct action on the part of elements of the middle and upper classes was reflected in the industrial lockouts of the day, and the fomenting of agitation such as resulted in the Curragh mutiny in 1914, when the commanding officer of the 3rd Cavalry Brigade and 56 of his subordinates elected to defy orders and sacrifice their careers rather than be involved in measures to force the Ulster Protestants into accepting Home Rule in Ireland. It was against this backdrop of social turmoil that Gilbert's distributist beliefs were refined and his commitment to them hardened, and that the history of the distributist movement now unfolded.

Doctrine

The emergence of distributism as a distinct doctrine dated from the appearance of Belloc's *The Servile State* in 1912. For all that there was extensive further discussion about what was involved in distributism, its fundamental character did not undergo significant alteration after that date. However, there was still no textbook or program to explain to the public what a distributist social order would look like, how it would be brought about and in what specific respects the lot of ordinary people would be improved. The omission was not rectified in the lifetimes of either Belloc or Gilbert Chesterton, for all their repeated undertakings to their associates that something would be done about it.

It was only Cecil who made some attempt to spell out the detailed information for which both supporters and critics of distributism were clamouring. Once Cecil was dead, and Belloc had become less active following — among other things — Elodie's death, Gilbert was left as effectively the main conduit through which the distributist idea could be brought to public attention, and the distributist movement inspired and energised. What then was it that he saw distributism as standing for? What alternative did it offer those of his fellow countrymen who detested capitalism but were neither socialists nor Liberals?

Hostile as Gilbert for his own part was to state socialism, he was no less hostile to capitalism. He was saddened and angered by what he saw as the consequences of capitalism — that, in Gilley's words, 'The poor, decanted from the countryside to vast and squalid cities, reduced to subsistence wage levels and entrapped in the soulless mechanical routines of the factory, had been re-enserfed, indeed were being re-enslaved'.[30]

'Capitalism', writes Dermot Quinn, 'was not a synonym for ownership or property, both of which Chesterton favoured. Rather, its chief characteristic was to deny property to most people, reducing them to servility'.[31] A notable passage from Gilbert's *What's Wrong with the World* reads: 'It is a negation of property that the Duke of Sutherland should have all the farms in one estate; just as it would be a negation of marriage if he had all our wives in one harem'.[32] So much did the harem analogy appeal to Gilbert that he frequently repeated it. 'It is my whole point', he wrote in a special pilot issue of *G.K.'s Weekly* in 1924, 'that to say we must have Socialism or Capitalism is like saying we must choose between all men going into monastries and a few men having harems'.[33]

For Gilbert, as for Belloc, state socialism, communism and capitalism were for all practical purposes the same system by different names:

> Capitalism and Communism are twin systems, resting as they do on the same idea — the centralisation of wealth and, its corollary, the abolition of private property. It is immaterial that they differ on where they wish to centralise this wealth — Communism in the state, and Capitalism in the hands of the most powerful plutocrats; both succeed in crushing the small individual by taking his property from him.[34]

'The truth', Gilbert insisted, 'is that what we call Capitalism ought to be called Proletarianism. The point is not that some people have capital but that most people have only wages because they do not have capital'.[35]

Gilbert also argued that 'The present system, whether we call it capitalism or anything else, especially as it exists in industrial countries, has already become a danger; and is rapidly becoming a death-trap'.[36] Like Hyndman and the SDF before him, he saw clearly the contradiction which would inevitably cause the system to fail:

> When most men are wage-earners, it is more and more difficult for most men to be customers. For the capitalist is always trying to cut down what his servant demands, and in doing so is cutting down what his customer can spend. As soon as his business is in any difficulties, as at present in the coal business, he tries to reduce what he has to spend on

wages, and in doing so reduces what others have to spend on coal. *He is wanting the same man to be rich and poor at the same time.*

'This contradiction in capitalism does not appear in the earlier stages, because there are still populations not reduced to the common proletarian condition', Gilbert concluded, 'But as soon as the wealthy as a whole are employing the wage-earners as a whole, this contradiction stares them in the face like an ironic doom and judgement'.[37]

The alternative — the establishment of a distributist social order — was an undertaking which Gilbert saw as being of truly revolutionary proportions. A memorable passage from his *What's Wrong with the World* in 1910 reads:

> The thing to be done is nothing more or less than the distribution of the great fortunes and the great estates. We can now only avoid Socialism by a change as vast as Socialism. If we are to save property, we must distribute property, almost as sternly and sweepingly as did the French Revolution.[38]

What then was Gilbert's vision of distributism — of 'the theory that private property is proper to every private citizen'[39] — and how was it to be brought about?

Over and above the origins of Gilbert's distributist convictions in his detestation of capitalism, they were squarely a product of his Christian faith. In as much as he saw all mankind as being of divine origin, of equal worth in the eyes of God and equally endowed with free will, it followed for him that they were also equally entitled to liberty and to the right to property through which alone liberty could be guaranteed. The Catholic social doctrine teachings of *De Rerum Novarum* to which Belloc introduced him were in this sense not new to him, but simply reinforced and clarified conclusions of his own, and showed him how they could be put into effect.

'The truth', wrote Gilbert, 'is this; and it is extremely, even excruciatingly simple':

> Either Private Property is good for Man or it is bad for Man. If it is bad, let us all immediately become honest and coura-geous Communists ... But if it is good for Man it is good for Everyman. There is a case for Capitalism; a case for Landlordism; a case for complete Despotism; ... there are

arguments for Trusts, for Squires, for big employers. But they are all arguments against Private Property. They are all more or less philosophical reasons why a man, as such, should not be an owner, as such; why the tenant should not own his house; why the workman should not own his workshop; why the farmer should not own his farm.

'The moment Private Property becomes a privilege', Gilbert summed up, 'it ceases to be private property'.[40]

Nor was Gilbert in any doubt that distributism had room for diversity:

> Even my Utopia, would contain different things of different types holding on different tenures ... There would be some things nationalised, some machines owned corporately, some guilds sharing common profits, and so on, as well as many absolute individual owners, where such individual owners are most possible ... Even while we remain industrial, we can work towards industrial distribution and away from industrial monopoly .... we can try to own our own tools ... In so far as the machine cannot be shared, I would have the ownership of it shared; that is, the direction of it shared, and the profits of it shared.[41]

One of the ways of achieving his distributist objectives which Gilbert favoured was by establishing co-operatives. As Quinn points out, 'Co-operatives were essential to the Distributist ideal. They combined ownership, labour for profit, reward for initiative, a degree of self-sufficiency, elimination of waste (as in duplication of equipment or use of unnecessary middlemen) and a strong commitment to reciprocal help'.[42]

Critics of distributism who held that the obstacles to it were insuperable tested Gilbert's patience. 'Why', he queried the writer Middleton Murry in 1932, 'do you say that there is no chance for this normal property and liberty?':

> You can only mean to say of our scheme exactly what you say about the Communist scheme. That it requires awful and inhuman sacrifices; that we must turn the mind upside-down; that we must alter the whole psychology of modern Englishmen. We must do that to make men Communists.

'Why', Gilbert asked Murry to explain, 'is it an answer to say we must do that to make them Distributists?'[43] What was needed most was to make a start. 'If we leave things as they are', Gilbert argued, 'there will almost certainly be a crash of confiscations. If we hesitate, we will soon have to hurry. But if we start doing it quickly we shall have time to do it slowly'.[44]

The debates

Meanwhile, what distributism meant was also clarified and publicised by the great debates between the distributists and the socialists with whom they differed so greatly but also had so much in common. The debates took place over a twenty-four year period, from 1903 until 1927. The main protagonists were Shaw and Gilbert. Hesketh Pearson — a leading literary critic of the day — sees Shaw and Gilbert as having been 'the debaters of the century'.[45] Their encounters shortly acquired the character of a distinctively British institution comparable with — if shorter-lived than — cricket, Morris dancing or the Proms.

The starting point of the debates was when Gilbert had 'a very pugnacious public argument' about religion in various periodicals of the day, with the veteran socialist leader, Robert Blatchford.[46] An arms-length exchange then took place at Cambridge in 1911, where Shaw initially addressed the Heretics Club at the Victoria Assembly Rooms on 'The Future of Religion' and Gilbert responded six months later at the Guildhall. Other highlights included their face-to-face confrontations in London at the Memorial Hall where Shaw and Gilbert spoke for the Fabian Society in 1911 on 'The Democrat, The Socialist and The Gentleman'; in the drawing-room of a family home where they debated privately — and thereby in the more frank and revealing terms — in 1923; and at the Kingsway Hall where the series culminated in 1927 with their debate for the Distributist League on 'Do We Agree?'

Interspersed with their appearances in person, there were further controversies between them in print, in which other leading political, literary and intellectual celebrities of the day also became involved. One key example was the controversy on the respective merits of socialism and distributism in Orage's *The New Age* from 1907 until 1909, which Shaw made memorable with his description of Belloc and Gilbert as a single monstrous entity, the 'Chesterbelloc'. The Chesterbelloc, Shaw claimed, was 'a very amusing pantomime elephant', the rear legs being Gilbert and the front 'Hilary Forelegs'.[47] This was not to say that the monster was necessarily benign or its influence on Gilbert beneficial. What Shaw meant when he created the Chesterbelloc is often misunderstood. The whole point was that the front and rear ends did not belong together and needed to be separated.

'Chesterton and Belloc', Shaw's account continues, 'are not the same sort of Christian, not the same sort of Pagan, not the same sort of anything intellectual. And that is why the Chesterbelloc is an unnatural beast which must be torn asunder to release the two men who are trying to keep step inside its basket-work'.[48] By 1923, Shaw's attitude had hardened. 'There dawned a day — a terrible day for you — when Hilaire Belloc came into your life', he told Gilbert in uncharacteristically acerbic terms when they debated privately in a London drawing room, 'Then indeed you were lost forever'.[49] He then listed the ways in which he believed Belloc had had an adverse influence on Gilbert, not least — as will be discussed in detail in Chapter 6 — by his anti-Semitism.

A second controversy appeared in *The New Witness* in 1916 and 1917, where what was initially another skirmish between Gilbert and Shaw drew in ultimately, in order of appearance, Belloc, Cecil, Hyndman and Wells. So much had Wells by then drifted away from the Fabians that he and Shaw directed their arguments as much at one another as at the distributists. As always, no matter who took part and whether they were on platforms or in periodicals, the main ingredients of these debates were Christianity, socialism and distributism. Only the proportions varied.

The flavour also stayed much the same, reflecting as it did the distinctive personalities of Shaw and Gilbert and their close relationship with one another. For all their more public differences of opinion — for all that the pantomime ostrich to which Shaw likened himself might fall out with the Chesterbelloc — Shaw and Gilbert were close friends who cared deeply about each other. In Shaw's view, Gilbert was 'a man of colossal genius'.[50] Shaw's admiration for Gilbert was given practical effect by encouraging Gilbert to develop the talents as a dramatist of which his play, *Magic*, affords so tantalising an intimation. Shaw regretted what he saw as Gilbert's failure to make greater use of his literary gifts. In as much as

Gilbert fell short of Shaw's hopes for him in this and other respects, Shaw laboured mightily to correct the deficiencies.

Such frustrations apart, when Gilbert died, Shaw was among those who mourned his loss most deeply. Shaw's were among the most laudatory of the innumerable tributes to his memory. 'It seems the most ridiculous thing in the world', Shaw wrote to Gilbert's widow Frances, 'that I, eighteen years older than Gilbert, should be heartlessly surviving him'.[51] Shaw also offered to help out Frances with any financial difficulties in which Gilbert's death might involve her. Gilbert, for his part, was admiring of Shaw. 'All the virtues he has are heroic virtues', he wrote. 'Shaw is like the Venus de Milo: all that there is of him is admirable'.[52]

He and Shaw each respected the other's fundamental sincerity and seriousness of purpose. Each acknowledged in the other a genuine and profound spirituality. They were united in their passionate condemnation of the capitalist social order which each in his own way sought to eliminate. 'To say I do not like the present state of wealth and poverty', Gilbert declared in the course of the debate in *The New Age*, 'is merely to say that I am not a devil in human form. No one but Satan or Beelzebub could like the present state of wealth and poverty'.[53] While Gilbert was critical of Shaw's predominantly state socialism, he acknowledged its moral character. To do otherwise, in his view, would have been 'as if one dismissed the sculpture of Michaelangelo and went on to his sonnets ... Socialism is the noblest thing for Bernard Shaw; and it is the noblest thing in him'.[54]

Shaw and his associates for their part saw distributism as differing only marginally from socialism, and sought to emphasise the common ground between them. For example, a key passage in regard to Gilbert and Belloc in Wells's contribution to the debate in *The New Age* reads: 'What we do all three want is something very alike':

> Our different roads are parallel. I aim at a growing collective life, a perpetually enhanced inheritance of our race, through the fullest, freest development of the individual life. What they are at ultimately I do not understand, but it is manifest that its immediate form is the fullest and freest development of the individual life. We all three hate equally and sympathetically the spectacle of human beings blown up with windy wealth and irresponsible power as

cruelly and absurdly as boys blow up frogs; we all three
detest the complex causes that dwarf and cripple lives from
the moment of birth and starve and debase great masses of
mankind. We want as much as possible the jolly life, men
and women warm-blooded and well-aired, acting freely and
joyously, gathering life as a child gathers corn-cockles in
corn. We all three want people to have property of a real
and personal sort, to have the son, as Chesterton puts it,
bringing up the port his father laid down, and pride in the
pears one has grown in one's own garden. And I agree with
Chesterton that giving — giving oneself out of love and
fellowship — is the salt of life.

'Differ as we may', Wells argued in extending his olive branch
to the distributists, 'Belloc and Chesterton are withall
Socialists in being on the same side of the great political and
social cleavage that opens at the present time. We and they
are with the interests of the mass of common men as against
the growing organisations of the great owners who have
common interests directly antagonistic to those of the
community and State'.[55]

Not least, Shaw and Gilbert were useful in practical terms
to one another. 'Shaw', writes the American scholar, William
Furlong, in his definitive account of the debates, 'welcomed
G.K.C. as a godsend':

G.B.S. was badly in need of a first-class debating opponent.
By 1911, G.B.S. had lectured and debated on at least one
thousand recorded occasions. He had achieved such
awesome proficiency that later he would describe his
speaking ability as analogous to the pugilistic ability of his
friend Gene Tunney, the heavyweight champion. Tunney
had declared it criminal for a professional fighter to
engage a layman in fisticuffs, and G.B.S. was to write 'I
never challenged anyone to debate with me. It seemed an
unfair practice for a seasoned public speaker to challenge
a comparative novice to a duel with tongues, of no more
value than any other sort of duel'.[56]

Gilbert — eighteen years Shaw's junior and still on the
upward trajectory of his fame — needed an opponent of the
skill and stature of Shaw in order to hone his skills, enhance
his reputation and further enlarge his following.

That Gilbert's hopes for the debates were at least in this
sense fulfilled is evident from an account of the atmosphere

at his final encounter with Shaw in 1927. The account — by Titterton, who was one of the organisers — reads:

> Despite our meagre means of advertisements, the great hall was packed long before the debate began. And throughout the proceedings wild hordes of men and women struggled in the corridors and hurled themselves against the shut doors of the hall. Once a door burst open, the shouts from outside became a pandemonium, and the hot lava flowed down every alleyway. Then the doors shut with a clang and the speakers could be heard again.[57]

How the fracas came about has been described by its instigator, Ellis Roberts. Roberts writes: 'As a fat lady in diamonds was giving every indication of fainting on top of me, and as I had a ticket and no intention of missing the fun, I just started a riot. It was a successful riot, because they had to let us in to keep us quiet'.[58]

Intense public interest also led the then recently established BBC to broadcast the proceedings. The broadcast has been described as 'one of the most notable events of the first few months of the Corporation's existence'.[59] Titterton has a pertinent comment on the effect on listeners of the noise of the crowds seeking to be admitted. He writes: 'I don't know how much of that was heard in the broadcast. It must have sounded like a revolution'.[60]

What the debates amounted to was a truly magnificent showcase for both socialism and distributism to display what they had to offer to the public. The opportunity was the more important for the distributists, who had fewer outlets than the socialists for getting across their message. It is therefore the more extraordinary that the distributists did not put the opening to better use. While Gilbert and his associates criticised the state socialists broadly along the lines which Belloc set out in his *The Servile State*, and argued persuasively on theoretical lines why distributism would be the better system, they failed for the most part to take up the opportunity to spell out what a distributist social order would look like and how it could be brought about.

'No remedy of a defined, immediate sort, applicable to the legislature', Belloc freely acknowledged in *The New Age*, 'is comparable in its efficacy to the proposals of the Collectivists'.[61] Belloc's rejection of any obligation to be specific was already as explicit and unbending as thirty years later in his *An Essay on the Reconstruction of Property*. The omission enabled the socialists to respond to the charges against them with countercharges that the distributists had not thought through their proposals properly or were covering up what was really intended.

The failure of the distributists to make better use of the debates was the more apparent for the intimation of a different approach which Cecil provided in a contribution to *The New Witness* shortly before joining his unit in France. Why the distributist cause needed Cecil so much, how much he might have done for distributism had he lived, and the huge setback his death inflicted on distributism were never more obvious. Unlike Gilbert and Belloc, Cecil saw clearly that ordinary men and women wanted to be told in plain terms what distributism would mean to them, in what ways it would be directly relevant to the circumstances of their lives and what practical measures would be necessary to give it effect. He also recognised the futility of distributists trying to win over to their side a largely urban and industrialised society such as Britain with arguments which were stated largely in terms of their application to agriculture and the land.

His presentation began with a precise statement of what he saw to be the difference between state socialism and distributism. It reads in terms similar to those of Belloc or Gilbert:

> A Collectivist or Socialist is one who desires the means of production to be the property of the community and to be administered by its political officers. A Distributist is a man who desires that they should, generally speaking, remain private property, but that their ownership should be so distributed that the determining mass of families — ideally every family — should have an efficient share therein. That is Distributism, and nothing else is Distributism.

'Distributism', Cecil then emphasised much more trenchantly than had either Belloc or Gilbert, 'is quite as possible in an industrial or commercial as in an agrarian community'.

Taking up, as had neither Belloc nor Gilbert, the claim by Shaw that distributism could not distribute a factory owned by a major engineering firm of the day among the firm's workers — that it could not 'distribute Armstrong's works among Armstrong's men' — Cecil rejoined in a prescient passage that 'If Mr Shaw means, as I suppose he does, that it cannot distribute the ownership of the works, it might be as well to inquire first whether the ownership is distributed already':

> I am writing far from books of reference, but I must confess that I shall be surprised to learn that Armstrong's works are today the property of a single man named Armstrong. Perhaps they are the property of half a dozen Armstrongs, but I should think that the chances are that by this time they are the property of a limited company of some sort. That means that while the works are one the ownership is already widely distributed.

'I do not see', Cecil concluded to crushing effect, 'why it should be harder to distribute it among Armstrong's men than to distribute it among a motley crowd of country clergymen, retired Generals, Cabinet Ministers and maiden ladies such as provide the bulk of the share-list in most industrial concerns'.[62]

Here at last, after ten and more years of argument, the practicalities of the distributist model had finally begun to be stated, the case which might have enabled distributism to emerge victorious from the debates to be outlined, and Antigonish and Mondragon to be foreshadowed. Unhappily, Cecil's intervention came too late. By the time his contribution appeared in *The New Witness* — on 3 May 1917 — he had barely a year to live, and was to spend most of it in the trenches. He was never able to explore further the direction in which his thoughts would now logically have taken him, or participate further in the debates where what he now had to say might otherwise have had so salutory an effect. Moreover, as has been seen, the public shortly ceased to take the debates seriously. It was in a sense Shaw who had the last word as to the outcome of the debates. 'We three', he wrote later, in regard to himself, Gilbert and Wells, 'roar louder, and over wider circulations, and much more amusingly than Ruskin, Marx or Henry George. But nobody marks us'.[63]

Alternatively, the last word can be seen to have been had by Belloc. Closing the final debate — entitled 'Do We Agree?' — in his capacity as chairman, Belloc said 'In I do not know how many years — five, ten, twenty — this debate will be as antiquated as crinolines are':

> I am surprised that neither of the two speakers pointed out that one of three things is going to happen. One of three things: not one of two. It is always one of three things. This industrial civilisation which, thank God, oppresses only the small part of the world in which we are most inextricably bound up, will break down and therefore end from its monstrous wickedness, folly, ineptitude, leading to a restoration of sane, ordinary human affairs, complicated but based as a whole upon the freedom of citizens. Or it will break down and lead to nothing but a desert. Or it will lead the mass of men to become contented slaves, with a few rich men controlling them.

'Take your choice', Belloc concluded; 'You will all be dead before any of the three things come off. One of the three things is going to happen, or a mixture of two, or possibly a mixture of the three combined'.[64] Which of Belloc's three alternatives it was to be was now very much in the court of the distributists. It was for the distributist movement to now determine by what means and with what effect the message of distributism was to be communicated to the public.

Father
Vincent McNabb

6

Putting Distributism on the Map: the Distributist League and the Weeklies

Advocacy and argument

'ABOUT fifteen years ago', Gilbert recalled in his *The Outline of Sanity* in 1926, 'a few of us began to preach, in the old *New Age* and *New Witness*, a policy of small distributed property (which has since assumed the awkward but accurate name of Distributism), as we should have said then, against the two extremes of Capitalism and Communism'.[1] The operative word was 'preach'. The activity which the distributists most enjoyed — and where they were seen to best advantage — was being involved in and generating controversy.

The cut and thrust of debate was what made them feel most at home. The downside was that the debate was as vigorous between rival groups of distributists as it was with their external adversaries. Not least, their deliberations were inconclusive. The issue of what the objectives of the movement should be and whether it was preferable to pursue them as a political or a social movement was never resolved. British distributism remained, until the day its few remaining activists effectively put it into cold storage, a movement effectively paralysed by indecision.

The conflict was reflected in the two main avenues the distributists used to bring their message before the public. These were distributist bodies such as the Distributist League which began in 1926, and the distributist weeklies: *The Eye-Witness*, *The New Witness* and *G.K.'s Weekly*. As has been seen, the weeklies in particular also reflected extraneous prejudices such as anti-Semitism on the part of some distributists, and fantasies such as that fascism — at least in its Italian and Falangist forms — was compatible with or conducive to distributism.

The distributist bodies

The Distributist League was the successor to two earlier distributist bodies, the National League for Clean Government, which was active from its inception in 1913 to the outbreak of the War, and the New Witness League, which replaced it in 1918 and lasted into 1920. Both bodies functioned as a means of enabling *The New Witness* to strengthen the loyalties of its current readers and attract new ones. While both included promoting distributism among their objectives, their energies, like those of the paper, were intended primarily for unmasking corruption.

'We decided', writes Ada Jones in regard to the first meeting of the National League for Clean Government, 'to open with the exposure of the sale of honours, which at that period were bought and sold like pigs and pumpkins':

> The hall was crowded and the interest was intense. For the first time the actual facts of the secret traffic were to be openly stated. The speaker set forth prices with admirable lucidity, he might have been an auctioneer describing the advantages of a desirable two-storey residence or a country house. 'A peerage can be bought for sixty to eighty thousand pounds', was the opening remark, and I remember the stir that ran through the hall ... The speaker continued to explain that the price of the peerage depended upon the repute of the buyer: those with a shop soiled past being charged more than those with a cleaner record. To become a Baron an aspirant had to plonk down thirty thousand to fifty thousand pounds, while a mere Baronetcy went for ten thousand and a Knighthood fetched five. Curiously enough, Dukedoms were not

included in the Government Bargain Basement; possibly existing Dukes objected.

'We held meetings all over the country and our membership continued to grow', she concludes. 'I think that the League could have been revived after 1918, but Gilbert had not the particular qualities necessary to make such a challenging body a success'.[2]

Ada was not alone in seeing that, as a leader, Gilbert had his shortcomings. 'Life to Gilbert Chesterton', Titterton wrote in 1908, 'is a thing one stands before and argues about; if necessary fights about, but which one does not live'.[3] That little had changed twenty years later was noted by a prominent Distributist League member of the day — later the British Consul in New York and Ankara — James Walsh. 'You felt', writes Walsh, 'that good works were not necessary. It was enough to think up a few good ideas. GK did not back practical experiments. He was a man who shrank from action'.[4] The deficiency was especially frustrating to those within the movement such as Father McNabb, who were impatient to get on with creating the new distributist social order which might in time replace capitalism from within. What was needed, McNabb wrote to Pepler at Ditchling in 1931, was 'a desperately serious attempt to make some of the Distributists turn their hands from merely writing to doing'.

Broadly speaking, by the time the Distributist League arrived on the scene in 1926, the movement had within it three main subsets. They were, in the first instance, those distributists who wanted distributism to be a political movement which modelled itself on the Fabian Society and which would perhaps ultimately become an actual political party in much the same way as Wells had favoured the Fabian Society becoming a political party; secondly, those who wanted to actively engage in giving effect to distributist principles by means such as the establishment of credit unions and other co-operatives, where possible in conjunction with other community groups; and finally those who were interested either mainly or exclusively in building a distributist social order from the ground up through rural resettlement.

In summary, the distinctions were between a mainly political distributist movement, a hybrid movement combining political and social attributes and a movement whose objectives were exclusively social and agrarian. By and large, the purely — perhaps purist — political element was associated with the Central Office of the league and the league branches in London, and the hybrid model with the branches in provincial centres, while the rural resettlement model had adherents in both London and the provinces as well as among distributists who chose to remain outside the league.

London

The Distributist League — and the predominantly Fabian approach of its Central Office and branches in London — were the creation of a former captain in the Royal Marines, H.S.D. Went. 'Toby' Went — 'a staunch Anglo-Catholic of High Tory outlook'[5] — proposed that the new entity should conform to clear principles and aims. They were in summary that '(1) It should not be too closely linked with the paper, so that it could have a life and function of its own. (2) Its aims should be (a) to expose and eliminate political corruption; (b) to restore the liberties of the subject; (c) to prevent the establishment of the Servile State; (d) to work for the establishment of the Distributist State'.[6] 'My view', recalls Went, 'was that our first task was to propagate the Philosophy of Distributism and inspire practical men to action. I think I had in mind the method of the Fabian Society'.[7]

Titterton took Went's ideas to Gilbert, who then approved them. The Distributist League was formally founded at two public meetings in the Essex Hall in the Strand, respectively on 17 September and 2 October 1926. Gilbert was made the president for life and Belloc the vice-president for life, and Went became — albeit briefly — the secretary. *G.K.'s Weekly* then announced, on 6 November, that it would henceforth be the organ of the league, and that its price would be reduced from sixpence to twopence in order to recruit new readers and members. 'The paper', the announcement continued, 'has sufficed to found the League, the League may suffice to circulate the paper'.[8]

The Central Office of the league was initially in Essex Street, and then at premises in Rolls Court, near Chancery Lane which it shared with *G.K.'s Weekly*. George Heseltine shortly took over as secretary, and was given a personal assistant, Michael Sewell — later Father Brocard Sewell — who was also the office-boy and general factotum for *G.K.'s Weekly*. At the peak of the league's affairs around 1928, there may have been as many as 24 branches and up to 2000 members.[9] The branches were in Scotland as well as in England.

A research committee of the league, founded in late 1931 or early 1932, was responsible for inquiring into 'questions of industrial organisation, population, education, machinery, co-operation and the rest'. There were league publications such as its 'Leaflets for Leaguers' — pamphlets on a variety of subjects which the league distributed at public meetings — and more substantial material such as Went's *The Drink Question*, *The Fairy Ring of Commerce* by Commander Herbert Shove, *War on the Weak* by K.L. Kenrick and most notably the 'Birmingham Plan' for smallholder land resettlement.

League speakers carried the distributist message to the public at Speakers' Corner in Hyde Park, and there were high-profile public debates such as between Gilbert and the millionaire London retailer Gordon Selfridge. As has been seen, the last of the great debates between Shaw and Gilbert, entitled 'Do We Agree?', in October 1927, was held under league auspices. The league was broadly supportive of the trade union movement up to and for some time after the General Strike in 1926, and of the Labour Party so long as the presence of Slesser as an MP kept alive the hope that the party might be induced to embrace distributism. It then became critical of the unions on the grounds that they had sold out their members in ways such as exploring consultative practices and profit-sharing with the employer bodies; and of the party because it had accepted the party system and in so doing become indistinguishable, in the respects that mattered, from its ostensible adversaries.

The league office and the Central London and North London branches of the league broadly adhered to Went's vision of it as being similar in function to the Fabian Society. League circles in London were mainly of the view that the proper business of the league was to engage in distributist propaganda to the exclusion of activities more geared to, say, establishing model distributist undertakings or otherwise trying to live in conformity with distributist principles. The affairs of the Central London Branch were conducted largely along Fabian lines. Branch meetings were held at the Devereux Tavern, where the attendance averaged around fifty, and could rise to as many as a hundred and fifty. The proceedings included private debates such as between McNabb and Shaw, and addresses by prominent speakers.

A case in point was an address on credit unions in 1933, by the leading American credit union activist of the day, Roy F. Bergengren, and his associate, Thomas W. Doig. Bergengren, a lawyer, had been hired by the founder of the credit union movement in the United States, Edward A. Filene, in 1921, to head Filene's US Credit Union Extension Board. As will be seen in Chapter 8, he entered into a long-lasting association with the Antigonish Movement in 1931, in bringing credit unionism to Nova Scotia, and largely drafted the credit union legislation which the province's legislature adopted in 1932. The Bergengren Credit Union — now the largest credit union in Nova Scotia — is named in honour of him.[10] It is unlikely that Bergengren failed to draw to the attention of his British distributist hosts the efforts of Tompkins and Coady to give effect to distributism, or that he was not struck, at least privately, by the contrast between talking about distributism as was in vogue in London, and the hands-on, down-to-earth approach which he had come to know and admire in Nova Scotia.

Be this as it may, his visit was an occasion of major significance for both bodies. Following the address, prominent British distributists such as Gregory MacDonald, later the head of the Central European Service of the BBC, showed much more interest in credit unionism. In Nova Scotia, leading identities in the Antigonish Movement such as Tompkins's biographer, George Boyle — also the editor of the Antigonish Movement journal *The Extension Bulletin*, which continues today as *The Maritime Co-operator* — stepped up their interest in British distributism. 'As I remember it back in the 30s', writes the one-time Extension Department organiser, Sister Anselm — today Sister Irene Doyle — in regard to distributism, 'George Boyle was enthusiastically reading everything he could find on it'.[11] Boyle's sources included *G.K.'s Weekly*. The Extension Department became a subscriber.[12]

'If there is any lesson in our experience in the development of co-operative credit in the United States', Bergengren told the league meeting, 'the first is that there is no such word as "can't".' It was a message that the audience could usefully have taken to heart, but signally failed to do so. The formal business of the league was followed by after-meetings in the general bar of the Devereux, where an account by one of the members describes pint pots banging on the tables and members 'shouting texts of St Thomas at each other, calling on the people of England for the overthrow of their taskmasters, and a return to the religion of their forefathers'.[13] There was also much singing. 'I have always', writes Titterton, 'regarded this singing as an essential part of Distributism'.[14]

Sadly, actually acting to give effect to distributist ideas and ideals and finding political allies with the clout required to establish distributism on the overall national political agenda were regarded as less essential, not least by Titterton. It was no accident that Bergengren's advice to the league that there was 'no such word as "can't"' fell on deaf ears. The time and energy of the Central Branch was frittered away on repeatedly revisiting topics as esoteric as whether a distributist social order would permit the use of machinery. Sewell recalls the machinery issue as turning in part on whether 'a dentist's drill was to be considered a tool or a machine, the difference being that the former aided human labour while the latter displaced it'.[15]

The provinces

The picture outside London was different. Branches sprang up in the provinces — in major cities such as Liverpool, Birmingham, Manchester and Glasgow — as quickly as in London. A representative monthly program for the Liverpool branch in 1932 reads: 'March 8 — Mr Murray "A Statistical Survey of the Food Problem"; March 15 — Mr Byrne "Taking Over the Land"; March 22 "Taxation of Land Values",' while a Mr T. Hanlon was to give an address on 'Distributism' to the Liverpool University Catholic Society at a date to be announced later.[16] The provincial leaders — activists such as were exemplified in the case of the Birmingham branch by the one-time school teacher, K.L. Kenrick, who later became one of the league's more able secretaries, the future leader of the Catholic Rural Land Associations, Harold Robbins, and F. Keston Clarke, a former school attendance officer and another of the league's secretaries — were notable for their determination and distinctive viewpoint on the league's affairs.

What was seen to be the insufficiently practical approach of the London distributists was frowned on in the provincial branches. The provinces had priorities of their own. It was here in the heartland of the industries which had made Britain great and were now declining — ship-building, coalmining, engineering and textile manufacturing — that the brutal impact of unemployment was being experienced most directly. What the provincial branches wanted above all was to identify ways of giving effect to distributism which brought about immediate improvement in the quality of life of their fellow citizens and gained new supporters for distributism. What this might mean in practice might be seen by different branches in different ways, and was open to negotiation, but the emphasis was on urgency.

The provincial branches believed that one key strategy ought to be for the league to reach out to other groups with which it would be possible to undertake distributist projects such as the establishment of the co-operative banks or credit unions, to whose success in the United States and Canada Bergengren provided such eloquent testimony. In this way, existing businesses could be relieved of their reliance on the commercial banks and other financial intermediaries, and wage-earners perhaps encouraged to go into business for themselves.

Ventures along credit union lines could also have the effect of bringing about a working relationship — even a partnership — between the distributists and bodies such as the trade unions and the co-operative movement. Becoming closer to the unions might in turn lead to the Labour Party interesting itself in distributism, and so for the first time give the distributists an effective political voice. The more outspoken advocates of the outreach strategy included Cecil's widow, Ada Jones, who generally reflected the course of action Cecil might have been expected to favour.

The provincial branches also favoured the preparation of detailed blueprints for distributist projects. An outstanding example was the proposal from the Birmingham branch for a 'working model of practical Distributism' — generally known as the 'Birmingham Plan' — which would alleviate unemployment by enabling the government to settle families on the land at a cost lower than supporting them through unemployment benefit. The plan envisaged families taking up rural blocks of around 25 acres, where they would be provided with the equipment, stock and seed needed for them to begin farming, and an income equivalent to unemployment benefit until the arrival of their first crops. 'While costing the community much less than the present unpro-ductive relief', the plan argued, it would also 'restore to the unemployed their dignity and independence'. Significantly, the Liverpool branch welcomed the Birmingham initiative as evidence of the willingness of some sections of the league 'to come to grips with the problems that face us'.[17]

Not least, it was the provincial branches which were most insistent that the League should publish a distributist textbook. The proposal for a textbook — a distributist manifesto and program — originated at the inaugural meeting of the league. Gilbert and Belloc had undertaken to get it done, but nothing more came of the project. There were insistent questions as to whether the textbook had been prepared, and, if so, what was delaying its appearance. 'During this period', recalls Robbins, 'Belloc was always saying that he must have a word with Gilbert on the point, and Chesterton was always saying he must have a word with Hilary. Naturally the Manifesto and Programme were not forthcoming'.[18] As has been seen, in describing the gap Cecil had left behind him, Ada Jones used as an example the fact that 'Neither G.K. nor Belloc seem to have produced a textbook formulating their belief, and in its absence, Distributism remains a creed without a dogma, evoking sympathy but lacking support'.[19] Here again, Ada's views largely echoed those of the provinces.

That the textbook was did not appear was put down in the provinces to 'the humbugging, hair-splitting nonsense' with which they saw London as being preoccupied.[20] More broadly, it symbolised for the branches a failure by the league to maintain its inital momentum and sense of purpose. The reluctance of the league to more energetically seek links with other bodies — and particularly with working-class bodies — as some of the branches so outspokenly advocated has been attributed to the class prejudices and insecurities of its largely middle-class membership.

A seminal article on the league by the British scholar, Michael Thorn, quotes one of its members as extolling the middle class as 'the bulwark of owning, responsibility and literacy', and as well, the source of 'the best minds in history'. The quotation continues that the league should not, under any circumstances, 'water down its views for the Proletariat'. 'In short', Thorn concludes, 'it was not for the League to win the confidence of the masses, but for the masses to win the confidence of the League!'[21]

The Land

Neither the metropolitan nor the provinicial approach satisfied those distributists, such as McNabb, for whom the whole point of distributism was to engage in land resettlement. McNabb — a one-time Prior of the Hawkesyard Dominican Priory in Staffordshire and, throughout the lifespan of the League, the Sub-Prior of St Dominic's Priory in London — was as much at home putting the case for Catholicism at Speakers' Corner in Hyde Park as in scholarly theological controversy. He followed in Manning's footsteps as Britain's leading exponent of *De Rerum Novarum.*

He was also among those of the distributists who most fiercely rejected the use of machinery. His colourful dress — the Dominican habit 'made by hand; spun in the Hebrides; woven in Sussex',[22] the ancient hat, the working-man's boots and the 'McNabb-sack' over his shoulder — made him one of London's more distinctive characters. 'Here', writes his biographer, Father Ferdinand Valentine, 'was a flaming personality which could fire the youth of England'.[23] Gilbert Chesterton recalls McNabb as 'one of the few great men I have met in my life'.[24]

McNabb based his thinking on the central role of the family. 'The Family, not the individual', he wrote, 'is the unit of the nation; the natural defence of Freedom is the Home; and the natural defence of the Home is the Homestead'. Saving England from itself — from an industrial social order which he regarded as a Satanic evil — required in his view that England should turn its back on industry, capitalism and urban society in favour of a wholesale reversion to agriculture. He argued:

> There is no hope for England except on the land. But it must be the land cultivated on a land basis, and not on an industrial basis. Nothing but religion will solve the land question. And nothing but a religious order seeking not wealth but God will pioneer the movement from town to land.

'Oh', McNabb concluded, 'that I could make religious men and women see what I see'.[25]

McNabb was not alone in believing that the basis of distributism should be agricultural rather than industrial. The 1930s saw the distributist movement give rise directly or indirectly to land settlement schemes as diverse as the Bosworth Guild project — the Birmingham Plan in a more highly developed form — which Kenrick proposed in 1935; the Marydown Farming Association farms in Surrey and Sussex; the short-lived Langenhoe Hall Estate Settlement which John Hawkeswell established in Essex; and the training farms — Broadfield Farm at Symington, Old Browns Farm at Chartridge, West Fields Farm at Market Bosworth, Grove Farm at Panton and Priors Wood Hall at Parbold — established by the Catholic Rural Land Associations. The Land Associations were a direct response to the case for land resettlement to which McNabb had so passionately given expression in his book *The Church and the Land*.

A summary of the thinking of the associations by their principal spokesperson, Robbins, reads: 'If men were taught to farm, primarily to feed their families, secondarily to feed neighbours grouped in social communities round them, and only finally to market their surplus co-operatively, it seemed not only would the marketing problem assume more modest proportions but the revival of social contacts would reverse the rural decline'.[26] The associations were given papal approval in 1933, in a letter over the signature of the then Secretary of State of the Vatican — and future Pope Pius XII — Cardinal Pacelli. Pacelli wrote:

> The Holy Father has heard with satisfaction of the progress already made by the five Catholic Land Associations of Great Britain, and prays this important work of restoring the sane and healthy life of the countryside may be abundantly blessed by God and result in a diminution of unemployment through the development of the agricultural resources of the country to the fullest possible extent. As an encouragement to persevere in this good work, His Holiness most gladly imparts his Apostolic Blessing to all who are engaged in helping to further this most praiseworthy enterprise.[27]

Unhappily, no comparable expressions of good will — much less more tangible support — were forthcoming from the Catholic authorities in England, either for land resettlement or distributism more generally.

The Catholic Social Guild — the major Church social doctrine body in England — was critical of the distributists for what it saw as their overemphasis on the importance of property and exaggerated anxieties in regard to the notion of the servile state. The Land Associations effectively had to discontinue their activities when the bishops refused to authorise an annual collection to pay for the properties the trainees were now ready to occupy. Meetings of the associations were suspended following the outbreak of the War in 1939. Robbins commented bitterly in regard to the attitude of the Church to distributism that 'The Catholic authorities in England have never shown any other sentiment than embarrassment to have their principles stated so eloquently'.[28]

McNabb favoured most of all the rural settlement which Gill and Pepler established at Ditchling Common. 'Ditchling', he wrote, 'was like music to my ear ... when I found it doing as well as preaching the things I could only preach to be done, I gave it something of the love I never gave a woman'.[29] The more senior founder, Gill, was incomparably the greatest English artist-craftsman of his time, and a worthy successor to Morris whom in many respects he so closely resembled.

He was also a highly original thinker whose hopes for the future centred on bringing about a reintegration of what he saw as a deeply fractured Britain. 'What I hope above all things', he wrote shortly before his death in 1940, 'is that I have done something towards re-integrating bed and board, the small farm and the workshop, the home and the school, earth and heaven'.[30] Ditchling enabled him to put his ideas into practice.

Ditchling was made up of artists and craftsmen who sought to escape from city life to the country, where they could live separately in houses of their own and produce their own food, while at the same time functioning as a tight-knit community. The Guild of St Joseph and St Dominic which they shortly formed was intended as a tertiary or third level unit of the Dominican order. Members of tertiaries were lay people who agreed to have their lives guided by the Dominican friars. It may be that life at Ditchling was more congenial for the men than the women.

The Guild, writes Pepler, was 'essentially a masculine conception of the good life; the men did not conspicuously dig, but the women were still expected to spin — in the intervals of producing children, baking bread, and curing ham'.[31] Ultimately Gill and Pepler fell out, in part over Gill's sexual idiosyncrasies, and Gill moved away to found new communities at Capel-y-ffin in Wales and later at Piggots in the vicinity of High Wycombe.[32] Ditchling survived the rift, and lingered on until it was wound up finally in the 1990s.

The various land settlement schemes demonstrated among other things that the enthusiasm for them among the distributists was greater in theory than in practice. While some distributists would have liked there to be more land projects, others wished there had been fewer. For example, reservations about the Birmingham Plan on the part of the league office in London were due in part to the conviction that agricultural communities were likely to be attractive to 'cranks, 'abnormals' and other undesirable elements.[33] Recalling his experiences in the distributist movement twenty years later for Maisie Ward, Desmond Gleeson — a further prominent distributist of the day and frequent contributor to *G.K.'s Weekly* — commented that 'One unfortunate feature of the League's history was the attempt to establish three or four little agricultural communities'.

'I call it "unfortunate",' Gleeson's account continues, 'because nothing was established — save only the proneness of certain Distributists to act first and think later':

> What happened was that on two or three occasions a band, not necessarily of Distributists, but rather of people who had been attending Distributist meetings, went off to form Land Settlements in different parts of the country. And when they set out, the only sure thing was that they would shortly be back in town. They were not the sort to dig themselves in; it was not land work so much that distressed them as work ... Worse still, some of the settlers were religious folk and instead of starting-in on the work of settlement, they must needs create a diversion by attempting to set up chapels and whatnot and generally show a much greater interest in devotion than in digging.

'Needless to say', the account concluded, 'none of these settlements settled anything, but the quality of the type of settler'.[34] Justified or not as Gleeson's strictures may have been, the Birmingham Plan was explicitly exempted from them.

'It is noteworthy', Gleeson recorded, 'that the only

realistic land scheme was launched from Birmingham. The rest foundered in folly'.[35] Unsurprisingly, the author of the Plan, Robbins, had a dim view of the league's attitude more broadly to land resettlement. 'The formation of the Distributist League', he wrote, 'revived hope only to mock it'.[36] In summary, what Robbins — and many others like him — were complaining about was more fundamentally the lack of interest of the league in acting on issues in any way other than discussing them. Gregory MacDonald insisted that the purpose of the league was exclusively 'the pooling of ideas, the formation of public opinion, and the definition of principle'.[37] 'That', as Cecil might have put the matter, 'is the Distributist League, and nothing else is the Distributist League'.

For all their failures, disappointments and apparent impracticability, the land resettlement schemes reflected the fundamental truth that distributism had to be implemented from the bottom up rather than imposed externally by legislation. There was a fundamental contradiction in distributists like Went believing that the league could model its activities on those of the Fabian Society and at the same time reject the parliament and the party system on which the Fabians relied to achieve their objectives. Nor was it inevitable, as distributists like Gregory MacDonald sometimes seemed to suppose, that a distributist social order would appear if it was talked about long enough.

What McNabb and his associates saw much more clearly than the League was that distributism required people to relate to one another in new ways which could only be learned by experience. Where they failed was in insufficiently appreciating that in urban and industrial societies such as Britain it would be less on the land than in the workplace that the necessary learning would have to occur. Significantly, it was not until 1927 that distributism formally caught up with Cecil in acknowledging the need for workplaces to be the property of their workers. The revised statement of objectives which the League then adopted reads for the first time 'Every worker should own a share in the Assets and Control of the business in which he works'.[38] It was a message to which the whole attention of the distributist weeklies could from then on usefully have been devoted.

The distributist weeklies

The original distributist weekly was launched in 1911. Its name was *The Eye-Witness*. Belloc was the editor, and Cecil his deputy. Cecil took over *The Eye-Witness* from Belloc in 1912, and renamed it *The New Witness*. Gilbert in turn edited *The New Witness* on a temporary basis during Cecil's service with the army in France, and permanently following his death there in 1918. By 1923, *The New Witness* had so much lost circulation and was experiencing financial difficulties of so great a magnitude as to require it to cease publication. It resumed in 1925 as *G.K.'s Weekly*. When Gilbert died in 1936, Belloc was again briefly the editor, before handing on the position to his son-in-law, Reginald Jebb. In 1938, there was a further, and final, change of name to *The Weekly Review*, and the paper appeared for the last time in 1947.

'*The New Witness*', wrote Shaw in 1916, 'ought now to be called *The Three Witnesses* — meaning not those whom some trinitarian forger foisted on St Jerome's Vulgate for so many centuries, but St Gilbert, St Cecil, and St Hilary'.[39] In journalism as in debate, Cecil's death two years later was a loss from which distributism never fully recovered. As Gilbert freely acknowledged in regard to his editing of *The New Witness*, 'I am under no illusion about myself as an ideal occupant of this position'.[40] The contrast between the brothers is captured in a notable firsthand account by Father Brocard Sewell, a one-time junior employee on the staff of *G.K.'s Weekly*, and today its only surviving member.

'Gilbert', writes Sewell, 'felt in honour bound to keep *The New Witness* going, but he lacked his brother's political instinct, and also his talent for detecting and exposing political corruption':

> Under Cecil's editorship *The New Witness* was in some respects a precursor of Richard Ingrams' *Private Eye* (though not of the *Private Eye* as it is today); but that kind of thing was not really GKC's *metier*. When GKC took over the editorship he told *The New Witness*' readers that he was probably the world's worst editor. That was a considerable exaggeration; but he was certainly not well equipped, either by nature or training, to be the editor of a weekly paper of national circulation ... When Cecil Chesterton was editing *The New Witness* he attended at the office every day

from Monday to Friday. GKC, however, was very much a non-resident editor. Cecil had been a complete master of all editorial processes, including the more technical ones of 'making-up' the paper and 'putting it to bed', the latter function being performed on the printer's premises. Chesterton did not enjoy this more 'typographical' part of an editor's duties, but he knew how to do it if required. Cecil had held a weekly editorial conference, rather like Punch's 'round table', at which the paper's directors were invited to be present.

'This', Sewell concludes, 'was not how the affairs of *G.K.'s Weekly* were conducted'.[41] It is less surprising that the rather dull paper that *The New Witness* was allowed to become under Gilbert's direction failed in 1923, than that it had lasted so long.

For all this, the Sewell thesis that Gilbert's decision to carry on *The New Witness* was an expression purely or even largely of what he thought Cecil would have wanted can be taken too seriously. Gilbert's situation was becoming one in which he was effectively black-listed from writing in any of the major dailies and weeklies by the proprietors whose characters and actions he had so repeatedly assailed. The proprietor of the Express group of newspapers, Lord Beaverbrook, advised his fellow tycoon, Lord Rothmere, in 1927, that he had 'given orders to the Express Newspapers that neither G.K. Chesterton nor Hilaire Belloc are to appear in the columns of those papers' on the grounds that 'They spend so much time writing abuse of me elsewhere, that I feel they have not got time to do good work for the newspapers with which I am connected'.[42]

The reality was that Gilbert and Belloc had largely been kept out of the Beaverbrook papers ever since the war. Their attacks on the third great press baron of the day, Northcliffe — who died in 1922 — had also caused them to be excluded from the Northcliffe papers. In as much as Gilbert wanted to write about the things which were closest to his heart, it was all but essential for him to have a journal of his own. That *The New Witness* survived was due at least as much to Gilbert's determination that he and his fellow distributists should have a paper to advance the distributist cause as to his grief for Cecil.

A key account of the distributist movement notes that 'The *Eye* and *New Witness* were not polite papers: they intended to shock readers by laying bare the rottenness of

British politics'.[43] Belloc and Cecil had written in *The Party System* that 'The political education of the democracy is therefore the first step towards reform. The first step is exposure'.[44] Their papers were intended to put the recommendation into effect. The strategy was to bring to public attention specific abuses such as where collusion between the front benches in parliament had resulted in benefits to the plutocracy or was in other ways detrimental to the public interest.

What was seen by some as the finest moment of *The Eye-Witness* and *The New Witness* — and by others as a characteristic excess — was the allegation by Cecil in 1912 of the involvement of prominent public figures — including such leading identities in the Liberal government as the Postmaster-General, Herbert Samuel, the Attorney-General, Sir Rufus Isaacs, and the Chancellor of the Exchequer, Lloyd George — in what was claimed to be an abuse of office arising from insider trading in Marconi shares.

The coverage gave heavy emphasis to the fact that three of the key offenders were Jews. Cecil was ultimately found guilty of libel in an action brought against him by a further party to the Marconi transactions, Geoffrey Isaacs. The judge commented in his summing up that those responsible for the offending material had been 'partly instigated by racial prejudice and partly blind to business matters'.[45] While Belloc was privately critical of aspects of Cecil's handling of *The New Witness*, he stood by his friend in public and was a defence witness at his trial. The affair was in his eyes one more confirmation of the connivance between the front benches and the plutocracy which he, Cecil and Gilbert so passionately detested.

Hindsight suggests a harsher judgment. For all the good *The Eye-Witness* and *The New Witness* achieved — for all their outstanding contributions to the development and advocacy of distributist thought, most notably in contributions by Belloc such as his seven-part series on the servile state in 1917 and his ten-part series 'The Reconstruction of Private Property' in 1919 — they also paraded to damaging effect the dark side of some distributists which so frequently brought distributism into disrepute and alienated potential supporters.

The tainting of the Marconi episode with anti-Semitism was in no sense an isolated occurrence in *The New Witness*, but rather reflected a pervasive prejudice among the paper's key contributors. Defenders and sceptics alike of the view that the leading distributists were in their varying degrees anti-Semitic usually base their arguments on such readily accessible material as their books, poetry and better-known public statements. The more conclusive — and deeply disturbing — evidence of anti-Semitism is in the largely neglected files of *The New Witness*.

The anti-Semitism which *The New Witness* featured so conspicuously was not limited, as is sometimes supposed, to Belloc and Cecil, but extended to Gilbert and even to Ada Jones. What the group thought they were doing — and their obliviousness to its dreadful significance — is conveyed graphically in the grotesque self-congratulatory passages with which Belloc and Gilbert celebrated the achievements of *The Eye-Witness* and *The New Witness* in — as they saw it — bringing the Jewish problem to public attention for the first time. Belloc trumpeted that '*The New Witness* was the first paper to tell an instructed public what the Jewish peril was, not only in England but in Europe'.[46] Gilbert concurred. 'Our notions do not always turn out to be nonsense,' he wrote. 'The Jewish Problem, once regarded as a fad, is now recognised as a fact; and a fact that fills the world'.[47]

Under Gilbert's editorial control, as under Cecil before him, *The New Witness* featured a broad range of anti-Semitic material, including the expressions of anti-Semitic opinion which featured from time to time in its leading articles. There was, for example, anti-Semitism of the petty, mean-spirited variety, as in an item in the 'Comments of the Week' column of *The New Witness* for 19 April 1918, which complained, in regard to rail travel, of 'hordes of Jews who congest the traffic between London and Brighton and overcrowd the trains to the Thames Valley'. 'It is nothing less than a scandal', the item continued, 'that while the Jews are allowed to overcrowd the trains on certain lines that the workman should be deprived of any trains at all, and should have to contemplate a long and dreary journey before he can get home'.[48]

A related item on an earlier occasion criticised Jews for taking shelter in the London Underground during air-raids, while supposedly more courageous sections of the population remained on the surface. What was objected to was — among other things — 'a Jew with a gold watch-chain grovelling on the floor of the tube'. The report originated from Ada Jones. 'Now that the unhappy "alien" by diving bodily under the earth, has come politically to the surface', wrote Gilbert in his regular column 'At the Sign of the World's End', 'I almost begin to have a humanitarian reaction in his favour'.[49] The implicit snigger or sneer — the failure to imaginatively get inside the head of a suffering fellow human being — was as uncharacteristic of Gilbert as it was unworthy.

At a second level, anti-Semitic material of an abusive, hysterical and overtly malevolent character appeared regularly in *The New Witness* over by-lines such as of O'Donnell. A representative extract from a contribution by O'Donnell to *The New Witness* for 13 November 1913 reads:

> Jews are still more discordant with, and destructive of, European civilisation than are Javanese, Mongols, Moors, Zulus or Malays ... the Zulu, the Mongol or the Malay is probably far less removed from European ideals than all these rodent and parasitic Asiatics who stammer our speech and imitate our exterior. At any rate, neither the Zulu, the Mongol nor the Malay has come in hundreds of thousands and in millions to batten on struggling populations of laborious men and pallid women whose livelihoods were scanty enough without the clutching fingers of the Arch-sweater, the Arch-monopolist, the Arch-usurer, the Arch-cheat.

'It is the tragedy of entire nations', O'Donnell concludes, 'which underlies the crawling, creeping, pustulate advance of the Universal Parasites'.[50]

O'Donnell's reference to 'the Universal Parasites' is from one of a protracted series of articles in *The New Witness* in 1913, about a supposed Jewish ritual murder of a Christian child in Kiev. The alleged perpetrator was a middle-aged clerk in a factory adjacent to where the body was found, Mendel Beiliss. As the prominent British historian Orlando Figes documents exhaustively, in his recent *A People's Tragedy: The Russian Revolution 1891-1924*, what achieved worldwide notoriety as the Beiliss Affair was a massive frame-up, perpetrated by the Russian authorities with the knowledge and support of the Tsar, in order to foment popular feeling against the Jews and so stave off the consequences of the regime's spectacular insensitivity and incompetence.[51] That *The New Witness* gave credence to the calumnies in its editorial columns — and allowed O'Donnell seemingly unlimited space for his increasingly hysterical justifications of them — is indicative of the propensity of those responsible to assume the worst where Jews were concerned.

While Belloc and Cecil are now generally acknowledged to have been anti-Semitic, Gilbert is sometimes exonerated on grounds such as that the leading Zionist of the day, Chaim Weizmann, would not have invited an anti-Semite to visit Palestine as he did in 1920, nor, if Gilbert had been anti-Semitic, would the invitation have been accepted.[52] It is at least as likely that Weizmann was not familiar with *The New Witness*, and had not had its more egregious excesses drawn to his attention. Nor would the dedicated journalist in Gilbert have allowed him to pass up an opportunity to see for himself a situation which was so frequent a subject of comment in *The New Witness*.

Exoneration is likewise sometimes claimed on the grounds that Gilbert had Jewish friends, including the Jewish writer, Israel Zangwill. It is at least open to question whether the friendship with Zangwill is likely to have survived the observation by Gilbert in 1920 that:

> Every Jew is at once National and International, working for his own race against the interests of the rest. This is precisely where the Jewish peril lies, and Mr Zangwill is a notable example; disintegration of European civilisation with the breakup of national frontiers is accompanied by a fierce and secret desire for the supremacy of the Jewish race.[53]

The demise of *The New Witness* and its reappearance as *G.K.'s Weekly* was accompanied by a shift in emphasis from the exposing of wrongdoing — from 'a sharp and illuminating criticism of happenings and persons, to throw a search-light on dark doings and drag obscure events into a proper publicity'[54] — to a much more active promotion of distributism. The new approach was signalled at the outset, in Gilbert's leading article for the pilot issue of *G.K.'s Weekly* which appeared in 1924. The article reads:

> I desire this paper to stand for certain very normal and human ideas. But though they are very normal and human, it is the cold and literal fact that they will not be printed in any other paper except this one. They are not fads; they are only human traditions that are treated as negligible while fads are welcomed as fashionable. They

are not eccentricities; they are only the central ideas of civilisation that are forgotten in a welter of eccentricities. But because they are neglected they are new, and because they are forgotten elsewhere they will only be found here. They are simply common sense in a world where sense is no longer common ... I believe it is possible to restore and perpetuate a reasonable just distribution of private property; and I will give my reasons for thinking so in this paper.[55]

The mix as Gilbert now determined it was much more congenial to him, and the paper recovered much of the zest of *The New Witness* as edited by Cecil.

Unhappily, there was no comparable improvement in the paper's financial position. The initial impact of the pilot issue — the publicity generated and the interest of potential readers and subscribers aroused — was largely lost when the paper did not begin to appear regularly until four months later. Chronically undercapitalised, lacking in business and managerial acumen and unattractive to most potential advertisers by reason of its hostility to the capitalist social order, *G.K.'s Weekly* then lurched from one financial crisis to another. Frequent appeals for donations from readers apart, the paper owed its survival to Gilbert's generosity.

Contributions from his own pocket in the six years prior to his death are estimated to have totalled some £5000. That the bills were paid was due at times to Gilbert's having raised the money by writing a new Father Brown story. The Catholic author and editor Douglas Woodruff writes in regard to the younger distributists who had now grouped themselves around Gilbert — most notably Gregory Macdonald and his distributist brother, Edward — that 'The truth is there was a virtuous circle: they said they must not let G.K. down and he said he must not let them down, and so he paid up when the paper made losses'.[56]

However, the financial difficulties which *G.K.'s Weekly* experienced were no more damaging than the deterioration of its ideological position on issues other than distributism which occurred in the 1930s. It is unlikely that *G.K.'s Weekly* could ever have wholly lived down the harm caused by anti-Semitism and other expressions of prejudice in *The Eye-Witness* and *The New Witness*, but its task was made much more difficult by its ambivalent attitude to the rise of the dictators.

While, with a very few disgraceful exceptions, the distributists had no time for the home-grown fascism of Oswald Mosley and his British Union of Fascists, their attitude to Mussolini and so-called 'Latin' fascism was much less clear-cut. The issue was brought to a head by what many supporters of *G.K.'s Weekly* saw — and roundly condemned — as its failure to adequately oppose the Italian invasion of Abyssinia. Gilbert appeared to side with the critics in the view that the paper had leaned over too far in the direction of the Italians, but he died before something more like a balanced view of the situation could be restored.

Following his death, the drift to the right accelerated, as those elements of the movement most sympathetic to Mussolini and Franco — and willing in some instances to turn a blind eye to the situation in Germany — established what was effectively an editorial stranglehold on the paper. The result was a vicious downward spiral in which more and more of the original distributists dropped the paper in protest against the new policies, and extremists such as Gilbert's second cousin, A.K. Chesterton — a one-time senior aide to Mosley and editor of the B.U.F. journals *Action* and *The Blackshirt* — featured much more prominently among its contributors. By the time what was now *The Weekly Review* finally ceased publication in 1947, it had become a travesty of the paper it had once been, and an embarrassment to its former ideals.

For British distributism — finding itself as it did by the middle 1930s with a public which was no longer interested in what it had to say, its journal compromised by the incessant, ill-disciplined parading of discreditable prejudices and polit-ical miscalculations, and its organisation so ineffectual as to be constantly haemorrhaging away its more practical and level-headed members — Gilbert's death was a blow from which it could only very slowly hope to recover. 'When the author of *The Outline of Sanity* died', Reckitt grieved, 'Distributism, being without sanity, died too. When England's greatest modern democrat laid down the flaming torch he had held aloft so long a night, the movement grouped around him spluttered out as a damp squib mid the showy and mechanical fireworks of Fascism'.[57] Reckitt was only half right. Distributism had not so much died as emigrated. It was alive and well in Nova Scotia, and being led forward there by Jimmy Tompkins and Moses Coady.

PART II

DISTRIBUTISM REBORN

Father Jimmy
Tompkins

7

The New Distributism in Nova Scotia: 'Jimmy' Tompkins, Moses Coady and the Origins of the Antigonish Movement

A new distributism

BELLOC had foreseen that a new mood and an integrated program would be needed to give effect to distributism. The challenge was taken up in the first instance in the Canadian province of Nova Scotia in the 1930s, with the promotion of what was effectively a 'new distributism' by the Extension Department at the University of St Francis Xavier in Antigonish. The instigators were two remarkable Catholic priests, Father 'Jimmy' Tompkins and Father Moses Coady. Tomkins and Coady used adult education to create Belloc's 'new mood', and co-operatives in the Rochdale mould as the vehicle for his 'integrated program'. Their aim was to combat poverty and enable local communities to become 'masters of their own destiny' by mobilising local and regional resources for economic development.

'We start with the simple things that are vital to human living and move on up the scale to the more cultural and refining activities that make life whole and complete', wrote Coady. 'Through credit unions, co-operative stores, lobster factories and sawmills, we are laying the foundations for an appreciation of Shakespeare and grand opera'.[1] Tompkins was a key source of inspiration for the establishment of the Extension Department. Coady was its long-serving inaugural director and intellectual driving-force.

What the Antigonish Movement wanted was a new social order — a 'Middle Way' between capitalism and communism — for Nova Scotia, and, through Nova Scotia, for people everywhere. A visitor from the Swedish co-operative movement is quoted as having responded patronisingly when Coady praised his country's then outstandingly successful co-operatives. 'Oh yes', the visitor said, 'we have a little program underway, but we don't say we are trying to do much. We are not trying to save the world or anything like that'. 'Well, Coady barked back at him, 'That's what we are doing around here. What else is worth doing?'[2]

Nova Scotia

The grinding poverty and social distress which prompted Tompkins and Coady to undertake their crusade was given eloquent expression by the Royal Commission which inquired into the fisheries of the Maritime Provinces and the Magdalen Islands in 1927. The Commission reported:

> We were given vivid word-pictures of fishing villages in which ageing men alone were left to man the fishing boats with little hope of adequate livelihood in the future years of their physical incapacity, and no hope of pension such as is possible to workers in other industries; of fishing communities from which the young men had emigrated in large numbers to another land, or were hoping to emigrate when they could gather sufficient means; of neglected boats with hulls ripe and rotten on the beach; of discarded gear once valuable and useful, but now falling to decay; of abandoned fishing vessels left hopefully equipped as they came in from the sea, to wait for a better season which never came; of wharves and breakwaters once staunch and busy, but now dilapidated and deserted; of once prosperous localities slowly but surely becoming the grave-yards of a dead industry; of fisher-folk despondent and

disheartened, struggling on against economic disabilities, eager to labour in one of the most hazardous of pursuits but unable to sell their products for a reasonable reward, always hoping for better luck, and clinging grimly and patiently to their calling, a tribute at once to their character and their courage; and of school-children psychologically distrustful of a future in their own country and planning to migrate at maturity to another land to make a living. Apart from the statements made to us we have taken every means and every opportunity to inform ourselves on the actual conditions, and we are convinced that these word-pictures were not overdrawn.[3]

Had the commissioners been asked to examine other aspects of the regional economy such as the small farms on which so large a part of the population depended for their livelihoods or the coal mines at Cape Breton, the picture would have been no less grim. The Maritime Provinces — Nova Scotia among them — were experiencing desperate times, with no apparent hope of improvement.[4]

Tompkins

All this was well-known to Tompkins because he grew up with it. He was of Irish descent, born in 1870 in the Margaree Valley of Nova Scotia, and raised by his maternal grandparents. The family had a mixed farming property, but two of Tompkins's uncles were teachers, and Tompkins initially followed in their footsteps. He was a pupil-teacher for his schoolmaster at the Margaree Forks school, received his provisional licence to teach when he was seventeen, and taught in fishing villages at Bruli near Cheticamp, and later at Salmon River. He also studied at the University of St Francis Xavier — then the St Francis Xavier College — in Antigonish.

The university — a former grammar school which had become a degree-granting body in 1853 — was chronically underfunded, with fewer than a hundred students. However, it was more forward-looking than most, having recently become the first Catholic institution in North America to grant degrees to women students, and having established the first engineering school in the Maritime Provinces. It also took modest pride in having produced, by 1893, no fewer than 'two bishops, fifty-five priests, nineteen seminarians, one judge, two senators, five Members of Parliament, two school inspectors, nineteen lawyers, nineteen physicians, and many teachers'.[5]

Tompkins received his teacher's certificate there in 1890 and his bachelor's degree in 1895. The university then employed him to teach junior Greek and intermediate mathematics. Meanwhile, one of his teacher uncles had entered the priesthood, and Tompkins decided that he too would become a priest. He was a seminarian in Rome from 1897 until 1902, and, following his ordination, resumed teaching as Professor of Greek and Higher Algebra at the university. The university made him in turn its librarian, the principal of its high school and its vice-president.

What Tompkins set out to achieve initially was to strengthen the financial position of the university and upgrade its faculty. Thanks to his efforts, major donors — notably a building contractor and a doctor who had made good in Boston — were recruited, and provided the university with a new science building, chapel, library, gymnasium and student accommodation. Tompkins was also able to interest the Carnegie Foundation in the university, with the effect in the first instance that a new chair in French — a major priority for the French-speaking or Acadian population — was endowed.

The improvements led the staff and students of the university — and community more generally — to feel that a new era was opening up in the history of the university and that their needs were being taken more seriously. Some of the best graduates were persuaded to return as teachers, and outstanding newcomers were recruited. Tompkins's main biographer, Boyle, describes an occasion when Tompkins met two of the university's Sisters of St Martha out for a walk on the campus. 'Pretty soon', said Tompkins, 'you won't have a place to walk. I'm going to have buildings all the way up to the graveyard'. The graveyard, Boyle writes, 'was about half a mile away'.[6]

Meanwhile Tompkins had become passionately committed to adult education as a means of enabling his deprived fellow countrymen to lift themselves out of their poverty and improve the quality of their lives. A Congress of Universities of the Empire which he attended in Britain in 1912 introduced him to the work of bodies such as the

Extension Department of the University of Wisconsin and the British Workers' Education Association.

He was also powerfully influenced by the example of the Danish Folk High School Movement and, closer to home, the agricultural extension work which was being pioneered in Nova Scotia by his former fellow seminarian, the Rev. Dr Hugh MacPherson — otherwise known as 'Little Doc Hugh'.[7] His imagination was fired by the arguments for making the resources of universities accessible to the wider community which the Bishop of Limerick, Edward O'Dwyer, set out in key addresses entitled 'A University for Catholics in Relation to the Material Interests of Ireland' and 'The Present Conditions of University Education in Ireland'.

'The University Question', Bishop O'Dwyer wrote, 'has more to do with the poverty in Ireland today than any other cause whatsoever; and whether one hopes to raise the industries of people in towns, or make existence possible for the agriculturists, in modern conditions, the first essential step is to bring the country ... to the same road by which every other prosperous country in the world has progressed in this century; that is, the road of higher knowledge'.[8] 'Few people realise how much Bishop O'Dwyer contributed to the awakening of St. F.X.', Tompkins was to recall. 'You probably remember his two famous addresses. I bought out the whole stock in Ireland and scattered them far and wide in this land and in Newfoundland'.[9]

'Why', Tompkins began to query, 'should the treasures of university knowledge be confined to boys and girls between the ages of eighteen and twenty-two?'[10] One avenue Tompkins used to advance his ideas was the Antigonish Forward Movement, a body of 'local Catholic and Protestant lawyers, merchants and clerics and successful farmers' formed in 1913 to advance the well-being of their town.[11] A second was the local weekly newspaper, *The Casket*. The Forward Movement and *The Casket* were forums where local problems could be raised, and solutions to them explored along lines such the scientific agriculture of which Little Doc Hugh was so passionate an advocate and the adult education and co-operatives which Tompkins favoured.

An exhaustive analysis of the content of *The Casket* by Professor Dan MacInnes of the Department of Anthropology and Sociology at the University of St Francis Xavier sees it as including 'agricultural production; the social consequences of the Industrial Revolution; lessons in economics; the use of statistics; the condition of the fisheries; and a variety of articles on programmes of action in other parts of the world, such as Vermont, Quebec, Denmark, etc.'[12] In particular, a new column established by *The Casket* in 1918 — 'For the People: Devoted Mainly to Social, Economic and Educational Affairs'[13] — carried the message that education was the means by which people could gain an understanding of the nature of economic processes and how they might be made to serve the best interests of the community. So great an importance did Tompkins attach to *The Casket* in raising the consciousness of the community that he arranged for the diocese to become its majority shareholder.

Tompkins's thinking about adult education was set out in detail in the seminal pamphlet *Knowledge for the People: A Call to St Francis Xavier College*, which he published in 1921. The pamphlet is widely regarded as having been among 'the great landmarks in the history of adult education' in Canada.[14] 'No other idea', Tompkins argued in his introductory passage, 'has so gripped the people of the whole world as the desire for more Knowledge, better intellectual training, and better organised effort in their various callings':

> It has gripped them *en masse*, and without regard to condition, class or circumstances. Men and women everywhere are clamouring for the equal opportunity that education and intellectual training give ... Subjects like Literature, History, Economics and Philosophy, that were once studied by the privileged few, are being sought by a rapidly increasing number of grown-up men and women who in their teens were not in a position to pursue such studies ... Disabilities and unjust inequalities, scarcely realised in times past by the very victims, or if realised borne with dull resignation, have now come to the attention of all and they must be redressed.

'University Extension', wrote Tompkins, 'implies an organised effort to give to the people not in college some of the advantages enjoyed by the one-half of one per cent who are able to attend college. It reaches out to the farmer, the workman and the average citizen, and says to each "If you cannot go to your college, your college will come to you".' Tompkins continued:

We must take and follow the opinion of the people themselves. For us, what the people most need to learn must be what they most want to learn ... In order that they do this, the first step necessary is that a conference be held between our educators and representatives of agriculture and industry. 'We are at your service', our educators must say, 'tell us how best we may serve you'.

It was important in his view that no time should be lost:

It is the shrewder, as well as the more heroic policy, to make an independent beginning immediately, on however modest a scale. Let us establish ourselves on the ground; as soon as our work proves its value, we can count on recognition and assistance. By any other course, we risk indefinite delay.

The obligation to see that all this happened was on the university:

It will not become those who have so long preached to the masses the value of education to be confounded by the ardour of the people's sudden conversion. By the speed of their response to the new demand, the sincerity of our educators, and their devotion to the cause for which they stand, will they be judged.

'St Francis Xavier's has the message', concluded Tompkins; 'it is within its power to devise how that message shall be carried out to the people'. The university would need to perfect the executive details, and put the project into operation as soon as possible.[15]

An immediate outcome of Tompkins's campaign was the People's School which the university conducted over a two-month period from January to March 1921. Participants in the school were welcomed to Antigonish by the mayor and members of the faculty. There was no test for entry other than that of being at least seventeen years old, and no fees were charged. All told, there were fifty-five students, ranging in age from seventeen to fifty-seven. The subjects taken included English, chemistry, business finance, agriculture, veterinary hygiene, natural resources, arithmetic, economics, physics, public speaking, stock breeding and biology. 'It can be said', wrote the Bishop of Antigonish, Bishop Morrison, in a subsequent brochure on the School's objectives and history, 'that it was nothing less than a revelation to observe what an amount of latent intellectual talent has been lying around undeveloped, and thereby precluded from attaining its proper destiny both as to individual needs and for the country's best welfare'.[16]

Comparing the school with the WEA, Tompkins commented that 'In a smaller way the record of the students of our People's School is another proof that the grown-up man of little or no previous education is capable of remarkable development if he possesses ambition and average intelligence'.[17] A comment by Little Doc Hugh reads:

> On the agricultural side, the object of the school is not only to lay a broad foundation of exact knowledge such as is essential in the successful prosecution of any modern industry, but so to develop the application of scientific principles as to disclose in agriculture a field of endeavour of great possibilities and of wonderful interest and fascination.

'This in itself', Little Doc Hugh wrote in conclusion, 'is a big program and its accomplishment will require time, but no one who has stood up before the eager students who attended the first session of the People's School can have any misgivings as to the feasibility of its final accomplishment'.[18]

A second school, in 1922, had sixty students, and it seemed briefly that nothing could now stand in the way of further progress. Even so, for all the success of the schools — for all that they were so widely admired and praised — Tompkins was still not satisfied. It seemed to him that requiring people to leave their communities in order to attend the schools limited the number who were able to benefit from them. The university would be able to work with people more effectively if its services were delivered to where they lived. A different approach would be needed in order for the wider objectives which had prompted the establishment of the schools to succeed.

Unhappily no such novel approach could for the time being be adopted. It was also in 1922 that Tompkins suffered what seemed at the time to be his greatest setback. For a time, he appeared likely to have no further involvement in the adult education activities which he had so largely brought about. Ironically his difficulties arose indirectly from his outstanding success in interesting the Carnegie Foundation in both the University of St Francis Xavier and higher education in Nova Scotia more generally.

A resolution of the university's Board of Governors on 17 December 1920 had invited the foundation to undertake a survey of the university and its catchment area, with a view to 'determining its educational policy'. The foundation then incorporated the survey in a wider study of higher education in Nova Scotia which it had already committed itself to carry out. The report arising from the study — the 'Sills-Learned' Report[19] — recommended that the several independent universities and colleges in the Maritime Provinces should be confederated so as to eliminate costly duplication of staff and facilities such as plant, libraries and scientific laboratories.

The cost of the project was estimated to be about $4.5 million, of which more than half would come from the foundation. In the event, the strong support of Tompkins and the faculty for the proposal was unavailing in the face of the opposition from Bishop Morrison. In the course of the fracas, Morrison instructed Tompkins to leave his post at the university and go to Canso — by Boyle's account 'a fishing port difficult of access, cold, foggy and in an advanced stage of economic decline' — as its parish priest. The conventional wisdom has usually seen Morrison's action as indicating that he had come to regard Tompkins as a 'turbulent priest', whose stance in favour of confederation required that he be disciplined. Irrespective of Morrison's motives, the decision was a blessing in disguise for Tompkins, albeit one which at the time bitterly disappointed him. Wittingly or not, Morrison had done Tompkins the favour of a lifetime.

'Canso ... Canso!', Boyle quotes Tompkins as crying out, 'What if I do not go? What if I got away from here entirely? They're looking for priests elsewhere'.[20] For all his distress, he bowed to Morrison's authority. It was a fortunate submission. Canso caused Tompkins to develop — and give practical effect to — his thinking much more radically than at the university. In the course of observing the adult education movements in other countries he had also come across their co-operatives. Closer to hand, he was aware of local success stories such as of the British-Canadian Co-operative Society — a retail co-operative on the Rochdale model — which the miners in Cape Breton had established in 1906, and of the co-operative to assist smallholders in processing and marketing their wool — later the Canadian Co-operative Woolgrowers Ltd — which was established by Little Doc Hugh.

Not least, he was interesting himself in the credit union movement which Alphonse Desjardins had initiated in Quebec at the turn of the century, and Bergengren was now driving forward in the United States. A letter he addressed to the Director of the Carnegie Foundation, Dr Keppel, in 1924 reveals the direction in which his thoughts were turning. It reads: 'I have been looking into Co-operation and Credit Unions for some time and I believe that great work can be done for adult education through these movements and their leaders'.[21]

Tompkins now took every possible opportunity to draw instances of co-operation and how it worked to the attention of his impoverished parishioners. At the same time he was constantly persuading them to meet, in bodies such as the Holy Name Society, and talk over their problems and how to overcome them. His consciousness-raising at Canso — and consequent extensive publicity in the *Halifax Herald* for the plight of the fishermen — were major factors in bringing about the appointment of the 1927 Royal Commission on the fisheries of the Maritime Provinces and the Magdalen Islands. 'If the shore fishing industry is to succeed, co-operation among fishermen is absolutely and immediately essential', reported the commission; 'We recommend, therefore, that the establishment of co-operative organisations of fishermen be assisted by the Department as soon as possible, and that an organiser, experienced in co-operative methods, be appointed and paid by the Federal Government for the required period to initiate and complete this work'.[22]

Meanwhile, other influences were also having their effect. Tompkins might have been exiled from the university, but he and his supporters did not lack alternative forums in which to put forward their views and continue pressing for action. The key groups were, in the first instance, a new annual conference on rural life; secondly, the university Alumni Association; and, finally, the Scottish Catholic Society. A second priest Morrison had reassigned in the course of the confederation imbroglio, Father Michael Gillis, had a leading role in all three bodies.

Gillis had served as an army chaplain in France, and studied at the London School of Economics. He returned to Nova Scotia fired with a passionate conviction that the Church had an inescapable obligation to involve itself directly in enabling its people to improve the quality of their lives. He was also an outspoken advocate of rural co-operatives. Coady credits him with having been 'the creative mind behind all movements, the dynamic leader and inspirer'.[23]

The success of the People's School gave rise in part in 1924 to the establishing of an annual Rural and Industrial Conference which was devoted largely to the problems of rural life. A summary of the topics discussed, by one of the key historians of the Antigonish Movement, Alex Laidlaw, reads 'loss of population, vacant farms, agricultural education, immigration and land settlement, organisation of farmers, training of young women for rural life, rural high schools, and all such matters that had any bearing on the evident deterioration of the rural community'.[24]

The conferences regularly adopted resolutions calling for more extension work and adult education such as, for example, in 1928:

> That whereas the economic well-being of a people depends to a large extent on their acquaintance with economic history and economic and sociological forces at work in a country; and whereas it is believed that the common worker is exploited now, because of the lack of knowledge of these forces and principles; and whereas the time would now appear to be opportune for the adoption of Adult Education for the whole of Canada and particularly for the Maritime Provinces. Therefore it is resolved that we pledge our support to the organisation that would in the opinion of a committee to be appointed by the Conference best formulate a policy of Adult Education.[25]

There was solid support for the conference decision from the Alumni Association. The association resolved in 1928 to press the board of governors of the university to make the university responsible for adult education.

Pressure was applied finally by the Scottish Catholic Society of Canada — a body committed to preserving Scotch culture and identity and the Gaelic language — which resolved in 1928 to create a $100,000 fund for educational purposes. A resolution the following year provided that the income from the fund should be applied 'to support, or help support' the Extension Department which the board of governors had now agreed should be created. When a further year was allowed to pass without the university taking action, the society threatened to take its money elsewhere. At this point the university finally capitulated. Establishment of the Extension Department was approved by the governors in 1928, and it began operations two years later, with an annual budget of $10,000.

Coady

The man the federal government chose to implement the thinking of the Royal Commission on fishing co-operatives — and the university chose to head its new Extension Department — was Father Moses Coady. Tompkins and Coady were first cousins. Like Tompkins, Coady was a farmer's son, born in 1882 on his parents' farm in Northeast Margaree, and raised on the farm in the Southwest Margaree Valley to which they moved two years later. 'I was doing a man's work when I was ten', Coady recalls; 'we were carpenters, coopers, woodsmen, fishermen, farmers all in one'.[26] Up until he was fifteen, his formal schooling was limited to 'a few weeks after planting in the spring and a little longer after digging in the fall',[27] together with such lessons as his parents were able to teach him at home.

None of this in any way held him back. Studying for the first time on a full-time basis, at high school when he was fifteen, he acquired his first mentor — 'the most inspiring teacher of my life'[28] — in Tompkins' older brother, Chris J. Tompkins. Coady was shortly recognised as Chris Tompkins's most promising pupil. His second — and more important — mentor was 'Jimmy' Tompkins. He was then undertaking his studies as a seminarian in Rome, and used to send back to his cousin a steady stream of pamphlets and books. One of the gifts from Tompkins which Coady thought about deeply was a penny edition of the Gospel of St Luke. 'When in later life M.M. Coady looked back upon that hour', writes Boyle, 'he knew it was the one in which he had decided to become a priest'.[29]

Meanwhile, Coady had completed his high school course, studied at the Provincial Normal School in Truro for a year to become a teacher, and taught for two years as principal at the elementary school in Margaree Forks, where he had been a pupil. Tompkins encouraged him to study Greek and Roman history during his first year as a teacher, and in the second year coached him in Latin by correspondence. In

1903 Coady entered the University of St Francis Xavier. Following his graduation in 1905, the Diocese of Antigonish selected him to study theology and philosophy at the Urban College in Rome, where he was awarded degrees as Doctor of Philosophy and Doctor of Divinity. 'This', Coady writes, 'was an unprecedented opportunity for a poor boy from the country to see the world, to enjoy the inspiration of a five-year sojourn in the Eternal City, and to get the best in theological and philosophical training of the time'.[30] He was ordained as a priest by Cardinal Respighi in the St John Lateran Basilica on 10 May 1910.

Coady then taught for a further four years at the St Francis Xavier College and the St Francis Xavier High School before undertaking additional graduate studies at the Catholic University of America in Washington DC, where his Master of Education degree was conferred in 1915. In 1916 he succeeded Tompkins as principal of the high school, and resumed lecturing at the college. The near-moribund provincial teachers' union made him its organiser — and later secretary-treasurer — in 1920. In the course of a four-year term of office, he turned the union back into a flourishing organisation with a large, active and professionally minded membership.

When the university established a new Department of Education in 1924, Coady headed it as the Professor of Education. He was also made an advisor to the Superintendent of Education. A capacity for vision — and for his visions to sometimes fall short of the hopes he invested in them — was evident in proposals he put forward in 1926, to the effect that the Sisters of St Martha should establish a school for adults — 'a new type of school that would bring music and the arts to the people'[31] — at Margaree. While what eventuated — a high school with a room for teaching domestic science — was more mundane, the venture had an unforeseen and far-reaching spin-off. Coady wrote:

> I was struck like a bolt from the blue, by an idea that turned out to be the turning point in my life ... It suddenly dawned on me that the short, quick, scientific way to progress in the world, even in the field of formal education of the youth, was through the enlightenment and education of adults ... I called a dozen or so of the people of this rural community to a meeting. My speech was short, just two sentences.

It was this: 'What should people do to get life in this community, and what should they think about and study to enable them to get it?' I sat down and listened to the comments of this small group of people. This was July, in the middle of my long summer vacation. By the end of the Christmas vacation, we had about twenty meetings of this little group and here emerged the technique of adult education known as the Antigonish Movement. It was a small study club, issuing in economic group action. We had co-operation before in many parts of the country. We had academic adult education, too.

'But this formula put the two of them together', Coady concluded, 'and that's what was new about the Antigonish Movement'.[32]

Following the decision by the governors of the university to establish the Extension Department, and the appointment of Coady as its director, the chancellor asked Coady what he thought should be done. His reply was that 'We could universalise the Margaree program'.[33] One of his first actions in his capacity as director was to appear before the Royal Commission on the fishing industry which had now been secured. Coady's submission argued that it was only through programs of adult education and organisation along co-operative lines that the well-being of the industry could be assured. The commission in its turn not only incorporated his recommendations in its report, but so arranged matters that the Department of Fisheries asked him to put them into effect.

The announcement was widely welcomed. A newspaper editorial of the day reads 'No better man could be found for this important work — he is of the people and he has never lost the common touch with the people, their needs and ambitions'.[34] Coady's efforts were an outstanding success. The outcome in the first instance was the establishment of more than two hundred local fishery unions, representing some ten thousand fishermen. 'After ten months work', writes Coady, 'I brought together 208 delegates from the fishing villages to Halifax where we set up the United Maritime Fishermen, June 26, 1930'.[35]

Purest milk of the distributist word

Where Coady wanted to go was now clear to him. While the details might change, and he was forever experimenting with new ideas, the underlying principles were those to which he adhered for the rest of his life. What he believed is readily recognisable as the purest milk of the distributist word. Its key elements were, in the first instance, well-divided property and why it was important; secondly, how political and economic democracy were linked inseparably with one another to the point where neither could succeed in the absence of the other; and, finally, co-operatives as a means of embodying the ideals of property and democracy and making it possible for ordinary men and women to find solutions to their problems and fulfil their hopes. Underpinning and drawing together all this was the role of adult education as a lifelong process of consciousness-raising and the acquisition of new skills, knowledge and perspectives. Coady's objectives were summarised in two phrases to which he regularly returned. People should be 'the masters of their own destiny' and they had a right to 'the good and abundant life'.

Accounts of Coady by the associates who outlived him refer repeatedly to the importance he attached to property. 'Ownership', writes Laidlaw in his 1971 collection of Coady's speeches and writings, 'was an essential ingredient of his democratic formula, and he looked upon great numbers of people without real ownership as a threat to democracy. Make all people owners, he said, and they will defend and preserve democracy, but by the same token the propertyless masses in modern society are an impediment and constant menace to true democracy'.[36]

A former fieldworker for the movement, Ida Delaney, recalls in a moving memoir of her experiences that 'the acquiring of ownership was one of the most powerful themes of Coady's speeches and the idea was one of the most frequently discussed in the study clubs ... He believed that pride of ownership was essential to the dignity of the person. "There is no democracy without ownership" he repeated from many platforms'.[37]

Not infrequently, the terms Coady used in his championing of the ownership of property were indistinguishable for all practical purposes from those of the distributists in

Britain. Take away the attribution for any given passage and it is difficult to say whether it is by Coady or by Belloc or one or other of his British distributist associates.

'Our world', Coady told an audience in Wisconsin in 1958, in terms which *The Servile State* had anticipated and Belloc would heartily have applauded, 'has become industrialised and ownership is now concentrated in the hands of a few':

> The great majority of the people, who are labourers in industrial centres, have become proletarianised. They no longer own anything. This is happening not only in industrial centres but also at great speed now in rural communities. Rural North America, for some decades has been contributing millions of its people to the proletariat ... Surely we can diagnose this frightening evil — on the one side the proletarianism of workers and farmers, and on the other a subtle new type of feudalism, the dictatorship of business and finance. If we prize our freedom, we must not permit the peoples of the world to become completely proletarianised.[38]

Many of his speeches linked the ownership of property with issues which were then barely if at all being publicly discussed.

He was in many respects a man decades ahead of his time. This was nowhere more strikingly evident than in regard to the link he saw between property and the well-being of the environment. He was a dedicated enviromentalist long before the word was in general use. 'The great masses of the people', he said in an address to the United Nations Conference on the Conservation and Utilisation of Resources in 1949, 'lacked interest in the conservation of natural resources':

> This is due to the fact that they lacked ownership. Tenancy, sharecropping, the emergence of the rural proletariat, and the landlordism that is still so widespread have all tended to make the masses of the world's people feel that they have no stake in the world. The good earth was not theirs, so why should they care? ... The most difficult phase of this problem is to find a formula by which the undeveloped masses of the world's people, who have heretofore never had any interest, ownership or control of the good things of the earth may be made capable of the task.

'The problem', the address concluded, 'is to find a program

that will bring the underdeveloped people of the earth up the road of progress to the point where they can own and control the earth — their earth — and become "masters of their own destiny".'[39]

The link of property and ownership with democracy was no less inseparable. By Laidlaw's account, 'Coady was convinced that ownership by all the people was the lifeblood of democracy'.[40] A letter Coady wrote in 1953 to the secretary of the Co-operative League of the United States, E.R. Bowen, reads: 'When men who are otherwise brilliant, realistic and scientific resort to telling bedtime stories to lull the masses of intelligent human beings in the world into the belief that democracy is compatible with financial plutocrats, then it is time for all of us to get on our knees and say our prayers'.[41]

In a similar vein, Coady told the National Convention of Canadian Home and School Federations in Halifax in 1951: 'To identify democracy with the ability of a man or a small group of men to set up economic kingdoms which necessitate the subservience and, I might say, the slavery of the masses is to indulge in a pure myth'.[42] 'In his view', writes Laidlaw, 'political democracy was good and necessary, but not enough; it had to be buttressed with economic democracy. He saw participation in all the vital processes of society as a test of democracy, for without participation, he said many times, democracy becomes a sham'.[43]

The remedy was co-operation. 'He chose the co-operative way', Laidlaw maintains, 'because he saw in it the only road to ownership of business enterprises open to the masses of any nation'.[44] In Coady's words:

> The great majority of the human race in all past times have lived frustrated economic lives in a world of potential plenty. They had no plan or formula by which they could release their energies on worthwhile activities. Economic co-operation meets this need. The people don't have to wait around for a superman to take a plan out of some metaphysical cloud. Through this simple co-operative formula they can, from the illiterate peasant and prole-tarian worker to the highest intellectual and spiritual leader, begin immediately to build themselves a social order in accordance with the specifications of right reason, if they but will.[45]

'Here's where the co-operative movement comes in', Coady

wrote to Gillis in 1951; 'It's the way the masses of the world can finance democracy'.[46]

The means of introducing co-operation was adult education. 'Education', Coady said in an address in Saskatchewan in 1949, 'should be coterminous with human life':

> Consequently, if we are to achieve our manifest destiny — to be enduringly great — we have to become firmly convinced that education does not end with high school, but that it is a continuous mobilization of people for adult learning. Only if the people of this country can keep on all the time during active life acquiring new ideas, new integrated ideas, are they able to evaluate the 'isms' of the day, meet problems that come up from time to time, rise above the hurdles that life throws across our way.

'Only in this way', Coady assured his audience, 'can we rise from one level to another in our civilisation'.[47]

All these elements and more were summarised for Coady in the phrase 'the good and abundant life' which he used so constantly. 'It embraced', according to Laidlaw, 'several concepts embedded in his mind: plenty in the material sense, ownership for all people, democratic participation, rational use of natural resources, and a just and equitable economic system':

> That is what he dreamed of; not only dreamed of, but was convinced mankind could achieve. He regarded human progress as steps in a journey towards a social order which he thought of in terms of good living and abundance for all.

'The good and abundant life for all which he pictured may be a dream today', Laidlaw continues, 'but it must be a dream first before it can become a reality tomorrow'.[48]

Away and beyond establishing co-operatives on a piece-meal basis, Coady looked forward to the wider vision which he and his associates referred to as 'the Big Picture'.[49] Within the overall framework of 'the Big Picture', consumer co-operatives would source their requirements from co-operative wholesale societies. The wholesale societies in turn would be supplied by factories which were the property of the movement. Coady's ultimate objective was an integrated system of co-operatives which would comprise a 'Middle Way' or 'Third Sector' between capitalism and communism. The model was very much that of consumer co-operative movements such as in Britain, where the giant Co-operative Wholesale Society has grown or manufactured a wide range of products either at home or abroad throughout most of the movement's history, and played a key role in the movement's affairs.

Coady saw consumer co-operation as embracing 'a vast field of business — retailing, wholesaling, manufacturing, money and credit and the wide range of services necessary to life in a modern society'.[50] 'We owe it all', he acknowledged in a speech in St Paul, Minnesota, in 1950, 'to the old Rochdale Pioneers'.

> They found a technique whereby people in groups can safely and surely carry on the economic operations incidental to mass life on earth. They have given us a technique whereby this can be done, a technique that does not permit one man or group to profit unduly from their fellows in society ... A business technique that precludes all possibility of exploitation at the expense of fellow human beings seems to carry with it the character of justice; but more than that, it is an instrument that permits charity. The strong can take care of the weak because they have an instrument that makes this possible.[51]

'The co-operative dream', Delaney quotes Coady as stating, 'is to cover the Maritimes with co-operatives and set the wheels of industry turning in our factories'.[52] However, none of this meant that the social order Coady had in mind would consist exclusively or even largely of co-operatives. 'The good society of the future', he wrote, 'should be a mixed society. It should imply individual and personal ownership, a large measure of co-operative ownership, some socialism and an area of private-profit enterprise'.[53]

Not least, Coady saw the principles and program of the movement as being in close conformity with his Catholic faith. The influence of the great social doctrine papal encyclicals *De Rerum Novarum* and *Quadragesimo Anno* on the Antigonish Movement was freely acknowledged. In Coady's view, not only Catholic business leaders but the Church's philosophical and educational leaders had been deaf to the appeal for social justice set out in *De Rerum Novarum*. Nothing, Coady argued, had emerged since the publication of *Quadragesimo Anno* that harmonised so well with its principles and proposals as the co-operative way of life.

Successive popes shared Coady's opinion. The strong support of Pope Pius XI for the work of the Antigonish Movement was set out in 1938 in a letter over the signature of the then Secretary of State of the Vatican, Cardinal Pacelli. 'May the work undertaken grow and flourish', the letter reads, 'and, with unswerving purpose of mind and will, be carried on to a complete fulfilment'.[54] When Pacelli succeeded to the papacy as Pius XII, he reaffirmed papal support for the movement, by naming Coady as a Domestic Prelate with the rank of Monsignor. The appointment was announced in May 1946. 'Where churchmen preached endlessly about the social encyclicals, never daring even to hope that they would be translated into action', concludes Laidlaw, 'the Antigonish program said: "Here are ways in which the teachings of *Rerum Novarum* and *Quadragesimo Anno* can be put to work right away ... let's to the task".'[55]

*Father Moses
Coady*

8

The Antigonish Movement
and the Limits of Rochdale
Co-operation

Little Dover

I
N ALL Coady's efforts, Tompkins not only inspired him
but provided him with a proven model on which to build.
At the same stage in the late 1920s as Coady was getting
off the ground the university's new Department of
Education, engaging in his ultimately unsuccessful bid for an
art and music school in Margaree, testifying before the Royal
Commission and carrying out his great organising task for
the Department of Fisheries, Tompkins was achieving
remarkable results in his Canso parish. The focus of his
efforts — the impoverished fishing village of Little Dover —
was to feature as a much noticed, widely written about and
frequently visited object lesson in the meaning, purpose and
methods of the Antigonish Movement. 'Little Dover', writes
the American author Bertram B. Fowler, 'was, in a sense the
cradle of the movement. The men of Little Dover were
among the first to shake off the lethargy of poverty and
misery and take the first strong strides towards a better order'.[1]

Little Dover, as Tompkins first became familiar with it in 1922, had a population of around four hundred. The soil was so rocky and inhospitable as to make the people wholly dependent for their livelihoods on their fishing. Their lives were dominated by a system whereby their tackle and other requisites were sold to them at the highest possible prices by the same middlemen who then bought their catches from them for as little as possible. As individuals, they had no way of extricating themselves from their predicament.

'What made their case even more bitter', writes Fowler, 'was the fact that most of them did not get in cash even the starvation price. They were in debt to the local merchant, who usually acted as the agent of the buyer'.[2] It was this desperate situation that Tompkins now set out patiently to remedy. The task before him was, as he saw it, to stir his parishioners and their neighbours of other faiths out of their apathy, set them to asking themselves what was the cause of their troubles, and provide them with information — pamphlets, leaflets and clippings — they could put to use in determining how better times could be brought about.

The first sign of progress was when the community was successful in petitioning the provincial government for a new road into the village. The people then asked themselves 'What next?'; 'What do you want to do?', was Tompkins's response, 'What problem do you think is worst?' The answer he was given was for the fishermen to can for themselves the lobsters they were catching and so capture the profits of the commercial canneries. 'You want a lobster factory', Tompkins told them, 'Why not build and operate it yourselves?'[3] Tompkins advice was taken. The people of Little Dover devoted the winter of 1929 to constructing the factory.

The work involved cutting the timber for themselves and hauling stones for the foundations, so that only the nails and hardware had to be bought for a total outlay of $129. Tompkins lent $300 for the purchase of canning machinery from his own pocket, and arranged a further loan of $700 from a friend. The business was then organised as a co-operative, to which members supplied their lobsters at the same low price as a commercial buyer would have paid. The result, at the end of the first season, was that the co-operative was able to pay off its borrowings, and return to its members an extra two cents per pound on the lobsters it had received.

The original study group now moved on to new projects. The lobster co-operative began selling into the Boston market for twenty cents a pound the larger live lobsters which previously had fetched six or seven cents from the middlemen. The price of fishing requisites was slashed — 'a savings of $4 on a single fishing net, five cents per pound on rope, four cents per pound on nails'[4] — by establishing a buying club. Another co-operative built two new fishing boats. Cottage industries were established to turn into rugs and scarves the local wool which previously had been sold raw to the agents at starvation prices. A new school was built, and additional teachers secured. Night classes for adults were established, in reading, writing, arithmetic and book-keeping.

'Even here', an Extension Department field worker wrote in 1935, 'extraordinary results are recorded. For instance, three men over sixty years of age who were formerly illiterate are reading the newspapers intelligently today'.[5] Not least, milk supplies for the community's children were assured by bringing in a herd of goats in place of the cows the meagre local pastures had been unable to support. None of this should be read as meaning that Little Dover ceased to be poor. What the local people did gain was a modest increase in their incomes, a significant improvement in the quality of their lives, renewed hope for the future and the sense of becoming again — in the phrase the Antigonish Movement was shortly to make famous — 'masters of their own destiny'.

The movement

Other fishing villages — hamlets with names as evocative of their Acadian French origins as Grand Etang, Cheticamp and Judique[6] — soon followed in the footsteps of Little Dover. In Grand Etang, the local priest put up his insurance policy as security so that the loan for the canning factory could be raised. 'We had learned', writes Coady, 'the wisdom of starting something that would demonstrate that thinking pays'.[7] Coady was now building up around him in the Extension Department an able and committed team of lieutenants. His associate director Dr A.B. MacDonald — usually referred to simply as 'A.B.' — was a fellow graduate of the University of St Francis Xavier, who had also studied agriculture at the Ontario Agricultural College in Guelph.

Prior to joining the Extension Department, A.B. was engaged in organisational work among farmers, and then became an Inspector of Schools for the county government.

He was initially doubtful about exchanging his secure position in the public service for the uncertain future the Extension Department now offered him, but was won over by the argument that Coady was making a genuine attempt to bring about social change. His gifts as an administrator ideally complemented those of Coady as a charismatic leader. 'What a team they were!', writes one of their contemporaries; 'Dr Coady, learned, dynamic, impressive, yet humble, zealous and kind; A.B., charming, jovial and good-natured, but at the same time ambitious, practical, and with a rare genius for organisation. It will probably be a long time before such a combination will be seen in action again'.[8] Accounts of the Antigonish Movement widely portray Tompkins as the prophet who cried out in the wilderness, Coady as the messiah, and MacDonald as the organiser. In 1944, A.B. left the Extension Department to become secretary of the Co-operative Union of Canada.

A second key lieutenant, A.S. MacIntyre, was a one-time vice-president of the United Mine Workers' Union and county vice-president of the Canadian Labour Party, widely known among his fellow miners as 'Red Alex'. MacIntyre helped to lead the bitter strike against the Dominion Steel and Coal Corporation in 1925. The mining companies then black-listed him, and he for a time earned his livelihood as a door-to-door salesman of Watkins and Raleigh products. An address he delivered at the 1932 Rural and Industrial Conference implored his listeners to pay more attention to the appalling living conditions of the miners and their families. Coady then hired him to manage the office which the Extension Department established for the mining community in Cape Breton in 1933.

Coady and Tompkins valued MacIntyre highly for his understanding of the labour movement and his ability to get across their message to the miners and other industrial workers. He was instrumental in setting up large numbers of study clubs in the Cape Breton area, which in most instances resulted in the establishment of credit unions and co-operative stores. In later life, he was made the secretary of the Nova Scotia Co-operative Union. Another welcome recruit was the

Presbyterian clergyman, J.D.N. MacDonald. Two notable public servants — J.F.C. MacDonnell from the Federal Ministry of Agriculture and R.J. McSween from the Provincial Department of Agriculture — worked so closely with the Extension Department as to be regarded as being for all practical purposes members of the staff. By 1938 there were eleven full-time staff members, seven part-time members and thirty associate members with duties in the fishing communities.[9]

A conspicuous feature of the team for its time was the talented and committed women it was able to attract — women of the stature of Kay Desjardins, Zita Cameron, Sister Marie Michael, Ellen Arsenault, Ida Delaney and Sister Irene Doyle — and whose efforts, under what were often appalling difficulties, contributed so greatly to the success of its work. Delaney describes occasions such as when a group visiting Canso overnight for a meeting were snowbound there for a week while they waited for a snowplow to clear the road. 'While the experience of being snowbound indoors was unpleasant', writes Delaney, 'it was not as bad as being outside in the midst of a storm. Once we had to leave the car and stand outside for some time during which the weather changed from snow to rain and then to sleet. My stockings froze to my legs'.[10]

J.D.N. MacDonald has an account of a related incident, when staying with a local farmer after a meeting:

> There was no plumbing of any kind in the house, so when we got up I asked the farmer where the outhouse was. He pointed to the side of a hill which seemed to me to be about a mile away. There was about three feet of snow on the ground, and the path to the outhouse was filled in by drifts.

'If you slipped off the path', the account concludes, 'you were instantly up to your middle in snow'.[11]

A final key figure for the movement — albeit never a member — was Bergengren. Bergengren's association with Tompkins and Coady dated from 1931, when he stood in for Filene in response to an invitation to address a conference. A contemporary report reads that 'Bergengren, a gifted orator, convinced Dr Coady and others who heard him speak, that the philosophy of credit unions was sound'.

The credit union legislation he drafted for the province enabled any seven or more citizens from the same neighbourhood, occupation or institution to form a credit union. Bergengren was also associated with Coady and other leading Antigonish Movement identities in establishing credit unions on the basis of movement's study clubs:

> He, Dr Coady and A.B. MacDonald set out for Canso to organise the first credit union ... A snow-storm blocked the way of the three men, however, and they decided to return to the main highway and go to Cape Breton. Bergengren and A.B. went to Broad Cove and organised a credit union there that night. The next night they joined Dr Coady, who had gone to Reserve Mines, and the three of them had a hand in organising the Reserve Mines Credit Union. This latter group acted quickly and got the first charter from the Nova Scotia government.[12]

There was no lack of formidable obstacles to the formation of credit unions, not least due to the poverty of their prospective members. Delaney quotes the response of a miner leaving a meeting in Glace Bay where an Extension Department speaker had urged his listeners to start a credit union. 'How does that fellow expect us to start a bank?', the miner said to his companions, 'We did not have ten cents among us in the hall'.[13]

Credit unionism became a major driving force for the movement's activities, thereby in part anticipating the role it was to play twenty and more years later in driving forward regional and local economic development in Mondragon. Where a credit union was established, a co-operative store often followed. Tompkins summarised one aspect of the situation when he addressed the American Catholic Rural Conference in October 1935. He told the conference:

> Take credit unions. They make for the federation of man, and are great aids for Christianity. They, with co-operative stores, prevent the work of loan sharks, eye-gougers, graft, undue profits, exploitation, and give us honesty in quality and quantity of goods. These two movements alone would help greatly in building a world *naturaliter Christiana.*[14]

The economic development dimension was no less significant. 'The nickels and dimes collected for the credit unions', write the Canadian scholars, Jim Lotz and Mike Welton, in their 1997 study of Tompkins, 'provided capital for co-operatives, generating a sense in small communities that they could tackle their own problems with their own resources'.[15]

Principles

The movement was now codifying what it stood for in what became by the early 1940s an explicit statement of principles. The statement in its final form was drafted by the Professor of Economics at the University of St Francis Xavier University, Harry Johnston, in 1944, as a lecture about the movement for students at the Acadia University. 'I remember', writes Sister Doyle, 'the day Harry Johnston brought the draft of his lecture to Dr Coady to read. Although the principles had been part of the movement from its beginning, Johnston's crystallising of them as he did was a delight to Dr Coady. He praised Johnston to the highest'.[16] The statement reads:

> The essence of the philosophy on which the Antigonish Movement is built is contained in six principles. The first of these is *the primacy of the individual.* This principle is based on both religious and democratic teaching: religion emphasises the dignity of man, created in the image and likeness of God; democracy stresses the value of the individual and the development of individual capacities as the aim of social organisation.
>
> The primacy of the individual gives rise to the second principle: that *social reform must come through education.* Social progress in a democracy must come through the action of the citizens; it can only come if there is an improvement in the quality of the people themselves. That improvement, in turn, can only come through education.
>
> The third principle is that *education must begin with the economic.* In the first place, the people are most keenly interested in and concerned with economic needs; and it is good technique to suit the educational effort to the most intimate interests of the individual or group. Moreover, economic reform is the most immediate necessity because the economic problems of the world are the most pressing.
>
> The fourth principle of the Antigonish movement is that *education must be through group action.* Group action is natural because man is a social being. Not only is man commonly organised in groups, but his problems are usually group problems. Any effective adult education program must, therefore, fit into this basic group organisation of society. Moreover, group action is essential to

success under modern conditions; you cannot get results in business or civic affairs without organisation.

The fifth principle is that *effective social reform involves fundamental changes in social and economic institutions.* It is necessary to face the fact that real reform will necessitate strong measures of change which may prove unpopular in certain quarters.

The final principle is that *the ultimate objective of the movement is a full and abundant life for everyone in the community.* Economic co-operation is the first step, but only the first, towards a society which will permit every individual to develop to the utmost limit of his capacities.[17]

The method

The movement also now had a largely standard procedure for bringing on communities to the point where their first co-operatives could be established. What was involved was, in the first instance, a public meeting designed, as Coady saw it, 'to explode the intellectual dynamite that would break up apathy and prejudice, shock the people out of their complacency and fire them with the enthusiasm to rebuild society';[18] secondly, study clubs to identify problems and sort out how to solve them; and, finally, the initial co-operative itself — more often than not a credit union — as the means by which people could lift themselves by their bootstraps out of poverty, and thereby move forward towards the goal which Tompkins and Coady defined as 'the good and abundant life'.

Delaney has given a vivid account of a series of public meetings which she attended with Coady in the Counties of Antigonish and Guysborough. 'Coady, she writes 'inspired and challenged his hearers to unite in a program of adult education that would change their lives'. His speech at the outset invited the audience to be humble enough to acknowledge how little they knew about the economic forces that governed their lives, and thereby to open their minds to new ideas. Coady would wish aloud for a magic iron with which to iron out such crooked thinking as might be abroad in the hall, or a giant vacuum cleaner to sweep up misconceptions. The speech would then move on to vividly illustrate how ordinary people had forfeited their control of the retail and financial sectors of the economy.

As a result, Coady would argue, 'The economic system is built like a tower that is out of plumb':

> When a leaning tower rises high enough, it becomes menacing and attempts are made to prop it up with guy-wires. But no matter how many wires are used, the tower still leans. If the building process continues and the tower is allowed to rise high enough, the time will come when nothing will keep it from crashing down. Society is making feeble attempts to prop up the leaning economic tower with the guy-ropes of a skimpy old age pension, mother's allowances and the rusty old wire the dole. But the fact remains that the economic tower still leans, no matter how many attempts are made to hold it up. The only wise course is to rebuild the tower on a true foundation. Only in this way will people correct their great default.

The speech would recommmend at this point that listeners should set up study clubs.

The objectives of the study clubs would be described as being to enable their members to become personally efficient in their fields of work, and to work together on those activities which could not be carried on alone. It was not co-operative marketing which mattered most as farmers often supposed, Coady would explain, but consumer co-operation such as could correct the 'great default' whereby consumers had abdicated their rights and responsibilities in retailing and banking. He would argue that the scope for co-operatives was limited only by the imaginations of their members, and could readily take in such services as health care, housing, libraries and recreation. He would conclude by telling his audience the story of the Rochdale Pioneers, and urging them to follow the example of Rochdale. 'It was time' he would say, 'for them to come out of their humble state and do great things'.[19]

During and after the public meeting, local leaders were identified, and the study clubs formed. An account of the system which Coady delivered as a broadcast under the title 'Adult Education in Action' in 1938 reads:

> The small study club or discussion, composed of five or ten members, is our fundamental unit of organisation. These small groups select their own leaders who serve as contact men with our department and see to it that the clubs meet regularly once a week. The federation of the small groups

of a community into larger groups known as associated study groups gives the people the opportunity to discuss the common problems arising out of their studies. The groups are supplied with regular study material from the University. They have at their disposal a wide range of books, pamphlets and mimeographed material ... Another important phase of the work is the training of community leaders. Short courses of four weeks' duration are held yearly at the University, to which men and women are coming in ever-increasing numbers. Regional conferences are held from time to time and the annual Rural and Industrial Conference, which had a small beginning a few years ago, is now a permanent institution which supplies the dynamics for the whole movement.

'The hope of Canada', Coady concluded, 'is that we can find enough bold spirits who will dare to oppose reaction and vested interests, dare to be scientific in the social field, realistic enough to face the facts, and make the people free'.[20]

Outcomes

At the peak of the movement's activity, in 1938-39, the three Maritime Provinces had no fewer than 2265 study clubs with a total membership of 19,600. The movement had by then established 342 credit unions and 162 co-operatives of other kinds.[21] Meanwhile, the consumer co-operatives — the local co-operative stores — had been federating to source their stock from co-operative wholesale societies, and the credit unions were learning to provide themselves with shared support services through credit union leagues. Two thriving co-operative wholesale societies — Cape Breton Co-operative Services and Maritime Co-operative Services — stood out as shining examples of what could be achieved by individual co-operatives taking seriously their obligation to co-operate with one another.

The following the movement had by now attracted was evident: the Rural and Industrial Conference in 1938 attracted around one thousand people, and two hundred people attended a Co-operative Institute meeting after the conference, to discuss issues of special interest to co-operatives. Those taking part in both gatherings included 'educationists, clergymen, social workers, and others from thirty states in the United States and from every province in Canada'.[22] The breadth of the representation was indicative of the widespread attention the movement was now attracting, both throughout North America and internationally.

For example, the Co-operative League of the United States organised annual tours of the area for groups of around one hundred and fifty. Other early visitors included the future Prime Minister of Canada, Pierre Trudeau. As has been seen, Coady in his turn spoke widely from platforms outside Nova Scotia and the Maritime provinces. An outstanding example was when, in 1936, the Carnegie Foundation and the National Catholic Welfare Conference in the United States sponsored a lecture tour which saw him speaking in a dozen states, often to several audiences in a single city. 'His talks', Doyle reports, 'were headlined in the local newspapers'.[23]

The media more generally were no less responsive. Periodicals in which feature articles on the movement appeared included *The Times,* the *New York Times, America, The Commonweal, Le Devoir,* the *Montreal Standard, Coronet* and *The Reader's Digest.* 'How many of the educated and intelligent people who read this supplement have heard of Antigonish?', asked a writer in the *Times Literary Supplement* for 1 August 1936, 'yet amid a multitude of crowded experience ... nothing moved me so much as the extra-mural work of the University of St Francis Xavier at Antigonish'.[24] The movement had innumerable radio programs devoted to it, as, for example, in 1942, when Belloc's biographer, Robert Speaight, told its story to a worldwide audience for the BBC. There was a film about the movement made by the National Film Board of Canada, and two more made by the Harmon Foundation.

None of this meant that all the attention the movement received was necessarily to its advantage. An editorial in *The Extension Bulletin* for 18 October 1938 reads:

> Exaggerations concerning the Movement which have appeared in print outside the Maritimes from time to time do no good to the cause at home. The home people read these, or hear about them, and are not favourably impressed. It is not necessary to exaggerate the material achievements of the work — which are considerable. The idea of the Movement, however, the restoration of effective

ownership of the people and making clearer their way to participation in the heritage of our age, is one the need of which cannot be exaggerated.

'But no one should underestimate the difficulties in the way', the editorial warned; 'Wishful thinking is the pitfall of the enthusiast'.[25]

A major spin-off from the attention the movement attracted was the interest which began to be taken in whether — and if so how — its program might be used to expedite development in countries in the Third World. Following the Second World War, the countries most frequently sending visitors to the Extension Department included those such as India, Pakistan and Indonesia which had recently achieved their independence. As has been seen, following Coady's death in 1959, the Coady International Institute was established as a memorial to him. The objective of the institute was to provide training in the Antigonish approach for students from developing countries.

Coady's immediate successor as Director of the Extension Department, Monsignor M.J. MacKinnon, saw the possibilities for the application of the program to the emerging countries of the world as being 'unlimited':

> It is a program of self-help and mutual help. It takes the people where they are, even the illiterate, and leads them to the higher levels of human performance. It is inexpensive and easily applicable to large numbers of people over wide areas. It is also big enough philosophically and scientifically to appeal to the most fastidious. It is a program suited to democracy in this scientific and technological age.

'It is a program of adult education', MacKinnon concluded, 'that begins in the economic field, and fans out into every phase of human activity; it is a program which will give life to all nations and all peoples, and not just the favoured few'.[26]

A 1966 study of the Antigonish Movement and overseas development by Father Boavida Coutinho lists bodies which have sponsored foreign students for courses at the Coady International Institute as including the ILO, the FAO, UNESCO, the Colombo Plan and the Ford Foundation. 'The Movement', affirms Coutinho, 'is known universally and the efficiency of its methods and principles is widely accepted'.[27] In 1984, the Coady Institute had development agencies linked to it in eight centres in Africa, twenty centres in Asia and twenty-one centres in Latin America.[28]

Tompkins at Reserve Mines

Meanwhile, notable new initiatives continued to be taken, not least by Tompkins, who had moved from Canso to the industrial parish of Reserve Mines in the heart of the Cape Breton coalfields in 1935, and was now organising the miners and their families as effectively as he had previously the fishermen. A key example was the co-operative housing project which Tompkins instigated on land in his parish originally intended for a graveyard. 'Yes', Tompkins is quoted as saying of the site, 'it would make a nice resting place for the dead, but I think we should let the living have it for now'.[29]

Tompkins was fortunate in having an outstanding executive officer for the program in Mary Arnold. Arnold — in Delaney's words 'a true pioneer who opened an entirely new field of co-operative endeavour in Nova Scotia'[30] — was the treasurer of the Co-operative League of the United States, with hands-on experience of co-operative housing in New York. She and her companion, Mabel Read, came to Antigonish to attend a Rural and Industrial Conference, and were recruited by Tompkins to organise housing co-operatives for the Extension Department. Arnold recalls telling Tompkins 'We are leaving tomorrow'. However, her account continues, 'We were not to go back to the United States on the following day. Instead we were to spend two years at the University of Reserve Mines, sitting at the feet of Father Jimmy Tompkins'. A comment by Tompkins at his first meeting with Arnold summarises his overall approach and outlook. 'Go to the people', Tompkins told Arnold; 'Learn from them. Choose your ideas. Ideas have hands and feet. They will work for you'.[31]

When the members of the first of the co-operatives — by Delaney's account 'eleven families with a total of forty-eight children' and at one point 'not a twenty-five cent piece among them'[32] — moved into their new houses, they named the development Tompkinsville in honour of Tompkins. Each home was financed with $100 saved by the family while the project was in its preparatory stages, $400 contributed in the form of labour and a $1500 loan from the provincial

Housing Commission. The loans were serviced with a monthly payment of $9.65 over a twenty-five year period. At a later stage, the establishment of a reserve fund to cover repairs, upkeep and protection in case of illness lifted the monthly payment to $12.15.

'They aren't just workingmen's houses', a local journalist wrote incredulously, 'but houses anyone might care to live in'.[33] Tompkins quotes a member of one of the housing co-operatives as having told him: 'I learned more in the last year than I did in the other twenty-seven of my life'. 'He did not mean from books', Tompkins continued, 'but that people could get together, work together, help one another, raise money, learn how to plan, to carpenter, to own a home — and — and develop the virtues of community. *He did get an education he could never get any other way*'.[34] The co-operative housing program ultimately produced homes for some 6500 families who would otherwise have had no hope of decent accommodation.

Tompkins's new ventures were not confined to housing. 'Why, do you know, there's not a library around here for miles', he told his associates in Cape Breton; 'Heavens, man, why don't we start a library — a co-operative library?'[35] The library — the People's Library as it shortly became known — was initially stocked with books he donated from his own shelves, and housed in the front room of his rectory. As he had done previously on behalf of the university, Tompkins was then able to solicit donations for the library from his friends at the Carnegie Foundation. The library became an important means of stimulating support for co-operatives such as the Reserve Mines Co-operative Society, and in turn was supported by them. 'The bulletin board', reports Boyle, 'was always hung with slogans such as, "The man who reads is the man who leads".'[36]

Tompkins was indefatigible in urging people to read, and drawing to their attention books which might interest them, including those of the British distributists. A review of Belloc's book *The Restoration of Property* in *The Extension Bulletin* in March 1937 — unsigned, but almost certainly by Tompkins — reads:

This newest volume by Hilaire Belloc is a very reliable source book of principle for those who can accept neither Finance Capitalism as we see it today nor Communist collectivism as we may see it tomorrow. It is an admirably clear and realistic analysis of the economic basis of freedom by a man who is a master of analysis and one of the major defenders of freedom in the modern world.[37]

Tompkins was also recommending Belloc's work directly to his friends and associates. 'I shall certainly get hold of Belloc's *The Crisis of Civilisation*', the Director of the Canadian Association for Adult Education, Dr E.A. Corbett, wrote to him in December, 1937, 'and let you know what I think of it'.[38]

The example of Reserve Mines encouraged other communities to set up libraries, and in 1940 Tompkins was able to persuade the provincial government to legislate for a regional library system, under the direction of a Regional Libraries Commission. 'The chief instrument for promoting Adult Education', he had argued, 'will be the well-stocked Regional Library, the people's university of the future, supported as our public schools are'.[39] The Carnegie Foundation saw the Commission off to a good start, with the offer of a donation of $50,000.[40] When, shortly before Tompkins' death in 1953, his admirers looked round for a way to thank him, they settled on a new building to rehouse the original People's Library in Reserve Mines which had meant so much to him.

The Rochdale cul-de-sac

The pattern of the movement's activities in the 1930s was carried forward into the 1940s and 1950s, albeit with changes in its pace, intensity and emphasis. However, there was no change in the nature of the co-operatives. Coady was totally convinced that — as he told an audience in St Paul, Minnesota, in 1950, in so many words — 'Consumer co-operation is the only thing that can be called real co-operation'.[41] He further firmly believed that, in consumer co-operation, he had the philosopher's stone which would enable him to bring about the new social order — the Middle Way or Third Sector between capitalism and communism — of which he and his associates dreamed.

What Coady in this later stage of the movement's history understood by change was not introducing co-operatives of new kinds, but making those with which he was already familiar bigger, better and more numerous. That changes to the co-operatives of a more fundamental nature might be necessary in order for the movement to achieve its objectives appears not to have occurred to him. In putting his trust in consumer co-operation — in concentrating on the creation of consumer co-operatives including credit unions and marketing co-operatives, virtually to the exclusion of other kinds of co-operatives — he was not alone, but rather in the distinguished company of authorities such as Beatrice and Sidney Webb and perhaps G.D.H. Cole. For all that, he and they were mistaken. Faith in consumer co-operation is a necessary but not a sufficient principle for a mutualist strategy.

As hindsight now makes clear, what Coady was up against was the Rochdale cul-de-sac. The Rochdale cul-de-sac is the situation which arises where co-operatives pass from the second to the third or system stage of their lifecycle as social movements. As has been seen, the first and second stages of the lifecycle are characterised by members of the co-operative being actively engaged in providing themselves with a product or service which otherwise would be insufficiently accessible to them. A co-operative in the third stage of its lifecycle is effectively one where members limit themselves to consuming products and services, and delegate the delivery of them to employees.

In this way, the co-operative ceases to be a body where all principals are agents and agents are principals, and an agency relationship is created. The co-operative then becomes subject to the basic agency dilemma in the same way as its conventional counterparts, and forfeits the competitive advantage it has previously had available to it. The employees are in a much more advantageous position to further their interests in their capacity as agents than the members in their capacity as principals, and their well-being rather than the well-being of the members increasingly determines how the co-operative goes about its affairs.

One possible outcome is that consequent difficulties on the part of the co-operative in controlling its costs will ultimately cause it to go out of business. Accounts such as *A Middle Way: Rochdale Co-operation in New South Wales 1859-1986* by the Australian historian Gary Lewis are a chilling reminder of how, in the absence of adequate member involvement and scrutiny, complacent, incompetent or opportunistic manage-ment can cause once thriving co-operatives and co-operative movements to vanish virtually overnight, and be forgotten as completely as if they had never existed. Alternatively, where co-operatives are successful in commercial terms, there may be attempts to demutualise them by their boards or managements or external corporate raiders. Where members of a co-operative have lost the habit of seeing themselves as having property rights in it or otherwise actively looking after their interests, a determined takeover bid may well be successful.

That the danger is real is clearly evident from the recent near-death experience of the Co-operative Wholesale Society (CWS) in Britain. In 1997, the CWS — the oldest and biggest consumer co-operative in Europe, with 35,000 employees, over 500 stores, annual sales in excess of £3 billion and major subsidiaries in the Co-operative Bank and the Co-operative Insurance Society — narrowly escaped being taken over and having its assets stripped by a 28-year old entrepreneur, Andrew Regan, to whom it had previously sold substantial manufacturing interests. Had Regan's bid proceeded, it was his intention to sell the Co-operative Bank, the Co-operative Insurance Society and perhaps the co-operative funeral businesses, and appoint a chief executive officer for the more profitable parts of the food businesses — at a salary package of around £6 million plus bonuses — to run them on his behalf in competition with other conventional supermarket chains such as Tesco and Sainsbury's. Regan would have walked away from the transaction with holdings to the value of between £1.8 billion and £2 billion, for an outlay of around £1.2 billion.

That the takeover was thwarted was due largely to the success of the CWS in proving that Regan's company, Lanica, had obtained the information for its bid illegally. The judge in the High Court proceedings arising from the fracas, Mr Justice Lightman, described Regan's actions in receiving the information — and the actions of key senior managers within the CWS in giving it to him — as 'clearly dishonest' and 'the clearest case of a gross, wilful and disgraceful breach of confidence'. Regan was reported in the *Daily Mirror* to be facing imprisonment in a private criminal prosecution for 'aiding and abetting theft and receiving stolen goods'. His bankers, Hambros, and his solicitors, Travers, Smith and Braithwaite, made an 'abject apology' to the CWS, and, following an internal inquiry at Hambros, two of its directors resigned and a number of other staff were disciplined. One senior manager at the CWS was dismissed, and another retired.[42] The Plunkett Foundation, Britain's oldest and most influential co-operativist and mutualist think-tank and consultancy, summarises the whole distasteful episode with eloquent understatement in its annual publication *The World of Co-operative Enterprise for 1998*, as having 'raised doubts about the ethics of a number of City institutions'.[43]

While the CWS has survived to mend its ways, other mutuals have been less fortunate. For example, Australia's two largest mutual assurance societies, the Australian Mutual Provident Society (AMP) and the National Mutual Life Assurance Society have recently been demutualised, to the considerable financial benefit of managements whose prime responsibility should have been to uphold their mutualist status. The Board of the AMP is reported to have allocated its Managing Director, Mr George Trumbull, free shares to the value of more than $10 million over a three-year period following demutualisation. Mr Trumbull will also receive a base yearly salary of $2.7 million.[44] What the founders of the AMP — pioneers of the mutualist cause in a new country — would have made of so grotesque a betrayal of their hopes and so inflated a remuneration defies imagination.

More than half the permanent building societies in both Britain and Australia have similarly undergone demutualisation. The more conspicuous victims in Britain have included the Abbey National Building Society with assets totalling £94.3 billion, the Halifax/Leeds Building Society with £93 billion and the Woolwich Building Society with £27 billion. The consequence has been a feeding frenzy in which hundreds of thousands of new members — so-called 'carpet-baggers' — have joined the societies for the express purpose of participating in the parcelling out of their capital. What has also been witnessed is the establishment of vulture funds specifically targeted to promoting and profiting from the demutualisation of building societies.

Two cases in point are the Cairngorm Building Societies Trust and the Cairngorm Demutualisation Trust. Interests associated with a former royal butler, Michael Harden, have also figured prominently in attempts to profit from demutualisation. Following an unsuccessful bid to demutualise the Bradford and Bingley Building Society, Mr Harden — now widely recognised as a 'serial carpet-bagger' — has recently notified the Yorkshire Building Society that he intends to stand for election as a director and propose a resolution for the conversion of the society into a conventional company.

Mr Hardern was also prominent in a recent failed attempt to demutualise the Nationwide Building Society. At the time of the poll, it was estimated that some 600,000 of the society's 4.9 million members were carpet-baggers who had joined in anticipation of a windfall. A prominant friendly society director likens what has been happening to the shattering of a great taboo. He writes: 'It is as though the members of a cricket club had suddenly decided to sell their playing fields and pocket the proceeds — and to hell with cricket'.[45]

There are indications that Australia's credit unions — a movement totalling more than three million members, with assets of more than $18 billion — are also being targeted by would-be demutualisers. When Australia's first demutualisation of a credit union — the Sunstate Credit Union in Queensland — took place in 1997, fewer than 14 per cent of its members received anything in return for their interests in its assets, and the most conspicuous beneficiaries were a tiny minority made up largely of its staff and directors.[46]

Distressing as the effects of the Rochdale cul-de-sac will be seen to have been for Coady when he encountered them in the 1950s, they were barely a hint of its ravages forty years later. Demutualisation negates the fundamental principle of co-operatives and other mutualist bodies that each generation of their members adds to their assets in the expectation that they will be retained for the benefit of others still to come — that current members are trustees in effect for the intentions of the dead and the inheritance of the unborn. That windfall payments may accrue to the current members as a consequence of an abrogation of this principle of the conservation of mutualist capital in no way mitigates its ethical enormity.

Nor should it obscure its cost in terms of further compromising the element of trust on which depends not only the future availablity of mutualist self-help as a means of meeting pressing social and economic needs, but our capacity to function as communities. As Francis Fukuyama reminds us, the level of trust inherent in a society is the 'single pervasive cultural characteristic' which determines its well-being, as

well as its ability to comptete. In undermining trust, demutualisation strikes at the ties which bind society together.[47]

Malaise

Lacking, as Coady and his associates did, a theoretical basis
for understanding the malaise they were coming to detect in
the movement, their frustration was expressed in complaints
such as that members were disloyal or insufficiently far-
sighted. Coady, for example, told a United Maritime
Fishermen Convention in 1954 that 'There are certain groups
of individuals in various parts of the Maritimes who still shop
around from week to week to sell their lobsters to private-profit
dealers if they get an extra cent or cent and a half there':

> They forget that over the years, by and large, the co-
> operatives gave a better price. They should remember also
> that the U.M.F. is only in the initial stages of its existence
> and there is every reason to hope that as it grows in volume
> and power it can do an even better job. It cannot grow,
> however, if thousands of fishermen hold aloof with the
> stupid attitude of comparing prices. If this is the right way
> to do business, why are they hesitating?

'One moment's thought', Coady concluded, 'should
convince these canny in-and-outers that if there were no co-
operatives the prices would immediately snap back to where
they were in the old days'.[48]

It was not in the fishermen's co-operative alone that
backsliding caused concern. Delaney highlights the problems
of the retail co-operatives with 'dividend chasers' and those
who looked on the co-operative 'solely as a way of saving
money on their purchases':

> New members were attracted first by the promise of
> patronage dividends ... The co-op was just one way in which
> they thought they could save money and they purchased
> every other way they could. They shopped at the co-op
> when it suited them, but they shopped at other stores too
> ... The co-ops lost business because of the impatience of
> those members who had joined with expectations of great
> savings. They were hard to reach with an educational
> program. They were not in the study clubs and they did not
> appear at membership meetings.

'If the members did not remain loyal to the co-op', Delaney continues, 'it would surely fold up and the attractive deals offered by the co-op's competitor would end'.[49]

The study clubs — the rock on which the movement had been built — were also having their problems. Delaney's account notes that by the 1940s the number of clubs was declining:

> While the clubs were engaged in the work preparatory to the organisation of a credit union or a co-operative store there was a compelling reason for full attendance at the study club meeting. When these co-operative enterprises were finally established, interest in the clubs was likely to diminish. The clubs became more specialised and of particular interest to a smaller group, consisting of directors and committee members. They had been the most active members of the study clubs and were now responsible for the operation of the co-ops that had resulted from the study program.

'The decline of the study clubs', Delaney concludes, 'was a source of much concern to them'.[50]

The error in each of the instances quoted was to attribute to individuals failings which in reality were due to the system. It was not disloyal or short-sighted members who were at fault. The fault lay in asking more of consumer co-operation than it was by its nature able to deliver. 'When co-operation is reduced to personal fiscal benefits and nothing more', writes the Canadian scholar, George Melnyk, 'then it is doomed to imitating capitalist practice'.[51]

Eastern Co-operative Services

The debacle was nowhere more strikingly evident than in the case of the new co-operative wholesale society, Eastern Co-operative Services (ECS). 'Our most promising program', Coady wrote in 1957, 'is the creation of a new wholesale, Eastern Co-operative Services, which will be the synthesis of all the things we ever thought about. It may well be a pilot plant for the underdeveloped parts of the earth'.[52] A one-time colleague recalls Coady confiding in him, in 1957 or 1958, that 'the ECS was for him a dream come true'.[53] ECS — launched on 3 January 1957 — linked with one another what had previously been a system of autonomous co-operative bodies comprising, in the first instance, the regional apex co-operative wholesale society Maritime Co-op Services; secondly, two sub-regional wholesale societies — Eastern Co-op Services in Antigonish and Cape Breton Co-op Services — and, finally, the local consumer and producer societies.[54]

The basis for ECS was the belief that being bigger would enable it to acquire, store and supply on a year-round basis sufficient local produce to meet in full the requirements of the regional market. It was further anticipated that the additional demand so generated would cause local production to expand, thereby creating additional income for farmers and jobs for workers. A poultry killing plant, egg grading facilities and cold storage facilities for fruit and vegetables opened in 1959. Later additions included a hardware outlet, automotive sales and servicing and a restaurant.

Had Coady lived, he would have seen his vision for the venture shattered. Not only did the anticipated level of demand fail to eventuate, but local production did not expand as had been foreseen. Several of the subsidiary operations, including the car agency, were unable to pay their way. The upshot was that ECS closed its doors for the last time in 1965. Its assets were acquired by Maritime Co-operative Services, which then reinvented itself with a new identity: the current impressively large-scale Co-op Atlantic.[55] There was a further blow in 1988, when the United Maritime Fishermen — the body Coady had established as long ago as 1930 — also failed, and was handed over to receivers.

Explanations for the failures have to date centred on grounds such as that, in the first instance, Eastern Nova Scotia was not a market commensurate with the scale of the larger co-operatives; secondly, that the larger co-operatives required more sophisticated management skills — and more sophisticated directors — than the movement had available to it; thirdly that the forward planning was deficient; and, finally, that ideological considerations such as wanting to enable families to remain on the land were allowed to take precedence over economic and financial realities. More broadly, it is argued that wartime pressures denied the movement the continuity which was required in order for it to develop effectively. In the relatively prosperous postwar economic climate there was less incentive for people to go out at night to meetings and otherwise involve themselves in the movement's co-operatives and other activities.

Be the merits of each of these suppositions as considerable as they may, the debate fails to come to grips with the real issue. The lesson from all the consumer co-operatives and co-operative movements that have failed, either wholly or in part, is that the experience of consumption either of goods or services is insufficiently central to the lives of ordinary people to provide the foundation on which a lasting co-operative consciousness — and thereby an enduring immunity to the basic agency dilemma — can be established. As the account of Mondragon in the following chapters makes clear, the only experiences equal to the task of developing a lasting co-operative consciousness or culture are those of work and property. It is only through stakeholding in property and the exposure on a daily basis to workplace democracy that members can acquire the habit of seeing themselves as the masters of their own destiny, and fully accepting the entitlements and obligations consequent on their status.

Significantly, ECS — like all the other co-operatives the Antigonish Movement and the Extension Department established — had no provision for its workers to have membership in their capacity as workers. It appears not to have occurred to Coady and his associates that having a say in the affairs of a co-operative and sharing in the ownership of its assets might be as important for workers as for consumers. The likely benefits for productivity also seem to have been overlooked. There is no evidence of a capacity for lateral thinking such as led — as will be seen — to the great Eroski consumer co-operatives in Mondragon being structured as a partnership between consumers and workers, or the Mondragon agricultural co-operatives as partnerships between workers and farmers.

ECS seems in hindsight a curiously old-fashioned entity to have been established in same year as Arizmendiarrieta and his associates were setting up their credit union, the Caja Laboral Popular — a partnership between its workers and the primary co-operatives which source financial services from it — and so laying the foundation stone for Mondragon's subsequent spectacular success. Had Cecil Chesterton lived to see the ECS episode, he might well have raised an eyebrow over the incongruity of fellow adherents of *De Rerum Novarum* —

distributists by every criteria other than their own admission — uncomprehendingly establishing even at so late a date a business in which the workers had no stake.

Nor is it realistic to suggest, as have some, that a remedy could have been found through greater attention to co-operative education. It was not possible for education to be effective in the absence of adequate motivation, nor could freedom from the basic agency dilemma be maintained in the absence of adequate adherence to subsidiarity — of constantly forcing back the conduct of the co-operatives into the hands of those whose interests they served. Contrary to romantic opinion, the only genuinely effective co-operative education results from democratic interaction on a daily basis in a co-operative workplace. In co-operatives as elsewhere, education is a useful instrument but a risky panacea.

Disappointment

Six years after Tompkins's death in 1953, Coady joined him in the graveyard on the hillside above the university. That his death occurred when it did spared him the heartbreak of witnessing the ruin of his hopes. 'The Big Picture', Delaney acknowledges, 'was not completed in the Maritimes. The co-operatives were not drawn in. The future did not bring the realisation of the co-operative dream'.[56] Delaney's estimate understates the seriousness of the situation. What the movement was having to face by the 1960s was that not only had the prospects of making further progress been lost, but many of its earlier gains were now in jeopardy.

Within a few years, all that remained to remind Nova Scotia of what had once made it the subject of worldwide attention was reduced to a handful of large consumer co-operatives conducting their businesses along lines which were largely indistinguishable from their conventional competitors. Students from around the world have continued to be attracted to the Coady International Institute for its courses about the Antigonish Program. 'Significant elements of the Antigonish Movement' argues a one-time Director of the Coady International Institute, Dr Alex A. MacDonald in a paper presented to the People's School on the Economy in Antigonish in March 1998, 'continue to be reflected in approaches to human development and social reform in

Canadian and other societies'.[57] However, of the optimism and excitement the movement once engendered in the local community, little trace is now to be found.

What the Antigonish Movement and the Extension Department needed — but conspicuously lacked — was a means by which members could be motivated to maintain as effective an involvement in the affairs of large and necessarily complex modern co-operatives as in smaller bodies in the hard times in the 1930s. Any divergence of interest between members and their co-operatives — any emergence of the basic agency dilemma — had by all possible means to be avoided. Such a divergence was a cost in terms of competitive advantage — and therefore of commercial survival — that no co-operative could afford. That no method of achieving these objectives — of arresting the generation-degeneration cycle, and breaking out of the Rochdale cul-de-sac — was developed by Coady and his associates was Antigonish's undoing. It remained for Arizmendiarrieta and Mondragon to remedy their omission.

Above: Bernard Shaw, Hilaire Belloc and Gilbert Chesterton at the debate on 'Do We Agree?' in 1927.

Left: Shaw and Chesterton as drawn by Max Beerbohm. A possibly apocryphalreport of an exchange between them reads:

Chesterton: You look as if you've been in a famine.

Shaw: You look as if you caused it.

Shaw debates with Belloc in 1913. The sketch, by the expatriate Australian cartoonist Will Dyson, is captioned: 'Fabians at Home: Fabian Diabolans exorcising a mediaeval Christian Saint on the occasion of the debate between Belloc and Shaw. It is not officially supposed that the Millennium will be in any way delayed by this debate.' Edward Pease and Hubert Bland are on the left of the speakers and Beatrice and Sidney Webb to the right.

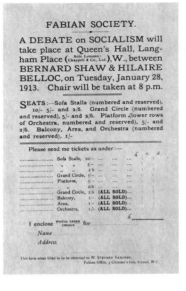

FABIAN SOCIETY.

A DEBATE on SOCIALISM will take place at Queen's Hall, Langham Place (Sole Lessees: Chappell & Co., Ltd.), W., between BERNARD SHAW & HILAIRE BELLOC, on Tuesday, January 28, 1913. Chair will be taken at 8 p.m.

SEATS:—Sofa Stalls (numbered and reserved), 10/- 5/- and 2/6. Grand Circle (numbered and reserved), 5/- and 2/6. Platform (lower rows of Orchestra, numbered and reserved), 5/- and 2/6. Balcony, Area, and Orchestra (numbered and reserved), 1/-

Please send me tickets as under:—

		£	s.	d.
Sofa Stalls,	10/-			
"	5/-			
"	2/6			
Grand Circle,	5/-			
Platform,	5/-			
"	2/6			
Grand Circle,	2/6	(ALL SOLD)		
Balcony,	1/-	(ALL SOLD)		
Area,	1/-	(ALL SOLD)		
Orchestra,	1/-	(ALL SOLD)		

I enclose Postal Order Cheque for £

Name

Address

This form when filled in to be returned to W. Stephen Sanders, Fabian Office, 3 Clement's Inn, Strand, W.C.

Left: Father Jimmy Tompkins congratulates members of the housing co-operative outside their new home in Tompkinsville.

Below: Father Moses Coady talks with his Deputy Director, A.B. MacDonald (right), and the then Premier of Nova Scotia, Joey Smallwood.

Right: Shopping in an Antigonish Movement consumer co-operative.

Below: Extension Department staff members Kay Thompson Desjardins and Ellen Arsenault pre-view a new issue of The Maritime Co-operator in 1956.

Don José Maria Arizmendiarrieta as commemorated by his statue in the garden at the university of technology in Mondragon, and (inset) in republican army uniform as a young journalist on the staff of the Basque army newspaper, Eguna (Today), before his surrender to forces under Franco in 1937.

Arizmendiarrieta among his graduating class at the Vitoria Seminary in 1940.

Arizmendiarrieta with staff and students of the Mondragon Escuela Profesional (Technical School) in 1945.

Ulgor: The original industrial co-operative in 1958.

The Olandixo hillside on which some of the emblematic buildings of the Mondragon Corporation are located. The Fagor industrial complex can be seen in the background.

Washing machines being manufactured by a Mondragon industrial co-operative.

Shopping in an Eroski worker/consumer co-operative supermarket.

*Don José Maria
Arizmendiarrieta*

9

Mondragon: The Role and Significance of José Maria Arizmendiarrieta

*The Mondragon Co-operative
Corporation*

THE well-judged distribution of property of which Belloc and Chesterton dreamed — the vision foreshadowed with Manning's encouragement by Pope Leo XIII in *De Rerum Novarum* and embraced in Antigonish by Tompkins and Coady — was brought finally to triumphant fruition in Mondragon in the Basque region of Spain in the 1950s by yet another remarkable Catholic priest, Don José Maria Arizmendiarrieta. What can be seen within the Mondragon co-operatives is both a distributist social order in the making — an evolved distributism in all but name — and a truly outstanding example for the world of the mobilisation of local and regional resources for local and regional economic development.

What has been known since 1991 as the Mondragon Co-operative Corporation (MCC) — the biggest business group in the Basque region and the ninth largest in Spain — is a major competitor in European and global marketplaces.

What began in 1956 as a handful of workers making oil-fired heaters and cookers with hand tools and sheet metal has now become a massive conglomerate of some 100 industrial, retail, financial, agricultural, construction, service and support co-operatives. Annual sales are now approaching $US6 billion. The MCC Annual Report for 1996 shows that sales were up on 1995 by 15.9 per cent, assets by 20.5 per cent and profits by 33.1 per cent.

All told, the MCC now provides jobs for roughly 3 per cent of the Basque region's 1 million workers. While the region has lost 150,000 jobs since 1975, and the level of unemployment is currently around 20 per cent, employment in the MCC has grown virtually every year since 1975 and in 1996 increased by a further 2684, from 27,950 to 30,364. The co-operatives expect to create a further 2000 jobs by the year 2000.[1] Fewer than 10 per cent of the co-operatives have failed to become going concerns, as opposed to a failure rate of around 60 per cent for conventional businesses. The co-operatives are constantly reinventing themselves in the light of new challenges and changing circumstances.

Export sales by the MCC's Industrial Group in 1996 were up on 1995 by 18.4 per cent, from 39 per cent to 44 per cent.[2] The MCC is Spain's largest exporter of machine tools and the largest manufacturer of white goods such as refrigerators, stoves, washing-machines and dishwashers. It is also the third largest supplier of automotive components in Europe — designated by General Motors in 1991 as 'European Supplier of the Year' — and a European leader in the supply of components for household appliances. Whole factories are designed and fabricated to order in Mondragon, for buyers overseas. Subsidiaries operated by the MCC in conjunction with overseas partners manufacture semi-conductors in Thailand, white goods components in Mexico, refrigerators in Morocco and luxury motor coach bodies in China.

MCC construction co-operatives carry out major civil engineering and building projects at home and abroad, including the building of key facilities for events such as the Barcelona Olympic Games. The steel framework for the new Guggenheim Museum in Bilbao — a building comparable in scale and significance to the Sydney Opera House — was fabricated by Mondragon's URSSA co-operative. The MCC also includes Spain's third largest and fastest growing retail chain, Eroski, currently comprising 37 Eroski and Maxi hypermarkets, 211 Consum supermarkets, 419 self-service and franchise stores and 33 travel agency branches.

The industrial and retail co-operatives source specialised support services from a unique network of secondary support co-operatives. Two of them — the Caja Laboral credit union and the Lagun-Aro social insurance co-operative — are among Spain's larger financial intermediaries. Others include Hezibide education and skilling co-operatives such as the José Maria Arizmendiarrieta Eskola Politeknikoa, the Ikerlan and Ideko research and development co-operatives, the Lankide Suztaketa (LKS) I and II management and engineering consultancy co-operatives and the Otalora management training co-operative.

A number of indicators suggest that the co-operatives have certain productivity advantages over their conventional counterparts. Absenteeism and other symptoms of workplace dysfunction are less prevalent.[3] In the view of the British scholars Keith Bradley and Alan Gelb, there is a distinctive Mondragon work ethic, stemming from 'the interaction of two factors: (a) the belief that success depends upon the efforts of the workforce, and (b) the shareholding of co-operators in their enterprises'.[4]

More generally, strong elements of a co-operative culture are evident, where MCC workers and their families and neighbours shop in co-operative supermarkets stocked in part with the products of agricultural co-operatives and manufacturing co-operatives; source banking and other financial services from financial co-operatives, educate their children in kindergartens and primary and secondary schools which are organised as co-operatives; prepare themselves for the world of work in a technical college co-operative or a co-operative university of technology; and enhance the quality of life of the local community through contributions paid by their co-operatives to local government.

Claims that the Mondragon model of co-operation is non-transferrable — that it is a one-off product of a uniquely Basque historical and sociological experience — are contradicted by the independent Mondragon-style co-operative group Grup Empresarial Cooperativ Valencia (GECV) which is now developing rapidly in Valencia. GECV currently has ten firms with some 4200 members and annual revenues of around $US575 million.[5] However, for all that Mondragon is the closest approach yet to putting distributism into effect, the process still has some way to go, and the challenges still outstanding are discussed in Chapter 10.

The basic principles of the Mondragon co-operative experience

The core values of the Mondragon co-operatives are set out in a ten-point statement of principles — 'The Basic Principles of the Mondragon Co-operative Experience' — which was adopted in its present form by a congress of the co-operatives in 1987. The ten points are, respectively, open admission, democratic organisation, sovereignty of labour, the instrumental and subordinate character of capital, participatory management, payment solidarity, interco-operation, social transformation, universality and education. The statement reads in part that admission to a Mondragon co-operative is available without discrimination on religious, political or ethical grounds or due to gender, subject only to applicants agreeing to be be bound by the principles and proving that they are professionally capable of carrying out such jobs as may be available. Members participate in the governance of the co-operative on a 'one member, one vote' basis, irrespective of their positions, seniority, hours worked or capital contributions. The co-operative recognises the primacy of labour in its organisation and the distribution of the wealth created; seeks to minimise the contracting of workers who are not admitted to membership; and seeks to provide work for all who are in need of it.

Capital is seen as being an instrument, subordinate to labour and subject to a maximum rate of return. The democratic character of the co-operative implies a progressive extension of opportunities for involvement by its members in business management, through mechanisms and channels for participation, freedom of information, consultation, implementation of social and professional training plans for members and the establishment of internal promotion as the basic means of filling positions of higher professional responsibility. Solidarity is to be observed, both internally among members of the co-operative so that the highest overall remuneration does not exceed the lowest by more than a ratio currently fixed generally at six to one, and externally so that rates for equal work are roughly the same within the co-operative as in the wider community.[6]

There should be co-operation by co-operatives, both within and between sectoral groups, and by the MCC with the Basque and international co-operative movements. The MCC should contribute to economic and social reconstruction and to the creation of a Basque society which is more free, just and expressive of solidarity; act in solidarity with all those working for economic democracy in the sphere of the social economy and champion the objectives of peace, justice and development, which are essential features of international co-operativism; and provide education and training in co-opera-tion for its members, management bodies and in particular the younger generation of members on whom its future depends. The Basic Principles broadly reflect — and in key aspects improve upon — those of the International Co-operative Alliance.[7]

The Basques

The essentials of the Mondragon story are simple. The Basques are a distinct people, speaking a language of their own, Euskera, and exercising a substantial measure of self-government within a region of Spain made up of the provinces of Alava, Guipuzcoa and Vizcaya.[8] As in Nova Scotia, the economic strengths of the region were once those associated with its proximity to the sea, such as fishing, shipbuilding and seafaring. The region also had extensive iron ore deposits, which were processed in local foundries and factories or exported. However, the importance of these traditional assets has now been radically reduced.

'We Basques', the then president of the Mondragon Polytechnic College, Juan Leibar, wrote in 1988, 'have used up all our natural resources and we have to sail thousands of miles for fish. Our only resources are human resources, so that education and technology are essential for our survival as a people'.[9] One key way of thinking about the development of the Mondragon co-operatives is as a struggle by the Basques to find ways of obtaining from their innate individual talents and capacities the livelihoods that the natural resources of the region can no longer guarantee. The lesson could not be more clear for regions in other countries where development will occur only through local people undertaking it for themselves.

Democracy, equality and social solidarity are important Basque values, reflected in the representative system of local and provincial government which emerged at an early stage in their history, and the guilds of professions and skilled crafts — health and welfare organisations as well as producer bodies — which operated in some instances well into the twentieth century. The Basques have also been committed Catholics and staunch supporters of their trade unions. Anarcho-syndicalism has been a significant influence within the union movement, and has imparted a distinctive flavour to its politics. Anarcho-syndicalist agricultural and industrial collectives were widespread under the republican government prior to the Civil War of 1936-38. Bloody conflicts between communist and anarcho-syndicalist elements of the Basque Left were a significant factor in weakening the region's resistance to the fascist insurgency of Franco and the Falange.[10]

Most of all, Basque history has to be understood in terms of an ongoing struggle by the region to protect its autonomy and identity against efforts by the authorities in Madrid to weaken or eradicate them. In terms of both identity and ideology, history has been on the side of the co-operatives. The co-operatives are expressive in part of a widespread and deeply felt hunger for ways to heal the divisions of class, ethnicity and conviction which have so deeply and tragically troubled the region, and so to unite its people in the face of the external pressures which are seen to threaten them.

That the Basques sided with the republican forces against Franco — and in so doing were supported by much of the local Catholic clergy — was due as much to nationalist as to party political motives. Following Franco's victory, the region was singled out by his government for reprisals. In Arizmendiarrieta's words, 'We lost the Civil War, and we became an occupied region'.[11] Large numbers of Basques were imprisoned, executed or forced to find refuge abroad. Use of the Basque language was forbidden. The regional economy was devastated, and poverty and massive unemployment remained endemic well into the 1950s.

The predicament to which the Basques had been reduced was exemplified by Mondragon, a small town in the Guipuzcoa province. What is striking from the perspective of the 1990s is less anything unique about the privation in Mondragon which resulted in the establishment of the co-operatives, than its close resemblance to that of the many other regions throughout the world which are now being devastated by the forces of headlong economic and technological change and globalisation.

The role and thought of Arizmendiarrieta

In the extremity of Mondragon's suffering in the early 1940s — at the height of 'the hunger period' as it is now widely remembered — Arizmendiarrieta set out to guide the community to a better future. Arizendiarrieta — an innovative social thinker with as distinctively hands-on an approach as Tompkins and Coady — had the key role in the establishment and development of the co-operatives. His own assessment of his contribution is in characteristically modest terms. It reads 'I was the one who reserved for myself the easiest task — to think aloud. All that I did was to raise ideas and provoke the young people, and nothing more'. 'We might add', write William and Kathleen Whyte in their magisterial study of the co-operatives, *Making Mondragon: The Growth and Dynamics of the Worker Co-operative Complex*, 'and nothing less'.[12]

Arizmendiarrieta grasped as clearly as had Belloc or Gilbert Chesterton the central importance of property. Co-operativism, in his words 'Here and now ... assigns a functional value to property. Property is valued in so far as it serves as an efficient resource for building responsibility and efficiency in any vision of community life in a decentralised form'.[13] He rejected capitalism no less categorically than had British distributism and the Antigonish Movement. 'It is a social monstrosity', he wrote, 'that a system of social organisation is tolerated in which some can take advantage of the work of others for their exclusive personal profit ... The co-operatist distinguishes himself from the capitalist, simply in that the latter utilises capital in order to make people serve him, while the former uses it to make more gratifying and uplifting the working life of the people'.[14]

As in the case again of those before him, his view of society was pluralist:

> In the mind of the co-operators is the idea that future society probably must be pluralist in all its organisations including the economic. There will be action and interaction of publicly owned firms and private firms, the market and planning, entities of paternalistic style, capitalistic or social.

'Every juncture, the nature of every activity, the level of evolution and the development of every community, will require a special treatment', his account continues, 'but not limited to one form of organisation, if we believe in and love man, his liberty, and justice, and democracy'.[15]

His recognition of the need for property to be built around the workplace was as clear as that of Cecil Chesterton. 'Don José Maria', wrote a key foundation member and subsequent senior manager of the co-operatives, José Maria Ormaechea, 'always insisted that the solution was not to be found in casual reforms but rather in structural reforms; that is to say, it was necessary to change the sovereignty of capital to the sovereignty of labour'.[16]

However, Arizmendiarrieta was also a gradualist. 'Advance a little each time', he urged, 'but without ceasing ... Step by step and without pausing'.[17] He rejected the idea that anything constructive could be achieved by revolution:

> Violence will prevail and power will pass from one party to another, but when the smoke has cleared and the bodies of the dead are buried, the situation will be the same as before; there will be a minority of the strong in power, exploiting the others for their own benefit.

'The same greed, the same cruelty, the same lust, the same ambition, and the same hypocrisy and avarice', he concluded, 'will rule'.[18]

Arizmendiarrieta took the idea of study clubs and used it to further distributism as effectively as Coady and Tompkins in Antigonish. The innumerable seminars he conducted in Mondragon were the counterparts of those in Antigonish. Like Tompkins and Coady, he saw in the combination of adult education with co-operatives the means by which his objectives could be given effect. Tompkins and Coady would have found nothing unfamiliar in his definition of the co-operative experience as 'an economic effort that translates itself into an educational action or ... an educational effort that employs economic action as a vehicle for transformation'. 'Co-operatives', Arizmendiarrieta wrote on another occasion, 'are schools and centres of training and maturation of those many men that the new order demands'.[19]

His committment to liberty and democracy was in every sense as fierce and unflinching as that of his British or Canadian counterparts. No less than Coady and Tompkins he wanted his fellow-countrymen and co-religionists to be in every sense 'masters of their own destiny' and enjoy 'the good and abundant life'. The idea of work was central to his vision of human happiness and a just social order. 'From Don Jose Maria', recalls one of his longterm associates, Alfonso Gorronogoitia, 'I learned that work was not a punishment — which I had been taught earlier — but rather a realisation of the Creation and collaboration with the plan of God'.[20]

Arizmendiarrieta is sometimes held to have been 'a simple priest' who was influenced less by external ideas than by his pastoral obligations to his parishioners. His modest personal library — now housed by the Otalora Institute in its Arizmendiarrieta Museum — tells a different story. Arizmendiarrieta's books included those of the key European Catholic philosophers of his day — thinkers of the stature of Maritain and Mounier — together with those of Marx, Marcuse and Freire, and works such as J.K. Galbraith's *The New Industrial State,* Jaroslav Vanek's seminal *Self-Management: Economic Liberation of Man* and — perhaps incongruously — *Socialism* by Ramsay MacDonald.

Maritain and Mounier in particular — adherents of the personalist school of philosophy — saw both capitalism and state socialism as being incompatible with personalist values. The personalists believed that businesses organised along mutualist lines would be more fulfilling for workers and give them greater control of their lives. Co-operatives and other mutualist bodies also served a more ambitious purpose. 'The central move of any personalist revolution', Mounier wrote in his influential *A Personalist Manifesto* in 1938, 'is not, then, to unite incoherent forces for an attack upon the coherent and powerful front of bourgeois and capitalist society. *It is rather to implant in the vital organs, at present diseased, of our decadent civilisation the seeds and the ferment of a new civilisation'.*[21]

Arizmendiarrieta embraced personalism. 'We are in total

agreement with the revolutionary formulation of the clear sighted Christian thinker Mounier', he wrote in 1966. 'The economic renewal will be moral or it will not exist. The moral revolution will be economic or it will not take place'.[22] Why his library included MacDonald's book, and not those of the British distributists — MacDonald's contemporaries — who also so largely shared the personalist views of Maritain and Mounier is unclear. It may be that, like Tompkins, he mostly read books and passed them on to friends and associates who were likely to benefit from them.

The breadth and eclecticism of his interests is strikingly evident in an anecdote told by the British scholar, Robert Oakeshott. Oakeshott describes having mentioned Mao Tse-tung to Arizmendiarrieta in the course of an interview with him in 1972. 'I can still remember the amused delight in his eye', wrote Oakeshott; 'He opened a locked drawer at the bottom of his desk and proudly produced for my inspection a copy of the Spanish translation of *The Little Red Book*'.[23] William and Kathleen Whyte interviewed Arizmendiarrieta on several occasions in 1975. By their account, 'He knew the Marxist literature much better than many ideologically committed Marxists, and he frequently used quotations from leading Marxist writers'.[24] Reading the Galbraith of *The New Industrial State*, Arizmendiarrieta also anticipated the Galbraith of *The Culture of Contentment*. 'Those who are satisfied', he wrote, 'will not build a new world, a new social order that is humane and just, nor will it be given us without risk and common effort'.[25]

For Arizmendiarrieta, as for British distributism and the Antigonish Movement before him, the starting point was the Church's social teachings. As a young seminarian and priest, he was profoundly influenced by *De Rerum Novarum* and *Quadragesimo Anno*. In later life, he seems to have decided that predominantly secular arguments were more persuasive. 'Religious themes', notes his principal biographer, Joxe Azurmendi, 'tend to disappear almost entirely from the writings of Arizmendiarrieta. The quotations from traditional authors, especially from papal encyclicals, markedly diminish, while at the same time there are increasing numbers of citations from people outside the Church, above all labour politicians, as he arrived at his own conception of the co-operative, in the 1950s'.[26]

Unlike his predecessors, Arizmendiarrieta had the added advantage of the example of the worker priests whose Christian Worker Movement took social Catholicism into factories throughout Western Europe — and most of all in Belgium and France — in the 1940s and 1950s. Like the Antigonish Movement, the worker priests relied heavily on study groups to get across their message and raise the consciousness of their members. The substance of the message was that workers should see work as less an imposition to be endured in order to earn their livelihoods than a means of achieving personal growth and development and contributing to the overall well-being of society.

The aim was to encourage workers to see themselves as agents for the transformation of industry — and through it the social order — in conformity with social Catholicism. Arizmendiarrieta ultimately arrived at a more radical solution. Rather than grafting social Catholicism on to existing firms, new ones should be created which embodied it from their inception. The means for bringing about the change was worker co-operation. It was through the study groups that the process could be started. 'We were disciples, recalls Gorronogoitia, 'who year after year educated ourselves, thanks to the teachings of Don José Maria, along lines of social concern and toward a translation of religious ideas into something that would link up with our real world'.[27]

Arizmendiarrieta's vision of co-operation recognised the limitations of consumer co-operation which Tompkins and Coady had overlooked, while at the same time embracing and celebrating its strengths. The debt to the Rochdale Pioneers which he so freely acknowledged was repaid many times over by providing the means to refurbish Rochdale and reinvigorate it for the twenty-first century. Thanks to Arizmendiarrieta, Rochdale has had lifted from its shoulders the burden of a century of intellectual baggage which in the most literal sense threatened to crush it to death. The Rochdale cul-de-sac has been reinvented as a modern freeway, whereby the co-operative movement to which the Pioneers gave rise can — if it so chooses — finally arrive at the destination they originally intended for it.

What Arizmendiarrieta saw in co-operatives was a pragmatic way of responding to the needs of ordinary people:

To build co-operativism is not to do the opposite of capitalism, as if this system did not have any useful features, when in reality it has been a very interesting experience in organisation and economic activity, and its efficiency cannot be doubted.

'Co-operativism', he went on to argue, 'must surpass it, and for this purpose must assimilate its methods and dynamism within the limitations and with the improvements necessary to support supreme human and personal values'.[28]

While regarding the co-operatives as 'an element in the vanguard of the labour movement', he rejected the view that the working class in isolation from other elements of society could achieve the objective of a more just social order. What was necessary was solidarity between classes:

It is not enough that the bosses undertake and do good things. It is necessary that the workers participate in those things, so that a real communion among them exists. It is not enough that the workers dream of great reforms, if the bosses or entrepreneurs do not contribute to their realisation, providing their zeal, their technical knowledge and skills, their experience. It is not enough that the authorities propose great objectives, because to reach them something more will always be missing than they have in their grasp, that is the enthusiasm, the zeal of subordinates. Where this fusion and spontaneous and generous collaboration has not been achieved, there is no real social life, and it will be difficult in such an environment to have fruitful co-existence.

'The existing peacable relations', Arizmendiarrieta concluded, 'will be superficial or fictitious'.[29]

Co-operation also attracted him because it was relatively free of ideological ties. Social Catholicism apart, he distrusted all ideologies, including the excessively rigid ways of thinking about co-operation which sometimes distorted the 'co-operativism' to which he attached so high a value. 'Ideas', he wrote, 'divide us but necessity unites us'. He was impatient with people who had preconceived ideas about what might or might not be possible. The only way of determining whether co-operatives could succeed in a capitalist society was by seeing how it worked out in practice. A recent study by the American scholar Sharryn Kasmir implies that there was a mystery about Arizmendiarrieta's convictions, or that he was in some sense not fully open and frank in expressing them.[30] The fact is that there was no mystery. Arizmendiarrieta was a committed adherent of social Catholicism, in the uniquely practical form of his own invention which was in all but name evolved distributism.

The Mondragon priest

Like Tompkins and Coady, Arizmendiarrieta was the son of a farmer, born in the village of Marquina, twenty-five kilometres northwest of Mondragon, in 1915. At the age of thirteen he entered the Catholic seminary in Vitoria, where he became known for his love of the Basque language and culture. His studies for the priesthood were interrupted by the Civil War in 1936. Following service with the Republican forces as a writer and editor on the trade union newpaper *Eguna*, he became a prisoner of war in 1937, and narrowly escaped execution.

The museum of the Otalora Institute in Mondragon includes among its exhibits the executioners' list on which the names of Arizmendiarrieta's fellow prisoners were crossed off as they were taken out to their deaths. Arizmendiarrieta's name was passed over. In all, sixteen Basque priests — among them Arizmendiarrieta's immediate predecessor in Mondragon, Father Joaquin Arin — were shot, and hundreds more were imprisoned in concentration camps, deported or driven into exile.[31] Those deported included the Basque archbishop, Mateo Mújica. His successor, Francisco Javier Lauzurica y Torralba, was a supporter of Franco. 'I am', Archbishop Lauzurica declared, 'one more general under orders from the Generalissimo to smash nationalism'.[32]

By 1938 Arizmendiarrieta had resumed his training as a seminarian. The subjects which interested him most deeply included — in addition to theology — social problems and the social movements which sought to grapple with them.[33] There was no lack of encouragement for him from his teachers. The seminary was noted for its sociological studies of working-class life and problems. Its Professor of Ethnology, Geology and Pre-history, Father José Miguel Barandiaran, was a distinguished scholar and dedicated researcher, whose example was not lost on Arizmendiarrieta.

As Arizmendiarrieta's ordination approached in 1941, he applied to the archbishop for permission to study sociology at the University of Louvrain. The archbishop refused, and instead sent him to Mondragon as an assistant to the more senior members of the local clergy. The episode — and its outcome — recalls Bishop Morrison's instruction to Tompkins, that he should leave his university and go to Canso. 'By denying Arizmendiarrieta's petition', write William and Kathleen Whyte, 'the monsignor deprived the Basque country of a sociologist with academic credentials and opened the way to a development of an applied sociologist whose extraordinary achievements would outweigh any set of credentials'.[34]

The situation in Mondragon was grim. 'In the postwar period', Arizmendiarrieta recalled in later life, 'the people of Mondragon suffered severely in the repression. I had known some people in Mondragon, but when I came after the war they all had either died, or were in gaol, or in exile'.[35] Arizmendiarrieta became the counsellor for the Church's lay social and cultural arm — Catholic Action — in Mondragon. The task he set himself was to find ways of enabling the local people to recover their confidence in themselves and take control of their lives. His initial focus was on the younger members of the community.

'The ideal of the youth of Mondragon', he wrote in 1941, 'is to make of the community a model among the industrial towns of Guipuzcoa'.[36] A start was made with proposals for the establishment of a sports club with its own soccer ground. Funds for the ground were solicited in part with posters on which club members painted slogans coined by Arizmendiarrieta. One poster read 'Sports unite us. Give us a field, and we will become champions'.[37] Three years later, in 1944, the club gained the championship of Guipuzcoa by defeating its rivals from a larger town. Arizmendiarrieta's community-building was not confined to sport. He was also responsible for the establishment of a medical clinic in Mondragon.

More importantly, he was interesting himself in enabling the young people to have better access to education. The only avenue for advancement open to young people in Mondragon was through the school for apprentices operated by the town's largest employer, the Unión Cerrajera foundry and metalworking company. Admission to the school was limited each year to children of the employees of the company and no more than twelve other applicants. The company invited Arizmendiarrieta to give religious instruction in the school, but rejected his proposals that the intake of students should be enlarged. Arizmendiarrieta's response to the rebuff was to propose a new school, independent of the company. Like Tompkins and Coady before him, he was intensely aware of the importance of education as a means of raising consciousness and enabling people to obtain jobs and lift themselves out of poverty.

A parents' association was formed to publicise the project and raise the necessary funds. The campaign culminated with the placing of boxes on street corners to receive pledges of cash or other contributions. Those responding were offered membership of the association, with the right to vote for its officials and determine its policies. In the event, pledges from some 600 well-wishers — roughly 15 per cent of Mondragon's adult population at the time — were received, and the new school opened in October 1943, with twenty students. Enrolments increased steadily, with the addition of new levels of instruction — first *oficialla*, then *maestria* and ultimately *peritaje industrial* — as the preceding ones were completed.[38] In 1948, the parents' association — to that point on informal offshoot of Catholic Action — was formalised as Hezibide Elkartea or the League for Education and Culture. The new body was notable in particular for a structure which foreshadowed the future shape of the Mondragon co-operatives as it was then evolving in Arizmendiarrieta's mind.

Hezibide Elkartea in its original form consisted of four groups of members: members who joined in their individual capacity; individual members who also either paid monthly dues or made contributions in kind such as teaching courses; sponsors such as small businesses who gave an annual donation of at least $US70; and local authorities which were required by law to be members. There was a General Assembly, to which ten members of each group were elected by and from its members. The assembly in turn elected fourteen members to a board which conducted the affairs of the organisation between assembly meetings.

What was taught at the school extended well beyond

purely technical subjects. The curriculum also included the social and ethical education to which Arizmendiarrieta attached so great an importance, and which was to lead ultimately to the establishment of the co-operatives. 'He taught classes in religion and sociology', a former student recalls, 'and his religion class was mainly sociology'.[39] The students were encouraged to involve themselves in all aspects of the school, not only studying but raising funds through events such as concerts and other cultural events which caused the school and the community to identify more closely with one another.

Arizmendiarrieta was putting in place foundations for the future. 'We must not devalue work', he argued:

> This temptation must not be put before new generations, particularly in a country in which we are at saturation point with speculative careers or bureaucratic employment. The road to self-improvement has to be open to all classes, but through a normal, social channel, that of serious and constant work. That is why we advocate technical training in stages because, while giving access to the truly talented, this will not hinder but rather give practical help in the placement of others.[40]

Students from the initial intake who completed the instruction available to them in Mondragon and took jobs with the Unión Cerrajera workshops were in some instances anxious to take their education further.

Arizmendiarrieta arranged for them to take correspondence courses from the School of Engineering at the University of Zaragoza, while working in Mondragon. Meanwhile, he continued to meet with them for seminars. The topics discussed most frequently included self-management, worker ownership, conflicts between labour and capital and the reform of private enterprise. Here again the parallel with Tompkins and Coady in Antigonish is obvious. 'We counted more than 2000 circles of study that he conducted', one of the participants later recalled, 'Some for religious and humanistic orientation; others for social orientation'.[41]

In 1952 eleven of the original group of twenty graduated from the university. The positions into which they were by then moving within the Unión Cerrajera were as foremen and section heads, but their sympathies were with the workers. Arizmendiarrieta's teaching had inculcated in them a deep commitment to democratising the workplace and engendering new attitudes on the part of management to its workers. An apparent opportunity for progress to be made presented itself in the early 1950s, when the Unión Cerrajera expanded its capital base by an issue of new shares.

Arizmendiarrieta's proteges argued with the management of the firm that the workers should be enabled to take up shares, but without success. The case was then taken to the authorities in Madrid, urging them to introduce a state-sponsored employee share ownership scheme, but again to no avail. It was plain at this point that efforts to reform and democratise private enterprise from within had no future. Management plainly was not about to in any way relax its control.[42]

What followed was a decision by five of the eleven graduates — Luis Usatorre, Jesus Larrañaga, Alfonso Gorronogoitia, José Maria Ormaechea and Javier Ortubay — to establish a business of their own which would embody the social and economic principles to which they were committed. 'This was no ambitious and well-considered project', one of their number later recalled; 'What we needed was to start something, to wake up, and see what would be the outcome'.[43] Initial inquiries suggested that the preferred structure — a firm embodying worker participation along the lines of the postwar German co-determination model — was not provided for by either the companies or the co-operatives legislation of the day, and it was decided that the business should be established as a conventional firm.

The name Ulgor — an acronym from the first or second letters of the surnames of the five founder members — was adopted. The founders agreed to pool such savings as they had, and an appeal to the community for loans resulted in pledges of some $US361,604 — 'An enormous sum', as has been said, 'at this time, in a working-class community of Spain'.[44] The final hurdle was that official permits for the establishment of new businesses were rigorously controlled and in short supply. The breakthrough came in 1955, when the bankrupcy of a private firm in Vitoria enabled the group to purchase its factory and equipment, complete with a licence for the production of electrical and mechanical home appliances. A year later, on 12 November 1956, Ulgor opened for business, with 24 workers manufacturing British-designed Aladdin paraffin stoves.

Meanwhile, Arizmendiarrieta and his associates continued to work towards a legal, economic and financial framework through which their vision of a new partnership between labour and capital could be given expression. The process has been encapsulated by Arizmendiarrieta. He wrote:

> In effect, formulas were found by which our enterprises' essential basis could be brought into line with current legal precepts, enabling the first industrial co-operatives to be set up in Mondragon ... to do this we had to overcome more than legal difficulties ... from the beginning we bore in mind the needs of a modern enterprise, and a formula was adopted which would make its development viable from all points of view: economic, technical, social and financial; not as a second ranking entity suitable only for a limited field of activity, but one which would be appropriate across a wide sector of the economy.[45]

A visit to Madrid enabled Arizmendiarietta to enlist a powerful ally and valuable source of advice in José Luis del Arco, who was an official advisor to the government agency responsible for the regulation of co-operatives, Obra de Cooperación.

Guided and supported by del Arco, Ulgor was able at last in 1959 to fulfil the aspirations of its instigators by being registered formally in the status of a worker co-operative. Nor at that point was it any longer alone. In the intervening period two further firms which now became co-operatives — the Ederlan iron and steel foundry and the Arrasate machine tools plant — had been established, and a consumer co-operative — San José — had become associated with the group. Even so, for all Arizmendiarrieta's painstaking preparation, the adoption of the co-operative model for the nascent businesses was not without its critics in Mondragon, or immediately accepted as a formula for their commercial success. 'In fact', Larrañaga — one of the five founder members of Ulgor — recalls in regard to the views of the sceptics, 'when Ulgor was constituted as a co-operative it was predicted that it would be short-lived'.[46]

Meanwhile, Arizmendiarrieta continued to play a key role in the evolution of the co-operatives, bringing forward suggestions and constantly engaging his associates in discussion about the theoretical and practical implications of the novel and exacting experiences in which they were finding themselves involved. However, he refused to accept any formal position other than advisor, either with Ulgor or the other industrial co-operatives whose number was now multiplying rapidly. 'He sees the future', it has been said of him, 'and makes us face it'.[47] His work continued on that basis until his death in 1976. The MCC in its modern form is his memorial.[48]

10
Mondragon: The Structure and Operation of the Co-operatives

Industrial co-operatives

THE development of the Mondragon co-operatives has fallen into two phases. The phases are, in effect, a Mondragon Mark I dating from the establishment of Ulgor in 1956, and the Mark II model which replaced it, with the establishment of the Mondragon Co-operative Corporation in 1991. In order to assess the success of the co-operatives in meeting their objectives and their relevance as an example for other communities and countries, it is necessary to understand both how the system works and the similarities between Mondragon Mark I and Mark II, together with why and how they differ from one another.

The basic building blocks of the MCC are its industrial co-operatives. The industrial co-operatives are owned and operated by their workers. The workers share in the profits — and, on occasion, losses — of the co-operatives in proportion to the work value of their jobs, and have an equal say in their governance. That they are able to do so is due to the unique structures and systems of governance and financial management which the Mondragon co-operatives have developed. In the case of governance, the workers in a co-operative have their say in the first instance through its General Assembly, where the performance of the co-operative is discussed and its policies determined. The General Assembly is the highest authority within the co-operative, is required to convene at least once a year, and often meets again for an information and discussion session.

The workers also elect a Governing Council, together with its president. The Governing Council conducts the affairs of the co-operative between assembly meetings, and oversees the performance of the co-operative and its senior management. Only members of the co-operative — all of them workers — are eligible to stand for the council, and voting is on a one member/one vote basis. Successful candidates hold office for a four-year term, but continue to be paid their normal salaries, and receive no compensation for their council responsibilities.

Council meetings are normally held before the working-day begins, and — other than in the largest co-operatives, where the position of council president can be a full-time job — members then resume their normal workplace duties. The council appoints a manager for the co-operative for a four-year period, which may be extended subject to a mandatory performance review by the council. The manager may attend council meetings in an advisory capacity, but is not a member and has no vote. There is a separate Management Council where the top executives and officers of the co-operative liaise with one another on at least a monthly basis. An Audit Committee — referred to by some as the 'Watchdog Committee' — monitors the co-operative's financial operations and its compliance with its formally established policies and procedures.

The separation of the Management Council from the Governing Council reflects the clear distinction which the co-operatives draw between the governance function which is properly the prerogative of their members, and the carrying on of operations for which management is responsible. This situation in this respect is no different from that in a conventional company. 'Management', as Roy Morrison points out in his *We Build the Road as We Travel*, 'is "free to manage" — that is, to implement the plan agreed to by the co-operators'.[1]

A key difference is that there is no place in the co-operatives for negligent shareholding such as by external investors — and in particular institutional investors — who either fail to vote or allow management to vote on their behalf. Worker-members have the advantage over conventional shareholders of being able to to see for themselves whether management is adequately protecting their interests, and whether, and if so how, improvements can be achieved. The co-operatives aim at operating on what is effectively an 'open book' basis, so that members are constantly kept up to date with detailed information about their financial status, productivity and future prospects.[2] Full disclosure of information to members is seen as being both a right consequent on their ownership of the co-operatives and as a means of encouraging them to work on the problems of the businesses and lift their performance.

A final body — the Social Council — is elected annually, by and from departments or shopfloor groups of from twenty to thirty workers. Members of the Social Council hold office for two-year terms, and may offer themselves for re-election. The Social Council is a unique structure, with a highly distinctive contribution to the well-being of the co-operative. Whereas the Governing Council represents the members of a co-operative primarily in their capacity as its co-owners, the Social Council represents them primarily as workers. The Social Council's character in this respect reflects in part the fact that the co-operatives were established during a period when trade unions had been outlawed by the Franco government.

Franco's negation of workers' rights was unacceptable to Arizmendiarrieta and his associates. In effect, the Social Council had built into it the union function of enabling members to monitor, question and — if necessary — oppose the policies of the Governing Council and management.[3] A further function of the Social Council is as an important means of communication between the members of the co-operatives and their decision-makers, contributing new perspectives to the discussion of key issues such as the redesign of work and facilitating feedback and the achievement of consensus. The Social Council is required to give advice to the Governing Council on industrial and personnel issues — for example, working hours, the evaluation and classification of jobs, and occupational health and safety — which the Governing Council must consider before its decisions on them are finalised.

In so doing, the Social Council fulfils the hopes expressed

by Arizmendiarrieta in the monthly journal of the Mondragon co-operatives in 1966. 'From the point of view of membership', wrote Arizmendiarrieta, 'we are all represented in the Governing Council, but if that were the only organ of representation, our participation in the firm would be very little, at least regarding the ordinary matters of working life. To avoid this passivity and to facilitate direct experience with many problems, what we call the Social Council came into existence'.[4]

While the Social Council is intended to serve mainly as a mechanism for transmitting information and ensuring that the shopfloor interests are adequately protected, it also can, and will, take up any issue of importance to the co-operative and, at the least, make sure that the shopfloor view is properly listened to and taken into account. In practice, senior managers in the co-operatives rarely make major decisions other than after the Social Council has been consulted and given its consent. In recent years, some co-operatives have mandated their Social Councils to bargain formally on behalf of members with their Governing Councils and Management Councils.

The earnings of a Mondragon co-operative — other than those assigned for business purposes to its collective reserves[5] — are the property of its members. In place of wages, members are paid monthly advances — referred to as *anticipos* — against the income their co-operative expects to receive. Two further advances required by Spanish custom are made available, at Christmas and for the summer holiday period. The co-operatives observe a 'principle of external solidarity', under which no advance should exceed by more than a narrow margin the wages paid for comparable work by nearby private sector businesses. The basis of advances for all but the most senior members of the co-operatives is the labour value ratings assigned to them by a committee made up of the human resources director of the co-operative and seven members chosen by the Social Council.

Factors the committee takes into account in arriving at its ratings include the measure of decision-making responsibility which a job requires; the levels of experience, skill or training required; and occupational health and safety considerations such as exposure to noise.[6] The committee then makes recommendations to the Governing Council, which can accept or reject them. Members have a two-week period to appeal the decision. If an appeal is lodged, the committee issues a new recommendation and the Governing Council makes a final determination. A manual of ratings for all the co-operative's jobs is issued as a public document. Members may also in some circumstances receive bonuses, which can have the effect of increasing the aggregate annual value of their advances by up to half. Overall, however, incomes are kept as equal as possible.[7]

A further share of the co-operative's earnings is credited to the members as capital. The capital structure has been designed to produce the greatest possible consciousness on the part of the members that they are stakeholders in their co-operative. The identification is achieved initially by requiring as a condition of entry to the co-operative that each member should make a direct personal contribution to its capital. There is an entry fee which currently stands at about $US12,500.[8]

Payment of the fee can be made on the basis of a 25 per cent initial contribution, followed by monthly instalments. The co-operative then establishes individual capital accounts for the members, to which 75 per cent of the initial contribution is credited. The capital accounts earn interest at an agreed rate, and are credited each year with, say, 45 per cent of the co-operative's surplus, apportioned among members on the basis of their salary grades and the hours worked. Members may draw on the interest accumulated in their accounts, or use the accounts as collateral for personal loans, but the principal cannot normally be touched until they resign or retire.

Payouts from the capital accounts of longer-serving members currently retiring in Mondragon — over and above their superannuation entitlements — are in some instances in excess of $US100,000. A further 45 per cent of the co-operative's surplus goes to its collective reserves, while Spanish law requires 10 per cent to be set aside for social and educational purposes. A co-operative which incurs a loss may require its members to reinvest the extra Christmas or summer holiday advances which they would otherwise have taken in cash. Alternatively, they can forgo the interest which would otherwise have been paid on their capital accounts. In extreme cases, the value of capital accounts can be written down or even written off.

Consumer-worker co-operatives

Mondragon's initial focus on industrial co-operatives has been expanded in recent years to include a major presence in consumer co-operation. The small consumer or retail co-operative, San José, became associated with the group almost inadvertently in 1959, when it joined with the Ulgor, Arrasate and Funcor industrial co-operatives in establishing the Mondragon credit union, the Caja Laboral Popular (CLP or CL). The admission of further consumer co-operatives to the group in the late 1960s prompted a study of the merits of a systematic and much more extensive involvement in retail trading. Members of the study team inspected consumer co-operatives in France and Switzerland. The report resulted in the creation of Eroski in 1968, as a major addition to the Mondragon family, bringing together the existing consumer co-operatives within a single organisation.

Reflecting the overall Mondragon approach, Eroski — unlike traditional consumer co-operatives, including those established by the Antigonish Movement — is not limited to consumer members. Instead, the membership falls into two categories: the workers who operate its supermarkets and other outlets, and the consumers who buy from them. The Governing Council has equal numbers of worker and consumer members, with the position of chairman always being held by a consumer. Eroski currently has around 12,000 workers. Consumer members are charged a $US75 annual subscription. In place of the traditional Rochdale dividend, there is a 5 per cent discount on all purchases, and the co-operatives emphasise low prices, healthy and environmentally friendly products and consumer education and advocacy. Consumer education courses, seminars, debates, discussions and presentations offered by Eroski in 1997 attracted 288,000 participants. Eroski has a key role in the Spanish Confederation of Consumer Co-operatives, and speaks for the confederation in its dealings with government and the media. It is also active in the affairs of the Consumer Advisory Council in Brussels.

In 1992, Eroski was joined within the MCC by the independent Valencian consumer co-operative Consum. Key functions of Eroski and Consum, including purchasing, marketing and distribution, were merged, but the co-operatives retained their separate identities, with the Eroski and Maxi-Eroski names reserved for the larger hypermarkets and Consum for supermarkets. The consumer co-operatives are also developing shopping malls in conjunction with a new financial intermediary — Lagun-Aro Interco-op — established for the purpose by the MCC. The outlets operated by Lagun-Aro Interco-op include sixteen supermarkets and one hypermarket in France, where a subsidiary — Sofides — plans to open a new hypermarket every year.

Eroski also has a 50 per cent interest in two Spanish retail chains outside the Basque region. While the status of employees in the new acquisitions remains unchanged, a new entity to encourage worker ownership, GESPA, was established in 1998. GESPA will be owned 50 per cent by Eroski and 50 per cent by those of the workers in its subsidiaries who choose to participate. Workers will make the traditional up-front membership investment, and, in return, will collectively elect half the members of the GESPA Governing Council, as well as enjoying job security and other entitlements similar to those of members of the MCC co-operatives. Early counts suggest that around 80 per cent of those eligible to participate in GESPA are doing so. It is now the policy of the MCC that all the new hypermarkets Eroski expects to open in areas adjacent to the Basque provinces should be structured as co-operatives.

Eroski-Consum stocks its outlets in part through agricultural co-operatives associated with the MCC, including the Udala dairy products co-operative, the Behi-Alde cattle co-operative, the Artxa pig co-operative and the Barrenetxe market-gardening co-operative. The memberships of the agricultural co-operatives are made up of the farmers who deliver produce to them and the workers who process it. Their surpluses are distributed, in the case of the farmers, in proportion to the product delivered, and of the workers according to the value added to it by their labour.

The Mondragon agricultural co-operatives are a pointer to how practical effect could be given to agrarian aspirations such as those of the original distributists, and most notably of Father McNabb. That distributism must now necessarily address itself to the needs of a predominantly urban society in no sense means that its agrarian elements are dead. It is at least possible that, given appropriate guarantees of dignity and security such as the infra-structure of a distributist social order would provide, significant numbers of the urban workforce — and particularly skilled and motivated workers facing permanent or long-term loss of employment — might prefer lives built around rural self-sufficiency.

The Caja Laboral credit union

Stakeholding and democratic governance apart, the success of the Mondragon co-operatives is also due largely to the unique system of secondary or support co-operatives from which the primary co-operatives — the manufacturing and retailing co-operatives — source key specialist services. The core and nerve centre of what is now the MCC was originally the Caja. As will be seen shortly, the Caja is also the co-operative which has been changed most radically in the course of the replacement of Mondragon Mark I by the Mark II model.

Arizmendiarrieta realised at a very early stage in the life of the co-operatives that expanding the existing businesses and creating new ones would require reliable access to capital on affordable terms. 'A co-operative', he wrote, 'must not condemn itself to the sole alternative of self-financing'.[9] His insight resulted in 1959 in the establishment of the Caja in order to mobilise capital for the co-operatives from the local and regional communities. The initial response to the proposal among his associates was unenthusiastic. 'We told him, yesterday we were craftsmen, foremen, and engineers', recalls one of them, 'today you want us to become bankers. This is impossible'.[10] As recalled by another, 'Our initial reaction was one of annoyance, and we literally sent Don José Maria packing'.[11]

Arizmendiarrieta was undeterred. Unable to persuade the group to participate in the preliminary meeting required by law for the establishment of a credit union, he submitted minutes of a meeting which had not taken place and to which names had been signed without authorisation. The strategem was a success. Those whose names were used unbeknown to them were largely unconcerned: 'They were upset momentarily, but they didn't think that the Caja would ever amount to anything, so it was not worth bothering about'.[12] Nothing could have been further from the truth. The Caja was to become not just the financier of the co-operatives, but the major force in driving forward and shaping their development and holding them together.

The slogan used by the Caja in the early stages of its development was 'savings or suitcases', indicating that local savings were necessary in order for there to be local jobs.[13] While Spanish law allowed credit unions the advantage of offering savers an interest rate marginally higher than those of commercial deposit-taking institutions, the real attraction of the Caja was that — as in Antigonish — the local people knew their money would be working on their behalf, to bring about development from which they would directly benefit.

The Caja in its original form was also the means whereby the co-operatives managed the capital held in their permanent reserves and individual capital accounts, so enabling them to retain within the group all of their surpluses other than the 10 per cent allocated by law to community projects. The effect overall was to free the co-operatives from the capital constraints which otherwise would so drastically have curtailed their development. The co-operatives were able to borrow from the Caja at interest rates which were 3 to 4 per cent below those of conventional financial intermediaries.

From functioning purely as a source of capital for the co-operatives, the Caja then moved on to become the mechanism through which their association with one another was formalised and their activities integrated. The individual co-operatives were linked to the Caja through a contract of association which set out in detail their respective obligations and entitlements, including a set of by-laws that governed their internal structure and system of individual capital accounts. For example, it was a requirement of the contract of association that an affiliated co-operative should adhere to an agreed system of wage levels and ratios. Returns to members on their capital contributions should be at a fixed rate of interest.

Each co-operative should invest in the Caja and the surplus cash and liquid assets of the co-operative should be held for it on deposit by the Caja. The co-operative's deposits with the Caja should also include all holdings on behalf of its members, such as pension funds, social security funds and workers' share capital. Each co-operative should adopt a five-year budget and report on it to the Caja at monthly intervals. The financial affairs of the co-operative should be subject to audit by the Caja at intervals of no more than four years.[14]

The Caja lastly had a key role in developing new co-operatives, advising and otherwise helping out co-operatives which were experiencing difficulties and, more generally, providing an integrated mix of services for co-operatives in all stages of their development. These functions of the Caja were performed by its Empresarial Division. 'The Empresarial Division is a "factory factory",' writes the American scholar David Ellerman: 'It, together with the Caja Laboral Popular as a whole, is the prototype of a new kind of economic development organisation which institutionalizes the function of the small business entrepreneur'.[15] The division consisted of seven departments: Advice and Consultation; Studies; Agricultural and Food Promotion; Industrial Promotion; Intervention; Auditing and Information; and Urban Planning and Building. These employed a staff of around 120 worker-members.

Where new co-operatives were concerned, a group of workers who were interested in establishing a new venture had first to find a product or service for which they believed there was a market, along with a manager. They were then in a position where an approach could be made to the Empresarial Division. If the division believed that the proposal was sound, it assigned an adviser — sometimes known as the 'godfather' — to the group. The group in turn registered as a co-operative and accepted a loan to cover a salary for the manager while pre-feasibility and feasibility studies were conducted. The studies usually lasted between eighteen months and two years. In the course of that period, the group's preferred product might be discarded in favour of an alternative drawn from the ideas bank which the division maintained from its own market research. Attention then focused on factors such as factory design, production processes, marketing strategies and export opportunities.

The completed study was presented to the Operations Committee of the Banking Division of the Caja, which determined whether the venture should be approved. Where a co-operative proceeded, the Empresarial Division godfather usually went on working with its manager until the break-even point was reached. The co-operative and the division then remained in touch through the monthly return of operating and financial information the co-operative agreed to provide as a condition of its contract of association. The information was stored in an electronic data bank — in its day a notable innovation — so enabling the division to at any time call up a comprehensive account of the status of the co-operative and the trends currently being experienced.

Where an established co-operative experienced difficulties, the Empresarial Division had the capacity to help out through the professional services of its Intervention Department. The data-base compiled from the monthly returns of the affiliated co-operatives enabled the department to have emerging problems brought to its attention, in some cases earlier even than the managers of the co-operative directly involved. An intervener was then appointed, who assessed the situation of the co-operative in terms of three categories of risk. The categories have been summarised as follows:

1. High risk: The life of the co-operative is threatened. The intervener reviews every aspect of operations and in effect takes over management on a full-time basis until a reorganisation plan is approved or the co-operative must be closed. Interest payments on outstanding loans are suspended until the plan is in place.

2. Medium risk: Bankruptcy is not imminent but could occur in the near future. In such cases the intervener spends at least one day each week at the co-operative during the reorganisation but does not take over the management of the firm. Interest on loans is reduced temporarily by, say, half, but returns to the full rate as the reorganisation progresses.

3. Warning or alert level: Here the threat of failure is not imminent but current trends are negative, suggesting a need for remedial action that may be beyond the capacity of the co-operative. No interest rate concessions are offered, as it is anticipated that the intervention will make the interest burden manageable.[16]

Once the seriousness of the situation has been determined, the intervener had the task of working out with the co-operative a new business and reorganisation plan.

The plan might require changes in the marketing strategies, manufacturing methods or product mix of the co-operative. Other changes might involve the organisational structure of the co-operative or the appointees currently occupying its key management positions. Members might be required to accept reductions in their *anticipos* or contribute additional capital. Where in extreme cases a reduction in the workforce was necessary, it fell to the Social Council to identify in conjunction with management those members who were to be retained in their current positions, those who were to move to new positions and those who were required to leave, normally by transferring to another co-operative in which business was expanding. Once agreement on the plan had been reached, the co-operative was responsible for securing approval from the Financial Division of the Caja. The Financial Division was required to determine whether interest on the co-operative's loans should be suspended or reduced or in what other ways, if any, the co-operative should be assisted.

Overall, no more than a handful of the more than one hundred primary co-operatives started to date have had to go out of business.[17] In all other instances of co-operatives finding themselves at risk, timely action by the Intervention Department of the Empresarial Division was successful in putting them back on their feet. In the view of David Ellerman, 'Just as the systematised innovation of the modern scientific research laboratory represented a major advance over the garage inventor, so the institutionalisation of entre-preneurship in the Empresarial Division of the CLP repre-sents a quantum leap over the isolated and unorganised small business entrepreneurs of the capitalist world'.[18]

The mutuality of interest between the Caja and the primary co-operatives which are linked with it through their contracts of association — together with its functions in regard to the co-operatives of capital mobilisation and management, integration and support — are entrenched in its structure and governance. Forty-two per cent of the delegates to the General Assembly of the Caja are from its workers and 58 per cent from the affiliated co-operatives. Seven seats on the Board are for the affiliated co-operatives, four for workers in the Caja and one for a representative of wider sectoral groupings of co-operatives. Rather than the Caja's workers having allocated to them a 40 per cent share of its annual surplus, as is the case in the affiliated co-opera-tives, their capital accounts are credited with the average of the amounts credited to members of the affiliated co-operatives.

The Caja has succeeded so spectacularly as to have now become effectively the fourteenth or fifteenth largest bank in Spain. The assets of the Caja are now so large that loans to the co-operatives account for no more than 25 per cent of its overall lending — or 10 per cent of its capital — with the balance available for regional economic development and other investment projects, often in partnership with the Basque government. The Caja triumphantly vindicates Arizmendiarrieta's faith in the capacity of working people to provide for themselves through co-operation and economic solidarity — through distributism in its evolved form — the jobs for which they can no longer rely on others.

Lagun-Aro social insurance co-operative

A second support co-operative, the Lagun-Aro social insurance co-operative, began as a division of the Caja. Being co-owners of the businesses where they work, instead of employees, meant at the time that members of the Mondragon co-operatives were ineligible for health and retirement benefits under the Spanish social security system. What was originally the Social Insurance Division of the Caja was established to remedy the deficiency, by providing a fund to which the co-operatives could subscribe through payroll deductions and from which benefits for their members could be drawn. In 1967 the division became independent of the Caja as Lagun-Aro, with a Governing Council which included representatives of the co-operatives affiliated with it. Lagun-Aro currently provides cover for around 18,554 members and their families, from 120 co-operatives.[19]

The functions and service-mix of Lagun-Aro have varied over time, reflecting in part that members now enjoy the same social security entitlements as other citizens. The health care clinic the co-operative conducted at Mondragon for many years was taken over by the Basque government in 1987, as a model for other towns in the province. Rather than administering pensions as previously on an in-house basis, Lagun-Aro now contracts out the function to a fund — Mutualidad de Autonomos — conducted by the state. At the same time, a general insurance subsidiary, Seguros Lagun

Aro, and a life insurance subsidiary, Seguros Lagun Aro Vida, have been established, as have subsidiaries for leasing and consumer finance, Aroleasing and Arofinance, and Lagun-Aro Intercoop (Max Centre), a subsidiary for the development of shopping malls in conjunction with the Eroski-Consum consumer co-operatives.

Hezibide Elkartea education and training co-operative

As has been seen, the third support grouping, the Hezibide Elkartea, stemmed from the establishment by Arizmendiarrieta of the training school for apprentices in Mondragon in 1943 and of the League of Education and Culture — a body to promote and co-ordinate education on all levels for all children and adults — in 1948. The apprentice school and the league played a key part in the consciousness-raising through which the establishment of the first of the industrial co-operatives, Ulgor, was instigated. The Hezibide Elkartea has come to cater for some 6000 students, with programs ranging from day-care to adult education.

The one-time apprentice school, the Eskola Politeknikoa José Maria Arizmendiarrieta, has now attained the status of a fully fledged and highly regarded private university of technology, the Mondragon Unibertsitatea, with an overall enrolment of around 2000 students, of whom about 1400 are studying engineering and the remainder taking humanities and education courses. Over and above its mainstream teaching programs, the Hezibide Elkartea brings together specialist bodies such as the Goeir centre for the co-ordination and promotion of overseas postgraduate engineering and technical studies; the Eteo school of business management; the Iraunkor centre for continuing education and in-company training; the Ahizke-CIM centre for language studies; and the Otalora centre for co-operative research, education and management training.

Students at the Mondragon Unibertsitatea have a co-operative of their own, called Actividad Laboral Escolar Cooperativa or, for short, Alecoop. In 1966 Arizmendiarrieta recognised the need for new arrangements which would enable students to support themselves financially during their courses, while at the same time obtaining a hands-on experience of how co-operatives work. Alecoop was his answer. The venture was launched initially as a department of the Eskola Politeknikoa, and experienced its share of financial difficulties prior to becoming an independent co-operative in its own right in 1970. The co-operative's products are mainly electrical components for household appliances, electrical wiring for motor vehicles and teaching equipment for technical and engineering education. It has operated profitably since 1971, and currently has around 600 members, whose time is divided more or less equally between work and study.

A further network of educational co-operatives offers a bilingual education in the Basque and Spanish languages at the preschool, primary and lower secondary levels. Funds for the schools are drawn in part from the social allocations of the Caja and its affiliated industrial co-operatives. Their General Assemblies include staff, parent, student and affiliate members. A comment by a visitor from the United States should be noted. The visitor wrote: 'To jaded eyes used to the dilapidated buildings, gang graffiti, violence, truancy, drugs, jingoistic patriotism and "dumbing down" curriculum of so many schools in the USA and Hawai'i, what we heard and saw in the classrooms, corridors, laboratories, cafeterias and grounds of the MCC institutions was inspiring'.[20] Faced in 1993 with demands by the Basque government that schools receiving government funds should join the government system, 80 per cent of the schooling co-operatives voted for rejecting the government's money and retaining their independence.[21]

Ikerlan and Ideko research and development centres

A fourth support co-operative, the Ikerlan research and development co-operative, reflects the high priority which the Mondragon co-operatives have always attached to keeping abreast of modern technology. This pattern, like so much else about Mondragon, was shaped by Arizmendiarrieta, through his initial choice of technical education as the means of bringing the community together and instigating change, and his insistence throughout that by mastering technology it would be possible to bring about higher forms of human and social development. 'Our people', he argued, 'require of our men the development of the means to scale the heights of scientific knowledge, which are the bases of progress'.[22]

Arizmendiarrieta's advice caused research and development to be pursued vigorously from the start by individual co-operatives and the Mondragon Polytechnical College, but this allowed insufficient scope for interdisciplinary problem-solving and cross-fertilisation within the overall scientific and technical workforce. Ikerlan was hived off from the college in 1974 as a separate support co-operative, in order to overcome these shortcomings, and further strengthen the competitiveness of the industrial co-operatives in the export markets where their future was seen to lie. As in other support co-operatives, the General Assembly consists of the worker-members of the co-operative and representatives of the affiliated primary co-operatives and other member co-operatives.

A staff of 133 highly qualified engineers and technicians enables Ikerlan to provide contract research and development services for co-operatives affiliated with the MCC, private sector businesses other than those in direct competition with the co-operatives, and agencies of the Basque government. For example, in 1993, sixty-six industrial research and development projects and forty-two study or service projects were carried out on behalf of fifty businesses, and the co-operative was a participant in ten international projects, including projects conducted under the auspices of the European Union through its ESPRIT III program. The international projects included the Biospace Separation Spacelab experiment — purification of proteins under microgravity conditions — carried out by a European consortium in conjunction with NASA, with an electronic control unit designed and built by Ikerlan.[23]

Ikerlan is also an active member of the European Association of Contracted Research Organisations, and offers competitive research fellowships for visiting scientists and engineers under industry revitalisation programs funded by the Basque government. The focus of research is currently on three basic areas: electronics; computer-assisted design and manufacturing (CAD/CAM); and energy systems and renewable sources of energy.[24] A second research agency, Ideko, specialises in machine tools and a third, Maier, in thermoplastics and product and process design, mainly for co-operatives producing automotive parts or those associated with them.

Co-operative groups

Over and above its unique support co-operatives, Mondragon was reinforced by a structure of groups or divisions which linked individual co-operatives together, both geographically on the basis of their proximity to one another, and by similarity of the activities in which they engage. Geographically, there were twelve regional groups of co-operatives. The structure stemmed from the rapid growth of the original household appliances co-operative, Ulgor, in the early 1960s. The co-operative had by then outstripped by far the limits within which the advantages of growth could be achieved without succumbing to the bureaucratic rigidities and other social problems associated with large organisations. Arizmendiarrieta and his associates developed a policy of spinning off those sections where a high level of efficiency was achieved in order to enable them to function successfully as independent entities.

In this model, the components manufactured by the new co-operatives had an assured market in Ulgor, but could also be sold to other buyers. In order to balance the interests of the new co-operative with those remaining behind in the parent body — and to avoid loading the new co-operative with costs such as the establishment of marketing and other specialist divisions of its own — a co-operative group, ULARCO, was formed from Ulgor itself, with the Arrasate co-operative (which supplied machine tools for Ulgor) and the Copreci co-operative (which supplied Ulgor with parts for its gas stoves and heaters). A fourth member, Ederlan, resulted from a private sector foundry being taken over and combined with the foundry at Ulgor. Fagor Electrotechnica became the fifth member when it was formed as a spin-off by the three foundation co-operatives, as an independent co-operative manufacturing electronic components and equipment.[25]

ULARCO adopted a structure similar to that of the individual co-operatives. Its General Assembly comprised the members of the Governing Councils, Management Councils and Audit Committees of the affiliated co-operatives, and was responsible for determining the policies of the group, making decisions about admissions to, and exclusions from, the group, and approving all accounts and budgets. There was also a Governing Council, made up of one member from each of the affiliated co-operatives, a General Management Committee chosen by the Governing Council, and a Central Social Council comprising one representative from each of the Social Councils of the affiliates. Similar structures were adopted by the other groups.

The groups enabled key planning and co-ordinating functions to be undertaken in the interests of their affiliates. From 30 to 100 per cent of the surpluses earned, or losses incurred, by individual co-operatives were pooled through their regional groups, so providing further protection for the co-operatives against the problems to which short-term market fluctuations might otherwise expose them. The groups facilitated the exchange of members between co-operatives for which markets were expanding and those which were experiencing contractions. Dialogue between the Governing Councils and Central Social Councils of the groups — reflecting in part discussion within and between the affiliated co-operatives — in some instances played a major part in enabling the co-operatives to implement the repositioning and restructuring forced on them by Spain's entry into the European Community and the economic stringencies of the 1980s and 1990s.

The Mondragon change process linked education, on-the-job training, research, product development, design, new production technologies, new organisational forms of work, financial restructuring, and domestic and export marketing. 'Technological change', an observer concluded, 'was an important part of these developments, but the accomplishment was not a triumph of hardware or engineering: the program succeeded because of a co-operative effort to implement the co-operators' choices'.[26]

Mondragon Mark II

A series of congresses of representatives of the Mondragon co-operatives between 1987 and 1991 agreed on the replacement of Mondragon Mark I by the Mark II model. The changes reflect the capacity of the co-operatives for constantly reinventing themselves, which is among their most impressive strengths. They also demonstrate an impressive capacity for dealing with differences of opinion and resolving conflict. The changes have in some instances been viewed by some members as prejudicial to fundamental points of principle. For all the seriousness of the differences which have arisen and debates which have occurred, the co-operatives have been able to move forward into a phase in which the new arrangements are being consolidated, while at the same time notable further improvements in the overall performance of the co-operatives continue to be achieved.

The key decisions of the congresses were, in the first instance — as seen in Chapter 9 — to codify the governing philosophy of the co-operatives in an explicit ten-point declaration known as 'The Basic Principles of the Mondragon Co-operative Experience'; secondly, to group co-operatives on the basis of their functions (market/industry) rather than their locations; thirdly, to establish the Mondragon Co-operative Corporation (MCC) and transfer to it the responsibilities for overall co-ordination and strategic planning previously exercised by the Caja; and, finally, to reposition the Caja as a conventional co-operative financial intermediary.

Structural changes

Since the 1991 Congress, individual co-operatives have been required to become members of one of three sectoral groups, these being the Finance Group, the Industrial Group and the Distribution Goods Group. The Industrial Group in turn has seven divisions: Capital Goods I, Capital Goods II, Automotive Components, Domestic Appliance Components, Industrial Components and Services, Construction, and Household Goods. The structure provides that the General Assembly of each co-operative in a group sends a delegate to a Group General Assembly. The group also has a Governing Council, usually made up of the chairperson of each co-operative together with a further member of the co-operative's board, and a Management Committee consisting of the managers of the co-operatives. Subject to the approval of the Governing Council, the president of the MCC appoints a group managing director, who also becomes a vice-president of the MCC.

The aim is for the co-operatives within each group to have experienced senior staff to engage in in-depth and continuous strategic planning, to search for and exploit economies of scale and business synergies, and to operate within a common business strategy. The groups have also had devolved to them significant elements of the intervention function previously carried out by the Caja. As has been seen, another of their key responsibilities is looking after workers whose positions are no longer required. Workers so affected are normally relocated — and where necessary retrained — for positions in co-operatives which are expanding. Figures for 1996 were: nine members unemployed and receiving payments equal to 80 per cent of their normal *anticipos* from Lagun-Aro; 144 temporarily relocated, thirty-four permanently relocated, 155 retired early, and four resigned.[27] There was a sharp fall in 1997, with a total for all categories of 175.[28]

A second resolution of the 1991 Congress established the MCC. The MCC has taken over the responsibility for co-ordination and overall strategic planning from the Caja. In the sphere of corporate governance, members of the co-operatives affiliated with the MCC elect delegates to a Mondragon Co-operative Congress, which is effectively its General Assembly. The congress meets at intervals of not more than two years, to consider the philosophy, policies and operation of the MCC. A Standing Committee — in many ways an internal board of directors — looks after the affairs of the congress between meetings. The seventeen members of the Standing Committee are elected from each of the co-operative groups and divisions, and in turn elect one of their number to serve as their president, and also as president of the congress.

In the sphere of management, the Standing Committee approves nominations from the president of the MCC for a fifteen-member General Council, and appoints a chief executive officer, who becomes the president of the council. The council members are one vice-president/director for each division or group within the MCC, together with the directors of the six central departments of the MCC. The high level of integration within the overall structure of the MCC — the tight linkage between its corporate governance and manage-

ment functions — is evident in the requirement of its constitution that, in order for a decision of the congress to be binding
on the co-operatives, 'it must be proposed by the Governing
Council, be presented by the Standing Committee and be
approved by the full Congress by an absolute majority'.[29]

What has been created is in effect an 'inverted conglomerate' where member co-operatives participate in the MCC by
decision of their General Assemblies, retain their legal
autonomy and are free at any time to disaffiliate. The
relationship reflects the fact that the structure of the MCC —
as of the groups and divisions within it — has been shaped
not by any desire to centralise operational control of the
member co-operatives, but rather by the need for them to be
supported more effectively.[30]

Functional changes

The introduction of the MCC and the changes to co-operative
groups have involved major changes in the role of the Caja.
The Caja has for all practical purposes become a conventional co-operative financial intermediary. Its responsibility
for co-ordination and strategic planning has been transferred
to the MCC. The Caja has also devolved the functions of its
Empresarial Division, in part, as has been seen, to the co-
operative groups, and in part to one or another of the six
central departments of the MCC. Other functions of the
Empresarial Division have been been assumed by the two
new consultancy co-operatives, LKS-Consulting and LKS-
Engineering. The changes reflect in part that where the MCC
has undertaken new activities in recent years it has been
mainly through joint ventures with external partners. Other
investment has focused on the consolidation and expansion
of its existing businesses.

In as much as new co-operatives continue to be created,
the main vehicle is Saiolan — at this stage a relatively small-
scale entrepreneurship training and small business incubator
program operated by a consortium which includes the
Basque government, the provincial government of
Guipuzcoa, the municipality of Mondragon, the MCC and
eight other area companies. Saiolan specialises in helping
younger people to establish businesses, which are not necessarily required to be co-operatives.[31]

INTERNAL STRUCTURE –
A Mondragon Cooperative Company

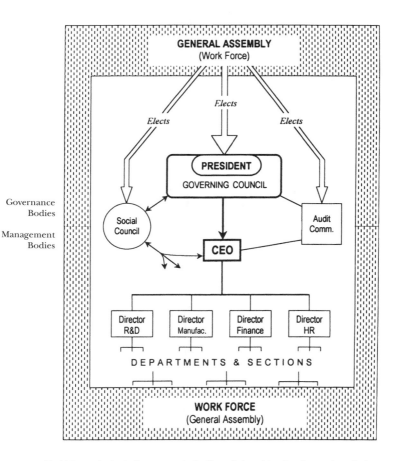

The highest authority in the company is the **General Assembly** of worker-members. It elects a **Governing Council** and the Council **President**, who serve as an internal board of directors. The Governing Council appoints the **CEO** and must approve his or her choices for division directors, who, together, are responsible for managing the company. Worker-members also elect an **Audit Committee** to monitor the firm's finances, and departmental representatives to a company-wide **Social Council**. The Social Council facilitates communication among the worker-members, management and the Governing Council and generally represents frontline workers' perspective.

Source: Freundlich, 1999

The Mondragon Cooperative Corporation
(MCC)

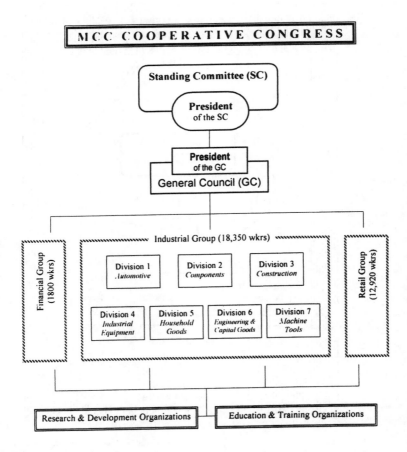

*This first chart is adapted from one used by MCC's Otalora Training Center.

Another key change is that the Caja now lends largely to private sector businesses. The move reflects in part new requirements by the Bank of Spain such as that financial institutions should not have an exposure in excess of 40 per cent of their overall lending to any single institution or group of institutions. In addition, the Caja has wanted to explore new business opportunities. 'The old strategy of risk diversification', writes the American scholar Melissa Moye, 'was one in which the CL helped the co-operatives to expand into new product markets. Now, the CL is diversifying in a more direct and traditional way — by moving its investment growth away from the co-operatives'.[32] So much is this the case that the associated co-operatives have been asked to obtain at least 30 per cent of their external finance from sources other than the Caja — a far cry from the requirement in their original contract of association that all their banking should be with the Caja.

The change of emphasis has involved, among other things, marketing the Caja much more widely than when its main focus was on funding for the associated co-operatives. The Caja's Annual Report 1992 reads: 'The quality of service required by the Co-operatives, and which Caja Laboral offers, is now also available to all our customers. We are now offering the following services to small business, in an attempt to increase our share in the non-associated company market'.[33] Legislative changes have lifted the geographical limits which applied to credit unions, and so enabled the Caja to operate on a national basis. What the changes to the Caja amount to in summary is that it has ceased to be the driving force and source of co-ordination and forward planning for the co-operatives, but remains a major profit centre and source of revenue for their overall activities and development.

The impact of the changes has been softened by the introduction of new sources of capital for those of the associated co-operatives which have special needs. The 1987 Congress established a special fund — the Inter-co-operative Solidarity Fund (FISO) — to help out co-operatives in economic difficulties with resources over and above those available from the Caja, and so avoid job losses. Subsequently, FISO has been subsumed in a Central Co-operative Fund (Fondo Central de Intercooperacion, or FCI) which comprises two legal entities. These entities are, in the first instance, the MCC Foundation

— an education and training arm which also subsidises certain business activities such as feasibility studies for new activities, marketing and sales networks overseas and assistance for co-operatives which are merging, restructuring or retooling — and, secondly, a venture capital fund, MCC Investments, for expanding existing businesses and starting new ones. FCI is funded by an annual contribution from the co-operatives of 10 per cent of their profits, together with 18.4 per cent of the profits of the Caja. By 1996 FCI had received about $US80 million, representing payments of around $US55 million to the MCC Foundation, and investments through MCC Investments of around $US25 million.

A further fund — the Fund for Education and Inter-co-operative Development (Fondo de Educacion y Promocion Intercooperativo, or FEPI) — was established by the 1989 Congress, to assist participation by smaller co-operatives in larger and longer-range projects, with funds drawn from the statutory 10 per cent of surplus social and community initiatives contributions of those which are larger or better off. FEPI also funds non-profit educational and research projects, mainly with institutions affiliated with the MCC or of which its affiliates are members. Whether co-operatives participate in FEPI is up to their General Assemblies. Those that do so then assign to FEPI a percentage of their contribution. On average the Caja has assigned 50 per cent of its contribution to FEPI, and the other participating co-operatives around 20 per cent. By 1996, FEPI's holdings totalled around $14 million.

Overall, the 1991 Congress marked the culmination of a radical overhaul of the co-operatives which has seen them reposition themselves to survive and prosper in the global economy. It remains now to assess the significance of what has been achieved to date, both for the co-operatives and their members and for the wider community which stands to benefit so greatly from their example.

Upside

That the advantages of the co-operatives are highly appreciated by their members is apparent from attitudinal studies which were carried out in the mid-to-late 1980s and early 1990s. The studies were, in the first instance, participative action research undertaken within Fagor — the principal regional sub-group in Mondragon — in the late 1980s under the leadership of Davydd Greenwood, a Cornell University anthropologist, and the then Director of Human Resources at Fagor, José Luis González; secondly, a survey of attitudes of members to their co-operatives conducted for Ikasbide — the predecessor of the Otalora Institute — in 1990 by the Director of its Office of Sociological Research, Mikel Lezamiz; and, finally, research conducted by the American scholar Sharryn Kasmir between 1987 and 1990, and reported in her largely critical account of the co-operatives in 1996.[34]

What the studies disclose is the more remarkable because their timeframes coincided with what has been, in terms of overall economic stress and structural adjustment, the most difficult period the co-operatives have so far encountered. Due largely to the global economic slumps which Spain has experienced with exceptional severity, the industrial co-operatives traded at a loss between 1980 and 1985 and again in 1992 and 1993, and the overall business was effectively kept afloat by the profits from its financial and retail co-operatives.

It was necessary in these circumstances for the co-operatives — and particularly for the industrial co-operatives which comprise so large a proportion of the overall Mondragon workforce — to take hard decisions, in some cases involving reductions in the level of *anticipos* paid to members, drawing down of individual capital accounts to cover deficits, transfer of members from unprofitable to profitable co-operatives and mergers between co-operatives to promote productivity and profitability. That the co-operatives ultimately did what had to be done and have emerged the stronger for it — that the transition from Mondragon Mark I to the Mark II model was successfully accomplished, and that the profitability of what is now the Industrial Group within the Mondragon Co-operative Corporation (MCC) has been restored — should not obscure the difficulty of getting there or downplay the headaches and heartaches which have been experienced.[35]

For all the trauma which was being suffered in the industrial co-operatives while the researchers were carrying out their investigations, the studies show that members attached a high value to their co-operatives, would not have wished to work other than in co-operatives, were prepared to make significant sacrifices where necessary in order for their co-operatives to remain in business, and were strongly committed to seeing that the principles of the co-operatives were adhered to in their entirety. 'When the point of reference is the rest of the world', Greenwood and González write in their report of the Fagor study, 'there is a nearly unanimous sense that the co-operatives offer a better social and working environment'.[36] Findings to similar, albeit less decisive, effect are reported in the Ikasbide and Kasmir studies.

'We steadfastly believed and continue to believe', Greenwood and González also report, 'that the co-operatives are strong and viable and that research did not need to confirm this':

> Rather the point was to understand the sources of conflict and difficulty in the co-operatives, to appreciate the heterogeneity of experiences within them, and to seek future action agendas that would continue the process of co-operative development ... The reader should not misunderstand this to mean that we developed a negative view of the co-operatives. The truth is the opposite.

'The co-operatives are strong', the report continues, 'because they can withstand conflict and because they build improvements out of gradual conflict resolution'.[37]

Not even the harshest critics of the co-operatives among their members would want to do without them. As Kasmir notes in regard to complaints that the introduction of additional shifts, in order for plant to be used to capacity on an around-the-clock basis, interferes with traditional Basque patterns of social life and political activism around the local bars, 'Without both the stable employment and temporary contracts created by the co-operatives, people in Mondragon would not have the money to frequent bars'.[38] A significant body of opinion within the co-operatives is exemplified in a comment quoted by Kasmir. 'One co-operator', Kasmir's report reads, 'wrote that she wouldn't prefer to work in a private firm, "but I would like it if things changed a lot in the co-operatives".'[39] The subtext of such disaffection as both the Fagor and Kasmir studies report is in almost all instances not to do away with co-operation but to make it work better and adhere more closely to its principles.

Downside

Even so, none of this means that Mondragon is Utopia, that the implementation of the spirit — as opposed to the letter — of what is in all but name an evolved distributism is as yet complete, that the co-operatives do not have significant problems or that there are not members who feel disappointed or aggrieved. Mondragon is vulnerable like other institutions to human frailty and error, if perhaps to a lesser degree by reason of its unique structure and processes. Not all the members of the co-operatives as yet fully understand — or have as yet fully availed themselves of — the opportunities which are open to them. Nor have the co-operatives always understood what is necessary in order for the system to deliver all the benefits of which it is capable.

That the co-operatives have their downside is evident from the persistent presence among a minority of members at the shopfloor level of what Greenwood and González describe as 'the discourse of "those above" and "those below".' What the researchers refer to is a perception by some members of a division between those in the co-operatives who make the rules and take the decisions, and those who are limited to complying with what is required of them. A comment by a participant in one of the round table discussions convened in the course of the Fagor research gives forceful expression to the sentiment. 'I believe', the participant states, 'that we are less equal among ourselves than the workers in a capitalist firm; being members, many of us often have to put up with things that workers in other firms would not tolerate'.[40]

The Fagor report quotes a second respondent to the effect that 'Power is found above ... although they say in the co-operatives we are all equal, it is not true, because I am here, below'. By a third account, 'We, the underlings, have neither voice nor vote. *Yes*, we vote, but since we aren't told everything, in the end we vote for what they want, for what the bosses want'.[41] Similar disaffection is reported in the Kasmir study. 'Control over work, job classification, ratings and perceived social distance', writes Kasmir, 'were significant markers of inequality and these differences were more significant to workers than the legal fact of joint ownership and their's and the managers' common formal class position of worker-owner'.[42]

What all this signifies is that the co-operatives have not as yet totally eliminated the basic agency dilemma, nor as yet do their practices at the shopfloor level in all instances fully comply either with their basic principles or with the require- ments of subsidiarity. The high cost of these shortcomings — of putting at risk the competive advantage the co-operatives enjoy by reason of their relative freedom from agency costs — is evident in responses to the Ikasbide research. Measures which were found to have majority support — albeit in some instances narrowly — included higher levels of *anticipos*, higher interest rates on capital accounts and payment in cash of a proportion of surpluses.

These measures would, if adopted, have the effect of reducing the amounts available for reinvestment by the co- operatives, and so restrict their ability to expand their activi- ties and create additional jobs. A third of the respondents also had yet to be persuaded that they owned the assets of their co-operatives.[43]

Greenwood and González report a comment which exactly captures the difference between the presence and absence of the agency dilemma — between those members who see themselves as sharing in a meaningful sense in the ownership of the co-operatives, and those who see themselves as being excluded. The comment reads that, in the past, 'if you saw a piece of scrap on the floor, you picked it up because it was worth a duro (a five-peseta coin). Today, you give it a boot, because today the co-operative doesn't belong to all of us'.[44]

Where the co-operatives are missing out is evident in another sense in a comment by a manager in 1991: 'We certainly don't do what the Japanese do, ie, stay after work to work out for ourselves the problems that arise, and then challenge the management as to why things are not done such-and-such way, in order to increase productivity. But we are not Japan, we are in Europe, and don't have the culture of that type of participation'.[45] The ability of the co-operatives to achieve at least as committed a culture as in Japan is the litmus test which will determine whether Arizmendiarrieta's hopes for them are to be fulfilled.

The malaise among some members at the shopfloor level likewise has its effect on the involvement in the governance of the co-operatives. While the Ikasbide material shows that a very substantial majority of respondents highly valued their right to participate in the General Assemblies of their co-operatives, even here dissident voices are audible. 'I only go to the annual meetings of the General Assembly because it is required', reads a comment quoted by Kasmir; 'Everybody goes because they have to. If we didn't have to, we wouldn't go'.[46]

While a majority of the members sampled also saw being able to serve on the Governing Councils of their co-operatives as important, the margin was significantly lower. Nor are attitudes on the part of some members to their Social Councils necessarily more positive. A respondent quoted by Greenwood and González comments 'The theory of the Social Council is fine, but without rhyme or reason we sometimes elect the most talkative person ... the most recent one who has joined to screw him; what happens is that we often don't take this whole business seriously'.[47]

Irrespective of how few the disaffected are, it is important for the MCC to listen to them. The danger is that the problem will not be correctly diagnosed and dealt with as being symptomatic of a lingering basic agency dilemma, but instead will be attributed — as previously by Coady and Delaney in Antigonish — to 'disloyalty' and 'short-sighted-ness' on the part of individual members. So fundamental a misreading of the situation could then mislead the co-operatives into adopting inappropriate solutions which compound the difficulty rather than remedying it.

For example, a significant cause of disaffection appears to be that the 'open book' policy of fully disclosing information about the performance and financial status of the co-operatives to their members is failing to fully meet its objectives. Effective implementation of 'open book' information policies requires that — as well as simply making available information — the co-operatives should enable their members to acquire the business acumen and skills to interpret what they are told, empower them to act upon it and see that the link with increased surpluses and personal earnings is clearly understood.

Complaints such as that members 'aren't told everything' strongly suggest that these requirements are not in all cases being satisfied. It may be that there is a new role here for trade unions which in part reinvent themselves, so as to be able to respond to the distinctive needs of worker-owners, such as for professional assistance — through independent financial, legal and technical advice — in analysing the information the co-operatives are freely making available to them. There may also be a need for the role of the Social Councils to be further examined, and for some — perhaps all — of them to be better resourced.

Other areas of controversy within the co-operatives include their current strategy of building market share in key areas through strategic alliances with conventional companies, and the acquisition of private businesses which have not yet in all cases become co-operatives. MCC subsidiaries which are not co-operatives have been established in developing countries such as Egypt, Morocco, Mexico, Argentina, China and Thailand. Whether — and, if so, when — the non-co-operative businesses are converted into co-operatives or worker-owned enterprises of other kinds remains an unresolved and hotly debated issue. Interestingly, whereas all the Eroski retail outlets in the Basque region are co-operatives jointly owned by their workers and customers, and those in other parts of Spain and in France operate as organisations other than co-operatives, it is the co-operatives which consistently achieve the higher levels of performance and larger surpluses.

In addition, seasonal fluctuations in demand in some co-operatives have been catered for by the employment of significant numbers of contract workers. All told, the MCC workforce, on the most recent count available, included 4165 temporary employees and 4671 employees in joint ventures or non-co-operative corporate subsidiaries.[48] The challenge of dealing fairly with the temporary workers — often the sons or daughters of members of the co-operatives, and referred to optimistically as *eventuales* — has been alleviated in part by recent changes in MCC policy, which provide for a temporary member status. Under the new arrangements, co-operatives are encouraged to take on a proportion of their temporary workers as temporary members. Temporary members will have the same rights as permanent members for the duration of their employment, other than that they can be laid off if economic circumstances make it necessary. To what extent the changes will enable the co-operatives to fully comply with their Basic Principles is as yet unclear.

In the area of gender, women are relatively underrepresented in absolute terms — if not by comparison with firms in the private sector[49] — at the more senior levels of the co-operatives, perhaps reflecting in part the bias of the early co-operatives towards trades such as metal-working and engineering for which women were unlikely to have been prepared by a traditional Catholic schooling. Gender bias in the co-operatives is also likely to have been promoted by the fact that Arizmendiarrieta only in the later years of his life came round to strongly advocating the involvement of women in the co-operatives on an equal footing, after having believed initially that their place was in the home.

In the area of capital, the changes to the bank have met with an ambivalent response, reflecting in part a greater acceptance by the larger co-operatives which can readily access capital from other sources than the smaller co-operatives for which it is more difficult. 'The bank', in the view of the manager of one of the co-operatives, 'is still preferential to us. It is one more co-operative of the group. However, there used to be a stronger relationship when they had their own consulting and assessing staff'.[50] There is a question here as to whether the new reliance on external borrowings sufficiently takes into account Arizmendiarrieta's warning, as quoted earlier on: 'A co-operative must not condemn itself to the sole alternative of self-financing'.[51]

Acceptance of the changes to the Caja also may not have been helped by the fact that in 1992 — the most recent year for which figures are available — interco-operative aid totalled only 245 million pesetas, as opposed to an average of 1600 million pesetas in debt cancellation by the Caja in each of the previous ten years.[52] In addition, the increasing number of older members who are eligible to retire and cash in their capital accounts represents a significant charge against the capital resources of the co-operatives. Meeting the heavy demand for capital consequent on competing in global markets is a major challenge for the MCC in the years immediately ahead of it.

Concerns over the availability of capital are also in part a subset of a wider fear that something of the original solidarity within and between the co-operatives — and of the co-operatives with local communities — has been lost as a consequence of the recent changes, and, in particular, in the move from locational to functional co-operative groups. So strong was feeling along these lines in 1992, that the co-operatives in one of the valleys near Mondragon opted to become independent of the MCC in preference to surrendering their locational links.

'We do not want our Group to be divided', the American scholar George Cheney quotes the president of the breakaway co-operatives as telling him, 'with one co-op being linked to a sector somewhere else. We derive our strength from one another, and we share a commitment to the local community'.[53] Concern over the new basis for the groups also has another dimension. 'Workers and plant-managers', reports Kasmir, 'feel that important decisions are made outside of their control as the Groups become more powerful'.[54]

The future that works

That neither the difficulties nor the disaffection would have dismayed or deterred Arizmendiarrieta — that their significance in the overall context of Mondragon pales by comparison with what has been achieved — is plain from a passage which he wrote a few days before his death in 1976. The passage reads:

> Hand in hand, of one mind, renewed, united in work, through work, in our small land we shall create a more human environment for everyone and we shall improve this land. We shall include villages and towns in our new equality; the people and everything else: 'Ever forward'. Nobody shall be a slave or master of anyone, everyone shall simply work for the benefit of everyone else, and we shall have to behave differently in the way we work.

'This', Arizmendiarrieta concluded, 'shall be our human and progressive union — a union which can be created by the people'.[55]

Had Arizmendiarrieta lived until today, he would be encouraged in his confidence by references, in the Fagor and Kasmir reports, to a recent, reinvigorated upward trend in the involvement and participation of members in the affairs of their co-operatives. 'One of the long-term trends identified', Greenwood and González report, 'is a tendency in Fagor toward a broader and more differentiated view of participation':

> We conclude that Fagor has become an increasingly participatory system and that the problems and conflicts found in it now provide opportunities and energy for continuing

change in the direction of greater future participation.

'From this vantage point', the report argues, 'Fagor is, as members like to say, an organisation that attempts to change its own structure and prides itself on the ability to change in fundamental ways. There is as much fear of too little change as of too much'.[56]

'The "corporate culture" of Fagor', the report notes elsewhere, 'should be conceptualised as an arena, bounded by shared commitments to one set of process rules for all members, in which ways to embody basic values better are debated':

> For each member, an important part of the internal experience of Fagor's organisational culture is the continuing process of comparison and contrast between personal experience and larger goals that Fagor is supposed to stand for ... The corporate culture of Fagor focuses attention on the issue of solidarity and makes it controversial.

'It does not resolve the issue or homogenise opinion', the authors conclude, 'it tells the membership what is important to debate about'.[57]

Kasmir — albeit from a less benign viewpoint — likewise detects a new willingness to face up to and tackle difficulties even on the part of those shopfloor workers who previously had seen equality as 'a cynical managerial ideology' and 'felt manipulated by co-operativism'. 'Toward the end of my fieldwork in 1990', she writes, 'co-operative workers were discussing equality differently ... They began to talk about it as an important co-operative value':

> More significantly, they began to embrace it as their value, which they had to defend against managers, who were willing to forgo equality for the sake of efficiency. Even those who had been the most vocal critics of co-operativism began to use the words 'co-operation' and 'equality' as weapons, and embraced egalitarianism as a working-class philosophy.

A relatively greater open-mindedness on the part of managerial workers was also apparent to Kasmir: 'Managers who told me eighteen months earlier that syndicates (i.e. trade unions) had no place in the co-operatives began to respond more moderately to my question. They said that it might be appropriate for syndicates to operate in a limited way'.[58]

11

Evolved Distributism: The Performance and the Promise

Summing up

THANKS to Arizmendiarrieta, distributism has had a robust rebirth, and is now in a position where its merits can be revisited and reassessed. The key distributist objective of a well-judged distribution of property has been achieved in Mondragon. As the previous two chapters have demonstrated, members of the co-operatives have property of four kinds: firstly, ownership of their jobs; secondly, direct personal ownership of the balances held for them in their capital accounts, which earn additional income for them through interest to which they have regular access; thirdly, a shared ownership of the assets of their co-operatives, such as buildings, equipment and reserves, the governance and management of which they are directly responsible for; and, finally, a further shared ownership — albeit less direct — of the secondary support co-operatives in which the primary co-operatives are major stakeholders. Nowhere else in the world has ownership of property been established on so well-distributed, diverse and entrenched a basis.

What emerges from the foregoing account of British distributism, the Antigonish Movement and Mondragon is that, in key respects, distributist and mutualist bodies succeed to the extent that they adhere to subsidiarity. The success of distributism in its evolved form can be seen in this sense to have had its genesis when the members of the first Antigonish credit unions and other co-operatives began to take into their own hands the decisions and functions which had previously been discharged by higher bodies. However, neither credit unionism nor consumer co-operation proved to be a sufficient motivation for members to maintain their initial high degree of involvement in the co-operatives consistent with subsidiarity.

To the extent that responsibilities once again gravitated from those most directly affected by them to others, there was insufficient pressure on the co-operatives to adopt structures and processes which entrenched subsidiarity or reconciled it with the increasing scale and complexity of their operations and local market forces. Similarly, there was no scrutiny by an involved and alert membership such as would have insisted on adequate levels of managerial competence. When, in the 1950s, the co-operatives experienced increasingly fierce competition from conventional firms, many of them were neither sufficiently well managed, nor sufficiently valued by their members, to survive.

A similar fate could all too easily have overtaken Mondragon. As has been seen, it is sometimes suggested that Mondragon owes its success to advantages consequent on, and unique to, the time and place of its inception. Advantages nominated most commonly include Basque exceptionalism, Arizmendiarrieta's charismatic leadership, the role of groups such as Catholic Action in the formation and nurturing of Arizmendiarrieta's closest associates, the relative eclipse of competing ideologies such as those of the unions and political parties suppressed in the aftermath of the civil war and the relatively closed and highly protected character of the Spanish economy under Franco. So much is this at times seen to be the case, as for it to be suggested by some that, other than in these circumstances, Mondragon could never have happened.

Considerable as may have been the significance of any or all of these factors at the time, that Mondragon now exists —

that its success is so plainly evident — creates its own new and in key respects incomparably more propitious reality. In place of such advantages as Arizmendiarrieta and his associates may in their day have enjoyed, the world today has the dynamic driving force of Mondragon's example. Mondragon's existence radically revises the theory of the firm. Thanks to Arizmendiarrieta, it is now evident that businesses in the co-operative mould can equal or excel their conventional counterparts, given that there is the will on the part of the community for them to have the chance. The hurdle is no longer, as at the inception of the co-operatives, one purely of commercial or economic constraints. It is of political vision, imagination and determination.

What in reality enabled Mondragon to succeed where Antigonish had failed was the recognition by Arizemendiarrieta of the centrality of work and work organisations in modern human experience — of the fact that the most important exercise of subsidiarity was through those in need of employment providing it for themselves. So much more central than either saving or consumption was the ownership of a job and the acquisition of property in other forms that the Mondragon co-operatives have been able to maintain the high levels of ongoing member involvement and motivation which eluded Antigonish. Arizmendiarrieta further understood, as Antigonish had not, the importance of creating structures and processes which would assist and encourage members to discharge their functions consequent on adherence to subsidiarity, and of sparing members the impediments to participation of excessive bureaucratisation.

It is at least likely that, had Arizmendiarrieta lived, there would have been a much more urgent and sustained effort by the Mondragon co-operatives to replicate at the shopfloor levels their highly successful involvement of members in the sphere of corporate governance. In as much as the co-operatives have not as yet fully achieved their objective of a system where effectively all principals are agents and all agents principals — and thereby maximised the consequent competitive advantage — the deficiency is less by far in the exercise of corporate governance than in shopfloor practice.

The high priority the MCC is currently giving to upgrading worker participation at the shopfloor level was given forcible expression when, in 1997, it convened a major international symposium on the topic in Mondragon. The aim of the symposium was to expose the managers of the co-operatives to the views of panels of internationally recognised experts on workplace participation, and of the most senior MCC officials. The symposium also showcased best practice as exemplified by the most successful and participatory MCC co-operatives. The managers then took part in workshops and planning sessions to consider the implications for their own businesses.

What has been achieved to date at Mondragon can now be seen to have been much as was hoped for by Cardinal Manning and Pope Leo XIII in *De Rerum Novarum,* and by subsequent popes in their further development of the Church's social thought. Pope Leo's insistence on the need for ownership of property to be widespread was reiterated in if anything stronger terms by Pope Pius XI in the encyclical *Quadragesimo Anno* in 1931. *Quadragesimo Anno* reads:

> The immense number of propertyless wage-earners on the one hand, and the superabundant riches of the fortunate few on the other, is an unanswerable argument that the earthly goods so abundantly produced in this age of indus-trialism are far from rightly distributed and equitably shared among the various classes of men. Every effort should, therefore, be made that at least in future a just share only of the fruits of production be permitted to accumulate in the hands of the wealthy, and that an ample sufficiency be supplied to the workman ... Unless serious attempts be made, with all energy and without delay to put them into practice, let nobody persuade himself that peace and tranquillity of human society can be effectively defended against the forces of revolution.[1]

Nor was *Quadragesimo Anno* any less adamant on the indis-pensability of subsidiarity:

> 'Let those in power therefore, be convinced that the more faithfully this principle be followed, and a graded hierar-chical order exist between the various subsidiary organisa-tions, the more excellent will be both the authority and the efficiency of the social organisation as a whole and the happier and more prosperous the condition of the state'.[2]

The current Pope, John Paul II — like Manning before him a conservative in religious matters but a political radical —

has repeatedly reaffirmed the adherence of the Church to the social justice objectives spelled out by his predecessors. A key statement in the course of his visit to Cuba in 1998 sets the issues in their wider international context:

> Various places are witnessing the resurgence of a certain capitalist neo-liberalism which subordinates the human person to blind market forces and conditions the development of peoples to those forces. From its centres of power, such neo-liberalism often places unbearable burdens upon less favoured countries. Hence, at times unsustainable economic programmes are imposed on nations as a condition of further assistance. In the international community, we thus see a small number of countries growing exceedingly rich at the cost of the impoverishment of a great number of other countries; as a result the wealthy grow even wealthier, while the poor grow even poorer. For many of the political and economic systems operative today, the greatest challenge is still that of combining freedom and social justice, freedom and solidarity, so that no one is relegated to a position of inferiority.

'The Church's social doctrine', the Pope's statement concludes, 'is meant to be a reflection and a contribution which can shed light on and reconcile the relationship between the inalienable rights of each individual and the needs of society'.[3]

The Cuban homily reflects, reinforces and enlarges sentiments expressed by John Paul II on earlier occasions — most notably on the ninetieth anniversary of *De Rerum Novarum* in 1981, in his encyclical *Laborem Exercens* (*On Human Labour*) — and also by the Second Vatican Council in its 1965 document *Gaudium et Spes*. The Australian theologian Gordon Preece sees the council document as sharing in a broader personalist conviction — the legacy of Maritain and Mounier — 'that a third way, beyond the impersonal industrialism of capitalism and communism, is required for human flourishing'.[4] The aspirations of *Gaudium et Spes* — for workers and management sharing in administration, profits and decisions, and investment being directed towards ensuring the availability of jobs and a sufficiency of incomes — are very much those of Arizmendiarrieta and Mondragon. They likewise recall the passionate lifelong dedication of Coady and Tompkins to enabling communities and their members to become 'masters of their own destiny' and live 'the good and abundant life'. Not least, the affinities with British distributism are obvious.

Evolved distributism similarly can be seen to offer much of what was hoped for by the associative and communitarian socialism, which largely originated with Ludlow and his fellow Christian socialists in the 1840s, and was picked up subsequently by guild socialism and syndicalism. The associative and communitarian socialist dream of workers owning and managing their workplaces and sharing among themselves the value added by their labour has been fulfilled at Mondragon, on a basis compatible in every respect with the requirements of efficiency, productivity and profitability. As the then chief executive officer of the MCC, Javier Mongelos, told a journalist in 1994, 'Our form of socialism works. The workers who own this co-operative know their future depends on making profits'.[5]

In as much as Mondragon still has difficulties in this respect to overcome, they are largely those identified earlier on by Belloc. A representative passage from Belloc's *The Crisis of Our Civilisation* in 1937 reads:

> The task is impossible *unless there be still left in the mass of men a sufficient desire for economic independence to urge them towards its attainment.* You can give political independence by a stroke of a pen, you can declare slaves to be free or give the vote to men who have hitherto had no vote; but you cannot give property to men or families as a permanent possession unless they desire economic freedom sufficiently to undertake its burdens'.[6]

Belloc's point is linked with a wider associative and communitarian concern. 'As the principle of subsidiarity so well understands', the American scholar Thomas C. Kohler points out, 'individuals and societies become self-governing only by repeatedly and regularly participating in acts of self-government':

> No single subsidiary structure — be it club, fraternal organisation, or union — is likely to survive in the absence of other such bodies. All require and can inculcate the same habits of reflection, choice, personal responsibility, and self-rule. When people lose these habits, no single institution alone can restore them. The existence and decline of subsidiary structures is mutually conditioning; the loss or deformation of any threatens the rest.

'It is for this reason', Kohler argues, 'that *Quadragesimo Anno* calls for "a social reconstruction" and pays such close attention to the seemingly mundane institutions that should be a remarkably unremarkable part of a flourishing life'.[7] Clearly what Kohler and the encyclical see as being required is nowhere more readily and effectively available than in self-governing workplaces such as of the MCC.

Evolved distributism can be seen in this sense to have a central part to play in the current debate about social and economic directions for the new millennium. What is in question currently is the whole notion of the nature and role of society as it has come to be understood in the fifty or so years following the Second World War. More intemperate adherents of free market economics such as Britain's Margaret Thatcher have gone so far as to call into question whether society can in any meaningful sense be said to exist. As David Marquand so forcefully drives home, 'The heaving, masterless, community-destroying global economy of the 1990s may be a long way from its benign and stable predecessor of the 1950s and 1960s, but it is uncomfortably close to that of the nineteenth century and even to that of the interwar period'.[8] So widespread and intense is concern over where Marquand's 'capitalism off the leash' is taking us, that there has been a major revival of interest in just such mutualist, associative and communitarian ideas as evolved distributism broadly exemplifies.

The point is powerfully argued by Paul Hirst in his seminal 1994 study *Associative Democracy: New Forms of Economic and Social Governance*. 'The late twentieth century', writes Hirst, 'offers new conditions in which ideas marginalised for many decades can be redefined and developed to serve as an alternative, radical means of reforming and reorganising economic and social governance in Western societies ... another set of ideas about social organisation that was developed in the nineteenth and early twentieth century, associationalism, has once again become relevant after a long period of eclipse by state socialist and liberal democratic ideas'.[9]

Hirst's analysis singles out mutualism — 'that as far as possible the economy should be organised on mutualist lines, that is by means of non-profit financial institutions and co-operative firms in which both investors and workers have a significant say in their governance'[10] — as being one of three pillars of associationalism, alongside the transfer of the organisation of social affairs as much as possible from the state to voluntary and democratically self-governing associations, and decentralising political authority and having it perform as few functions as are consistent with its role.

Not least, evolved distributism is seen to address equity and justice. So unfashionable have both words become as for there to be a danger of losing sight of imperatives — at once moral and pragmatic — such as are stated by John Rawls in his influential book *A Theory of Justice*. Rawls writes that '... since everyone's well-being depends upon a scheme of co-operation without which no-one could have a satisfactory life, the division of advantages should be such as to draw forth the willing co-operation of everyone taking part in it, including the less well-situated'. Evolved distributism would grant Rawls his wish. 'The higher expectations of those better situated', Rawls continues, 'are just if and only if they work as part of a scheme which improves the expectations of the least advantaged members of society'.[11] Evolved distributism meets the test with flying colours.

Prospects

For all the strengths and attractions of evolved distributism — for all that Mondragon stands out as a beacon of hope in a troubled world — what outcome can be hoped for from it at present is necessarily an open question. In as much as distributism is an idea which leads by force of example, it requires a receptive audience. Given the current worldwide infatuation with free market economics, it is entirely possible that the message will go unheard. In this event, Mondragon will remain in the nature of a curiosity, a source of fascination for visiting scholars — and of useful insights for currently somewhat isolated forward-thinking business people, community activists and politicians — but without practical significance other than for those in and around the co-operatives whose lives have benefited from them.

This in no way makes Arizmendiarrieta's teachings less valid or his achievements less admirable. If Mondragon were to abandon co-operation and revert to a conventional corporate structure tomorrow, jobs would still have been created for tens of thousands of workers who otherwise would have been unemployed, and prosperity in the Basque region would have been maintained at significantly higher levels than would otherwise have been experienced. Over and above these advantages, there have been major transfers of technology, know-how and skills into the Basque region which otherwise would not have occurred. Services such as health care and education are at a higher level than would otherwise have been provided. Make of Mondragon what the rest of the world may, nobody can take away from the co-operatives that they have demonstrated beyond doubt the capacity of communities and regions to pull themselves up by their bootstraps through the use of locally controlled educational institutions to develop local skills and capacities, of credit unions to mobilise local capital for regional economic development and job creation, and of mutualist and co-operative principles to reinforce stakeholder identity and thereby enhance productivity, job satisfaction and democratic governance of economic life.

In a more ambitious scenario, more Mondragons would be created, but in numbers that fall short of the distributist ideal of a social order such as where, in Belloc's words, 'families composing it are, in a determining number, owners of the land and the means of production as well as themselves the human agents of production (that is, the people who by their human energy, produce wealth with these means of production)'.[12] In this scenario, the new Mondragons remain something in the nature of monasteries in the Dark Ages, preserving within their confines values and ideas of whose worth the wider community is as yet insufficiently persuaded.

The most likely way for developments along these lines to occur would be for the Mondragon idea to be adopted and talked up by peak bodies within the wider mutualist movement such as the International Co-operative Alliance and the World Council of Credit Unions, and supported at the grass-roots level from resources such as those of mutual assurance societies, permanent building societies, friendly societies, credit unions and co-operatives of other kinds. What this requires in the first instance is an acceptance by mutualist bodies that they are not chained to the provision of services for which the original justification no longer exists or is now less pressing, but rather should see themselves as pools of community capital which can be re-tasked in the face of new needs on the part of those for whose interests they are trustees.

A compelling demonstration of the capacity of mutualist bodies to reinvent themselves is evident in a major co-operative in the United States — Co-operative Services of Oak Park in Michigan — which was formed in the 1940s in response to a pressing community need for affordable, hygienic household milk delivery services. When the corporate dairies moved in with comparable services at a comparable price, the co-operative reinvented and repositioned itself so that the community capital it had accumulated was applied to meeting the need for affordable optometrical testing and the supply of spectacles. When this function in turn was taken up by the optometrical services corporations, a further reinvention of the co-operative took place. The co-operative at this point re-tasked itself to meet a pressing need for affordable accommodation and support services for older people. It now operates some 4000 apartments in twenty-five housing co-operatives spread out from Massachusetts to California, with more being developed. Each co-operative is now an autonomous entity in its own right, within the overarching structure of the parent body.

A second compelling case in point is the great Desjardins credit union federation in Canada. The Desjardins credit unions were originally established around the turn of the century, in response to a pressing social need for affordable loans to tide over working-class households in the face of emergencies from one payday to another, and so provide protection against the loan-sharks who were lending them money at grossly exorbitant rates. In the 1950s and 1960s the credit unions reinvented themselves as a source of affordable personal loans for major consumer durables such as cars, furniture and household appliances. They are now undergoing a second reinvention, so as to be able to respond to the current most pressing need on the part of their members: for the local and regional economic development which will provide them and their children with jobs.

It takes no great leap of the imagination to envisage a third step forward, whereby the Desjardins credit unions would begin to give preference in their allocation of development capital to co-operatives which could count on being advantaged like those in Mondragon by a relative freedom from the basic agency dilemma. Nor is it difficult to envisage the credit union movement more generally establishing structures and acquiring skills with which to support recipients of commercial loans through services such as those of the Empresarial Division of the Caja Laboral in the Mark I phase of Mondragon. There should not be any insuperable barrier to a repositioning along these lines by credit unions and other co-operative and mutualist financial intermediaries such as in Asia, Australasia, Europe and North America.

What this second scenario also calls for is for Mondragon to become much better known. The world has too few high-profile examples of mutualism in its evolved distributist form, such as where labour hires capital rather than capital labour, and working people are the owners of their workplaces and in charge of their working lives. More should be known about what Mondragon is, how it works and the distributist philosophy, in fact if not in name, to which it gives expression. It is remarkable, for a start, that there is no English language edition of the key account of Arizmendiarrieta's thinking, as set out in Joxe Azurmendi's massive study *El Hombre Cooperativo: Pensamiento de Arizmendiarrieta* (*Co-operative Man: The Thought of Arizmendiarrieta*). Nor is the monthly journal of the co-operatives, *TU/Lankide* (*Work and Unity*), the only regular source of up-to-date information on current developments within the MCC, available in other languages.

The Mondragon Web site, http://www.mondragon.mcc.es, provides a limited account of the co-operatives in several languages, but has not yet acquired the capacity to include posted material or exchanges of information or opinion. There is no body such as an international 'World Friends of Mondragon' or 'Mondragon Studies Association' which would put in touch with one another people from a wide range of backgrounds and with interests of many different sorts in Mondragon, and assist the Otalora Institute and the MCC in disseminating information about Mondragon, and acquiring feedback from those who care passionately about its well-being.

None of this reflects adversely on the co-operatives, whose first obligation is to their members, and who do the best they can with the limited time and resources they are able to allocate for dealing with inquiries. What it spells out is that the world at large has made insufficient provision for informing itself about Mondragon and assessing its lessons. There will shortly be an ideal opportunity to redress the imbalance. The twenty-fifth anniversary of Arizmendiarrieta's death, in 2001, would be a fitting occasion for both the MCC and its admirers to honour his memory and gain greater recognition for the importance of his achievements and teachings.

A final, and best case, scenario would see Mondragon also taken up much more widely, in the political sphere and by bodies outside the mutualist movement. Despite the current infatuation with free market economics, there is also widespread and profound questioning of it such as by environmental, welfare and ethnic interest groups, churches, centre and left political parties and some conservatives. What these groups have in common is that they offer no plausible remedy for the social fragmentation and deprivation they condemn. Evolved distributism on the Mondragon model has attractions for a wide range of interest groups which increasingly see government and the nation-state as being ineffectual in the face of pressures stemming from globalisation, and are in search of alternative sources for radical renewal.

In particular, evolved distributism is potentially attractive to groups such as the churches whose interests are poorly served by overt involvement in the party political arena. Nor are its attractions other than marginally less marked within the political arena, where parties are looking for ways of achieving their objectives and giving effect to their values which do not require higher taxes. All that evolved distributism asks of the state is moral support and that it removes existing legislative impediments to the establishment and growth of distributist and mutualist entities, and ensures an even playing field with adequate protection for smaller businesses against unfair practices by their larger competitors.

For example, it is ludicrous that governments should still be enacting or retaining legislation which restricts the purposes for which credit unions can make loans, or obstructs the establishment of employee share ownership plans (ESOPs). Current credit union legislation in countries like Australia — enacted ironically in some instances by social-democratic governments — would be a major impediment to development along Mondragon lines, as is much current employee share ownership legislation to the spread of ESOPs other than for listed companies. The potential gain from more effectively fostering ESOPs is evident from the US experience, where more than a thousand majority employee-owned companies are now pioneering changed work and management practices.[13] Businesses which begin as ESOPs may well evolve — over time, and in the light of experience and heightened consciousness — to the point where more democratic and participative structures in the Mondragon mould are adopted.

However, irrespective of the scenario which eventuates, distributism on the Mondragon model is not a panacea for the world's problems. Nor is it a formula for enabling governments to divest themselves of core functions, such as social insurance, where risk-pooling on the widest possible scale is paramount. Rather it complements government by opening up new options in areas of public policy, such as local and regional economic development and job creation, where government has been conspicuously ineffectual. That the initiative for taking action passes from government to the intended beneficiaries is an important step towards Coady's goal of enabling people to be 'masters of their own destiny'.

Living 'the good and abundant life' becomes an objective people expect to achieve, and define, for themselves rather than have it defined for them by others. 'The concept of the governance of social affairs through voluntary associations', writes Hirst, 'can enable groups to build their own social worlds in civil society'.[14] As Hirst further emphasises, the capacity for communities to build worlds of their own is as necessary in the economic as in the social sphere. People are reminded that — *pace* Margaret Thatcher — society actually does exist, and co-operation is as effective for some purposes as is competition for others. Meanwhile, governments would have energies freed up for thinking about proposed measures for coping with globalisation — Tobin taxes on foreign exchange transactions, controls on capital flows, limits on the creation of credit and the like — the feasibility of which might more usefully engage their attention.

New Labour

In all these respects, evolved distributism in the Mondragon mould speaks most directly to New Labour such as that of the Blair government in Britain. Where New Labour leads, parties of similar stamp in Europe and Australasia show every sign of following. Blair's debt to Christian socialism — to well-springs in key instances identical or closely linked with those of distributism — is a matter of record. His intellectual mentor, the Australian Anglican priest Peter Thomson — in Blair's words 'the person who most influenced me'[15] — is a deeply committed Christian socialist. It was through Thomson that Blair had his introduction to the communitarian ideals of the Scottish philosopher John Macmurray.

'Blair's idea of community', writes his biographer John Rentoul, 'derives directly from Macmurray'.[16] By Blair's own account:

> It seemed to me a sensible explanation of the human condition. There seemed a coincidence between the philosophical theory of Christianity and left-of-centre politics. I didn't work these things out very clearly at the time, but they were influences that stayed with me. They were formative influences.[17]

The outcome in part was the emphasis which Blair gave to stakeholder democracy prior to his sweeping victory at the 1997 elections.

Stakeholder democracy was in turn linked with a corresponding emphasis on reciprocal rights and responsibilities — with the notion that authentic communities cannot exist other than on the basis of mutual obligation. 'The importance of the notion of community', Blair argued in a seminal address in Wellingborough in 1993, 'is that it defines the relationship not only between us as individuals but between people and the society in which they live, one that is based on responsibilities as well as rights, on obligations as well as entitlements. Self-respect is in part derived from respect for others'.[18]

The argument was taken further in a speech later that year, which reads:

> It is largely from family discipline that social discipline and a sense of responsibility is learnt. A modern notion of society — where rights and responsibilities go together — requires responsibility to be nurtured. Out of a family grows the sense of community. The family is the starting place.[19]

'When you go back and read about Keir Hardie', Blair told a BBC interviewer in 1995, 'you understand that what a lot of people came to perceive as the great driving forces behind the Labour Party weren't the driving forces behind it at all.

He used to talk about self-help and self-improvement the whole time'.[20]

However, with New Labour now in government, stakeholder democracy has figured less prominently in the priorities of Blair and his ministers than the related issues of community and mutual obligation. An analysis of the record to date by the Professor of Social Policy at the London School of Economics, Julian Le Grande, sees the dominant values of the government as being 'community, accountability, responsibility and opportunity'. 'Unlike the neo-liberals', writes Le Grande, 'there is no automatic belief in the virtues of the free market':

> Unlike the social democrats, there is no special commitment to the public sector, to public expenditure or even to the mixed economy. Instead, this way incorporates a robust pragmatism: the best method is that which is most likely to promote the values of community, accountability and responsibility. What's best is what works.

Le Grande concludes that, at least as regards local government and the welfare state, 'There does indeed seem to be something of a pattern ... a true Third Way'.[21] Notable as the achievement of the 'true Third Way' of Le Grande's analysis may be, it leaves the observer with a strong sense that all is not in balance — that a key ingredient has been omitted.

The key question for New Labour is whether community defined exclusively in terms of where people live and the social groupings with which they identify is viable in isolation from its counterpart in the workplace. Is it likely that the key New Labour values of community, opportunity, responsibility and accountability will be adequately embraced so long as they are constantly contradicted in the sphere of work, which is where so large a part of most people's time is taken up, and so many of their most meaningful interactions are experienced?

That New Labour has so far promoted stakeholder democracy less zealously in office than from the Opposition benches has been attributed to a perceived lack of persuasive models. If so, evolved distributism in the Mondragon mould — and variations of it adjusted to local conditions — can fairly claim to answer the government's dilemma. Evolved distributism meets squarely the requirement stated recently by Blair, that his fellow countrymen should 'stop wringing their hands and start taking more responsibility for their lives'.[22] Stakeholder democracy is nowhere more authentic or effective than where workers are the owners of their workplaces and jobs.

It would create some nice symmetries if New Labour was to adopt evolved distributism as a means of delivering stakeholder democracy. Distributism would then have returned via Canada and Spain to the country of its origin. Christianity and socialism would as much have played their part in the acceptance of distributism into the political mainstream as they did in bringing about its inception. The socialist seedbed and the Catholic harvest would at long last and after many vicissitudes have fulfilled their mission. The efforts of the long succession of contributors to the distributist cause, from Manning to Arizmendiarrieta, would have been vindicated. That bringing to fruition so large an undertaking will be difficult need not deter making the attempt.

It is relevant finally — in times that cry out so urgently for a new vision and for a convergence of traditions of reform and social justice which, while differing in many respects from one another, also have much in common — to recall that, shortly before the reform-minded Catholic Robert F. Kennedy was assassinated in the course of the 1968 US presidential election campaign, he had begun incorporating in his speeches a saying which originated with the veteran socialist Shaw. The passage strikes an appropriate concluding note. 'Some men', Kennedy would say, as had Shaw before him, 'see things as they are and say "Why?". I dream of things that never were and say "Why not?".'[23]

BIBLIOGRAPHY
Primary sources

Contemporary periodicals

The New Age (Complete set on micro-film in the Baillieu Library at Melbourne University).

The Eye-Witness and *The New Witness* (Complete set in the State Library of New South Wales).

G.K.'s Weekly (Complete sets in the St Michael's College Library in Toronto and the National Library of Scotland, and an incomplete set in the Joint Theological Library at Ormond College at Melbourne University).

The Cross and the Plough (Complete set in the Archives of the English Chapter of the Order of Preachers at Blackfriars in Edinburgh).

The Casket (Complete set in the St Francis Xavier University Library in Antigonish).

The Extension Bulletin (Complete set in the St Francis Xavier University Library in Antigonish).

TU/Lankide (Complete set in the Otalora Institute in Mondragon).

Books

Arnold M.E. 1940, *The Story of Tompkinsville*, New York, The Co-operative League.

Arnold M.E., not dated, *Father Jimmy of Nova Scotia*, Chicago, Co-operative League of the U.S.A.

Belloc H. 1897, *Essays in Liberalism*, London, Cassell and Co.

Belloc H. 1899, *Danton: A Study*, London, James Nisbet & Co.

Belloc H. 1900, *Paris*, London, Edward Arnold.

Belloc H. 1901, *Robespierre*, London, James Nisbet and Co.

Belloc H. 1902, *The Path to Rome*, London, George Allen & Unwin.

Belloc H. 1906, *Esto Perpetua*, London, Duckworth and Co.

Belloc H. 1911, *The French Revolution*, London, Williams and Norgate.

Belloc H. 1912, *The Servile State*, London, T.N. Foulis, (Third Edition 1927), London, Constable & Co.

Belloc H. 1920, *Europe and the Faith*, London, Constable & Co.

Belloc H. 1922, *The Jews*, London, Constable & Co.

Belloc H. 1924, *Economics for Helen*, Bristol, Arrowsmith.

Belloc H. 1925, *The Cruise of the Nona*, London, Constable & Co.

Belloc H. 1932, *Napoleon*, London, Cassell and Co.

Belloc H. 1936, *An Essay on the Restoration of Property*, London, The Distributist League.

Belloc H. 1937, *The Crisis of Our Civilisation*, London, Cassell and Co.

Belloc H. 1940, *On the Place of Gilbert Chesterton in English Letters*, New York, Sheed & Ward.

Belloc H. and Chesterton C. 1911, *The Party System*, London, Stephen Swift.

Belloc Lowndes M. 1943, *'I Too Have Lived in Arcadia': A Record of Love and of Childhood*, London, Macmillan & Co.

Belloc Lowndes M. (ed. Lowndes S.) 1971, *Diaries and Letters of Marie Belloc Lowndes 1911-1947*, London, Chatto & Windus.

Bentley E.C. 1940, *Those Days*, London, Constable and Co.

Beveridge. W. 1953, *Power and Influence*, London, Hodder and Stoughton.

Blatchford R. 1895, *Merrie England*, London, Clarion Newspaper Co.

Blatchford R. 1903, *God and My Neighbour* (1934 Edition), Chicago, Charles H. Kerr & Co.

Blatchford R. 1906, *Not Guilty: A Defence of the Bottom Dog*, London, Clarion Press.

Blatchford R. 1931 *My Eighty Years*, London, Cassell & Co.

Blatchford R. 1940, *What's All This?* London, The Labour Book Service.

Booth C. 1891, *Life and Labour of the People in London* (Five Volumes, Revised Edition 1902), London, Macmillan & Co. Reprinted 1969, New York, Augustus M. Kelley.

Booth C. 1902, *Life and Labour of the People in London* (Final Volume) London, Macmillan & Co. Reprinted 1970, New York, AMS Press.

Champion H.H. 1887, *Social-Democracy in Practice*, London, Swan Sonnenschein & Co.

Champion H.H. 1890, *The Great Dock Strike in London, August 1889*, London, Swan Sonnenschein & Co.

Champion H.H. 1907. '*Quorum Pars Fui*: An Unconventional Autobiography' in Henderson L.M., 1973, *The Goldstein Story*, Melbourne, Stockland Press.

Chesterton A.K. 1965, *The New Unhappy Lords*, London, The Candour Publishing Co.

Chesterton C. 1912, 'Democracy and the Great State' in Wells H.G. (ed.) 1912, *The Great State*, London, Harper & Brothers.

Chesterton C. 1919, *A History of the United States,* (Everyman's Library Edition 1940), London, J.M. Dent & Sons.

Chesterton Mrs C. 1941, *The Chestertons*, London, Chapman & Hall.

Chesterton. G.K. 1904, *The Napoleon of Notting Hill,* London, John Lane: The Bodley Head.

Chesterton G.K. 1905, *Heretics*, London, John Lane.

Chesterton G.K. 1908, *The Man Who Was Thursday*, London, Arrowsmith.

Chesterton G.K. 1909, *George Bernard Shaw*, London, John Lane: The Bodley Head.

Chesterton G.K. 1910 *What's Wrong with the World*, in Marlin G.J. Rabatin R.P. and Swan G.L. (eds), *The Collected Works of G.K. Chesterton*, Vol. IV, San Francisco, Ignatius Press.

Chesterton G.K. 1911, 'The Ballad of the White Horse' in Chesterton G.K. 1927, *The Collected Poems of G.K. Chesterton*, (Eleventh Edition 1948), London, Methuen & Co.

Chesterton G.K. 1911, *Manalive*, London, Arrowsmith.

Chesterton G.K. 1914, *The Flying Inn,* London, Methuen and Co.

Chesterton G.K. 1915, *The Crimes of England*, London, Palmer & Hayward.

Chesterton G.K. 1919, 'Biographical Note on the Author', in Chesterton C. 1919, *A History of the United States* (Everyman Edition 1943), London, J.M. Dent and Sons.

Chesterton G.K. 1922, *The Man Who Knew Too Much*, London, Cassell and Co.

Chesterton G.K. 1925, *Tales of the Long Bow,* London, Cassell and Co.

Chesterton G.K. 1926, *The Outline of Sanity*, London, Methuen & Co.

Chesterton G.K. 1927, *The Catholic Church and Conversion*, in Marlin G.J. Rabatin R.P. and Swan G.L. (eds), *The Collected Works of G.K. Chesterton.*, Vol. IV, San Francisco, Ignatius Press.

Chesterton G.K. 1927, *The Return of Don Quixote*, London, Chatto & Windus.

Chesterton G.K. 1929, *The Thing: Why I am a Catholic*, in Marlin G.J. Rabatin R.P. and Swan G.L. (eds). *The Collected Works of G.K. Chesterton*, Vol. IV. San Francisco, Ignatius Press.

Chesterton G.K. 1937, *Autobiography*, London, Hutchinson & Co.

Chesterton G.K., Shaw G.B. & Belloc H. 1928, *Do We Agree?*, London, Cecil Palmer.

Coady M.M. (ed.) 1935, *How St. F.X. Educates for Action*, New York, The Co-operative League.

Coady M.M. 1938, 'Adult Education in Action', Radio Address over the CBC, February 10 1938.

Coady M.M. 1939, *Masters of Their Destiny: The Story of the Antigonish Movement of Adult Education Through Economic Co-operation*, New York, Harper and Row Publishers.

Coady M.M. 1945, *The Social Significance of the Co-operative Movement*, Antigonish, Extension Department, St Francis Xavier University.

Coady M.M. 1953, 'Through the Visible to the Invisible', address given at the closing of the Rural and Industrial Conference Celebrating the 25th Anniversary of the Founding of the Extension Department, 7 July 1953.

Coady M.M. 1957, 'My Story', Interview for CBC TV, Antigonish, Extension Department, St Francis Xavier University.

Corbett E.A. 1957, *We Have With Us Tonight*, Toronto, The Ryerson Press.

Delaney I. 1985, *By Their Own Hands: A Fieldworker's Account of the Antigonish Movement*, Hantsport, Lancelot Press.

Disraeli B. 1845, *Sybil, or The Two Nations* (Wordsworth Classics Edition 1995), Ware, Hertfordshire, Wentworth Editions Limited.

Doyle I. 1964, *The Antigonish Idea and Social Welfare*, Antigonish, Nova Scotia, St Francis Xavier University Press.

Doyle I. 1995, 'The Antigonish Movement Beyond the Atlantic Region', Research Paper, 4 October 1995, Antigonish, University of St Francis Xavier Extension Department.

Gillis M., not dated, *The Social Doctrine of the Church as Exemplified in The Antigonish Movement*, Le Seminaire.

Greenwood D.F., González J.L.G. *et al.* 1992, *Industrial Democracy as Process: Participatory Action Research in the Fagor Co-operative Group of Mondragon*, Assen/Maastricht, Van Gorcum.

Haynes E.S.P. 1951, *The Lawyer: A Conversation Piece*, London, Eyre & Spottiswood.

Hyndman H.M. 1911, *The Record of an Adventurous Life*, London, Macmillan & Co.

Hyndman H.M. 1912, *Further Reminiscences*, London, Macmillan & Co.

Irigoien J. 1984, *The Practice and Experience of the Mondragon Basque Co-operatives*, Scott Bader Common Ownership Lecture 1984, Scott Bader Commonwealth Centre, 12 May 1984.

Jebb E. & R. 1956, *Testimony to Hilaire Belloc*, London, Methuen & Co.

Kasmir S. 1996, *The Myth of Mondragon: Co-operatives, Politics, and Working-Class Life in a Basque Town*, State University of New York Press.

Lezamiz M. *et al,* 1990, *Estudio Sociologico Sobre Grado De Adeptacion De La Sociodad Co-operativa,* Mondragon, Ikasbide Hezkuntzetxea: Centro de Formacion.

MacDonald J.D. Nelson. 1986, *Memoirs of an Unorthodox Clergyman* Truro, Nova Scotia, Co-operative Resources.

Mann T. 1923, *Tom Mann's Memoirs.* Melbourne, The Labour Publishing Company.

Manning H.E. 1891, 'A Pope on Capital and Labour, the Significance of the Encyclical Rerum Novarum' in *The Dublin Review,* July 1891.

Manning H.E. 1947, *What One Work of Mercy Can I Do this Lent: A Letter to a Friend,* London.

Masterman C.F.G. 1909, *The Condition of England,* (Reset 1960), London, Methuen & Co.

Mounier E. 1938, *A Personalist Manifesto,* London, Longmans, Green & Co.

O'Connor J. 1937, *Father Brown on Chesterton,* London, Frederick Muller.

Ormaechea J.M. 1993, *The Mondragon Co-operative Experience,* Mondragon, Mondragon Corporacion Cooperativa.

Pease E.R. 1926, *The History of the Fabian Society,* New York, International Publishers.

Pius XI, 1931, *Encyclical Letter on Social Reconstruction,* Boston, Mass., St Paul Editions.

Ransome A. 1976, *The Autobiography of Arthur Ransome,* London, Jonathan Cape.

Reckitt M. 1941, *As It Happened,* London, J.M. Dent & Sons.

Rowntree S. 1901, *Poverty: a Study of Town Life,* London, Macmillan and Co.

Royal Commission Investigating the Fisheries of the Maritime Provinces and Magdalen Islands, 1928, *Report,* Ottawa, The Kings Printer.

Sewell B. 1966, *My Dear Time's Waste,* Aylesford, St Dominic's Press.

Sewell B. 1990, *G.K.'s Weekly: An Appraisal,* Aylesford, The Aylesford Press.

Shaw G.B. 1884, *A Manifesto,* Fabian Tract No. 2, London, The Fabian Society.

Shaw G.B. 1889, 'The Transition to Social Democracy' in Shaw G.B. (ed.) 1889, *Fabian Essays in Socialism,* London, The Fabian Society.

Shaw G.B. 1892, *The Fabian Society: Its Early History,* Fabian Tract No. 41. London, The Fabian Society.

Shaw G.B. 1931, 'Preface to the 1931 Reprint' in Shaw G.B. (ed.) 1950, *Fabian Essays in Socialism 1889*, London, George Allen & Unwin.

Shaw G.B. 1933, *The Political Madhouse in America and Nearer Home*, London, Constable and Co.

Shaw G.B. 1949, *Sixteen Self-Sketches*, London, Constable and Co.

Shaw G.B. (ed. Laurence D.H.) 1965-1985, *Bernard Shaw: The Collected Letters*. (Three Volumes), London, Max Reinhardt.

Speaight R. (ed.) 1958, *Letters from Hilaire Belloc*. London, Hollis & Carter.

Speaight R. 1970, *The Property Basket: Recollections of a Divided Life*, London, Collins & Harvill Press.

Swinnerton F. 1935, *The Georgian Literary Scene 1910-1935: A Panorama*, London, Hutchinson & Co.

Tillett B. 1931, *Memories and Reflections*, London, John Long.

Titterton W.R. 1936, *G.K. Chesterton: A Portrait*, London, Alexander Ouseley.

Tompkins J.J. 1921, *Knowledge for the People: A Call to St Francis Xavier's College*, Antigonish.

Webb B. (ed. Mackenzie N & J.) 1982-1965, *The Diary of Beatrice Webb* (Four Volumes), London, Virago.

Webb S. 1894, *Socialism: True and False*, Fabian Tract No. 51, London, The Fabian Society.

Webb S. & B. 1920, *A Constitution for the Socialist Commonwealth of Great Britain*, London, Longman.

Secondary sources

Academic theses

Alexander A.M. 1985, *The Meaning of Liberation in Adult Education as Revealed by Moses Coady and the Antigonish Movement*, PhD Thesis, University of Alberta.

Ayers T. 1986, *The National Catholic Rural Movement 1939-1955*, Honours Thesis, University of Melbourne

Hunt P.R. 1980, *Chesterton and Dickens*, PhD Thesis, Dalhousie University.

MacInnes D.W. 1978, *Clerics, Fishermen, Farmers and Workers: The Antigonish Movement and Identity in Eastern Nova Scotia 1928-1939*, PhD Thesis, McMaster University.

Sacouman R.J. 1976, *Social Origins of Antigonish Movement Co-operative Associations in Eastern Nova Scotia*, PhD Thesis, University of Toronto.

Schirber M.E. 1940, *The Antigonish Movement: Its Method and Meaning*, PhD Thesis, Harvard University.

Timmons H.P. 1939, *An Analysis of the Religio-Cultural Aspects of the Nova Scotia Adult Education Movement*, M.A. Thesis, Catholic University of America.

Books

Alexander A. 1997, *The Antigonish Movement: Moses Coady and Adult Education Today*, Toronto, Thompson Educational Publishing.

Anon. N.D., *Democracy Ensured: A Social Drama of the Canadian Maritimes*, New York, International Friends of the Antigonish Movement.

Arendt H. 1963, *On Revolution*, New York, The Viking Press.

Attwater D. 1969, *A Cell of Good Living: The Life and Works and Opinions of Eric Gill*, London, Chapman.

Auden W.H. (ed.), 1970, *G.K. Chesterton: A Selection of His Non-Fictional Prose*, London, Faber and Faber.

Azurmendi J. 1991, *El Hombre Cooperativo: Pensamiento de Arizmendiarrieta*, Mondragon, Otalora Institute.

Barker D. 1973, *G.K. Chesterton: A Biography*, London, Constable & Co.

Barker R. 1997, *Political Ideas in Modern Britain: In and After the Twentieth Century* (Second Edition), London, Routledge.

Barnett. C. 1972, *The Collapse of British Power*, London, Eyre Methuen.

Beilharz P. 1992, *Labour's Utopias: Bolshevism, Fabianism, Social Democracy*, London, Routledge.

Beilharz P. 1994, *Transforming Labour: Labour Tradition and the Labor Decade in Australia*, Cambridge University Press.

Beilharz P. 1994, *Postmodern Socialism: Romanticism, City and State*, Melbourne University Press.

Baum G. 1980, *Catholics and Canadian Socialism: Political Thought in the Thirties and Forties*, Toronto, James Loromer & Co.

Bettany F.G. 1926, *Stewart Headlam: A Biography*, London, John Murray.

Binyon G.C. 1931, *The Christian Socialist Movement in England: An Introduction to the Study of Its History*, London, The Society for Promoting Christian Knowledge.

Black A. 1984, *Guilds and Civil Society in European Political Thought from the Twelfth Century to the Present*, London, Methuen and Co.

Blake R. 1966, *Disraeli* (New Edition 1987), New York, Carroll & Graf.

Blasi J.R. 1988, *Employee Ownership: Revolution or Ripoff*, New York, Harper Business.

Bogardus E.S. 1964, *Principles of Co-operation*, Chicago, The Co-operative League of the U.S.A.

Boyd I. 1975, *The Novels of G.K. Chesterton: A Study in Art and Propaganda*, London, Paul Elek.

Boyle G. 1953, *Father Tompkins of Nova Scotia*, New York, P.J. Kennedy & Sons.

Bradley K. & Gelb A. 1983, *Co-operation at Work: The Mondragon Experiences*, London, Heinemann Educational Books.

Brandon R. 1990, *The New Women and the Old Men: Love, Sex and the Women Question*, London, Secker & Warburg.

Britain I. 1982, *Fabianism and Culture: A Study in British Socialism and the Arts 1884-1918*, Cambridge University Press.

Calvez J.Y. and Perrin J. (eds) 1961, *The Church and Social Justice: The Social Teachings of the Popes from Leo XIII to Pius XII*, London, Burns & Oates.

Camp R.L. 1969, *The Papal Ideology of Social Reform: A Study in Historical Development 1878-1967*, Leiden, E.J. Brill.

Campbell A., Keen C., Norman G. & Oakeshott R. 1978, *Worker Owners: The Mondragon Achievement*, London, Anglo-German Foundation for the Study of Industrial Society.

Campbell J. 1983, *F.E. Smith: First Earl of Birkenhead* (Pimlico Edition 1991), London, Jonathan Cape.

Canovan M. 1977, *G.K. Chesterton: Radical Populist*, New York, Harcourt Brace Jovanovich.

Cecil H. & M. 1991, *Clever Hearts: Desmond and Molly MacCarthy: A Biography*, London, Victor Gollancz.

Coates J.D. 1984, *Chesterton and the Edwardian Cultural Crisis*, Hull University Press.

Clayre A. (ed.) 1980, *The Political Economy of Co-operation and Participation: A Third Sector*, Oxford University Press.

Cole G.D.H. 1938, *Persons & Periods: Studies*, London, Macmillan & Co.

Cole G.D.H. 1948, *A History of the Labour Party from 1914*, London, Routledge & Kegan Paul.

Cole G.D.H. 1951, *The British Co-operative Movement in a Socialist Society*, London, George Allen & Unwin.

Cole G.D.H. 1955, *Beatrice and Sidney Webb*, Fabian Tract 297, London, The Fabian Society.

Cole G.D.H. 1959, *A History of Socialist Thought* (Seven Volumes), London, Macmillan & Co.

Cole G.D.H. & Postgate R. 1938, *The Common People*, London, Methuen and Co.

Cole M. 1948, *Makers of the Labour Movement*, London, Longmans, Green & Co.

Cole M. 1961, *The Story of Fabian Socialism*, London, Heinemann.

Cole M. 1971, *The Life of G.D.H. Cole*, London, Heinemann.

Coleman J.A. (ed.) 1991, *One Hundred Years of Catholic Social Thought: Celebration and Challenge*, Maryknoll, New York, Orbis Books.

Colloms B. 1982, *Victorian Visionaries*, London, Constable & Co.

Conlon. D.J. (ed.) 1987, *G.K. Chesterton: A Half Century of Views*, Oxford University Press.

Coren M. 1990, *Gilbert: The Man Who Was G.K.Chesterton*, New York, Paragon House.

Coren M. 1993, *The Invisible Man: The Life and Liberties of H.G. Wells*, New York, Atheneum.

Corrin J.P. 1981, *G.K. Chesterton & Hilaire Belloc: The Battle Against Modernity*, Athens, Ohio University Press.

Coutinho B. 1966, *Community Development Through Adult Education: The Story of the Antigonish Movement*, Rome, Institute of Pastoral Sociology.

Dale A.S. 1982, *The Outline of Sanity: A Life of G.K. Chesterton*, Grand Rapids, William B. Eerdmans Publishing Co.

Develtere P. 1992, *Co-operative Development: Towards a Social Movement Perspective*, Saskatoon, University of Saskatchewan Centre for the Study of Co-operatives.

Dixon Hunt J. 1982, *The Wider Sea: A Life of John Ruskin*, London, J.M. Dent & Sons.

Donahue J.D. 1989, *The Privatisation Decision: Public Ends, Private Means*, New York, Basic Books.

Duncan B. 1991, *The Church's Social Teaching: From Rerum Novarum to 1931*, North Blackburn, CollinsDove.

Ellerman D. 1982, *The Socialisation of Entrepreneurship: The Empresarial Division of the Caja Laboral Popular*, Boston, Industrial Co-operative Association.

Ellerman D. 1984, *The Mondragon Co-operative Movement*, Harvard Business School Case 1-384-270, Boston, Harvard Business School.

Ensor R.C.K. 1936, *England 1870-1914*, Oxford, The Clarendon Press.

Feske V. 1996, *From Belloc to Churchill: Private Scholars, Public Culture and the Crisis of British Liberalism 1900-1939*, University of North Carolina Press.

Ffinch M. 1986, *G.K. Chesterton: A Biography*, San Francisco, Harper & Row.

Figes O. 1996, *A People's Tragedy: The Russian Revolution 1891-1924* (Pimlico Edition 1997), London, Random House.

Fowler B.B. 1938, *The Lord Helps Those ... : How the People of Nova Scotia Are Solving Their Problems Through Co-operation*, New York, The Vanguard Press.

Fraser R. 1979, *Blood of Spain: The Experience of Civil War 1936-1939*, London, Allen Lane.

Fremantle A. 1956, *The Papal Encyclicals in Their Historical Context*, New York, The New American Library of World Literature.

Fremantle A. 1960, *This Little Band of Prophets: The Story of the Gentle Fabians*, London, Allen & Unwin.

Fried A. and Elman R.M. (eds) 1969, *Charles Booth's London: A Portrait of the Poor at the Turn of the Century, drawn from his 'Life and Labour of the People of London'*, London, Hutchinson & Co.

Fukuyama F. 1995, *Trust; The Social Virtues and the Creation of Prosperity*, New York, The Free Press.

Furlong W.B. 1970, *Shaw and Chesterton: The Metaphysical Jesters*, London, The Pennsylvania State University Press.

Gates J. 1998, *The Ownership Solution: Toward a Shared Capitalism for the 21st Century*, Reading, Massachusetts, Addison-Wesley.

Glass S.T. 1966, *The Responsible Society: The Ideas of Guild Socialism*, London, Longmans.

Henderson G. 1983, *Mr Santamaria and the Bishops*, Sydney, Hale & Iremonger

Himmelfarb G. 1984, *The Idea of Poverty: England in the Early Industrial Age*, London, Faber & Faber.

Himmelfarb G. 1991, *Poverty and Compassion: The Moral Imagination of the Late Victorians*, New York, Alfred A. Knopf.

Hirst P. 1994, *Associative Democracy: New Forms of Economic and Social Governance*, Cambridge, Polity Press.

Hobsbawm E. 1964, *Labouring Men: Studies in the History of Labour*, London, Weidefeld & Nicolson.

Hobsbawm E. 1968, *Industry and Empire: An Economic History of Britain Since 1750*, London, The History Book Club.

Hogan M. (ed.) 1990, *Justice Now! Social Justice Statements of the Australian Catholic Bishops 1940-1966*, Sydney, University of Sydney Department of Government and Public Administration.

Hunter L. 1979, *G.K. Chesterton; Explorations in Allegory*, London, Macmillan & Co.

Hutton W. 1995, *The State We're In* (Revised Edition 1996), London, Vintage.

Hutton W. 1997, *The State To Come*, London, Vintage.

Hynes S. 1968, *The Edwardian Turn of Mind*, Princeton University Press.

Jenkins R. 1996, *Gladstone*, London, Papermac.

Jones P. d'A. 1968, *The Christian Socialist Revival: Religion, Class, and Social Conscience in Late-Victorian England*, Princeton University Press.

Kenner H. 1948, *Paradox in Chesterton*, London, Sheed & Ward.

Koss S. 1973, *Fleet Street Radical*, London, Allen Lane.

Kristol I. 1983, *Reflections of a Neoconservative: Looking Back, Looking Ahead*, New York, Basic Books.

Laidlaw A.F. 1961, *The Campus and the Community: The Global Impact of the Antigonish Movement*, Montreal, Harvest House.

Laidlaw A.F. (ed.) 1971, *The Man from Margaree: Writings and Speeches of M.M. Coady*, Toronto, McClelland and Stewart.

Las Vergnas R. 1938, *Chesterton, Belloc, Baring*, London, Sheed & Ward.

Lauer Q. 1988, *G.K. Chesterton: Philosopher Without Portfolio*, New York, Fordham University Press.

LeBlanc U. and Teaf H.M. Jnr, not dated, *The Rehabilitation of a Nova Scotia Fishing Village*, Haverford, Pa., Haverford College Graduate Program in Social and Technical Assistance.

Lewis G. 1992, *A Middle Way: Rochdale Co-operation in New South Wales 1859-1986*, Sydney, Australian Association of Co-operatives.

Lewis G. 1996, *People Before Profit: The Credit Union Movement in Australia*, Kent Town, South Australia, The Wakefield Press.

Lotz J. and Welton M.R. 1997, *Father Jimmy: Life and Times of Jimmy Tompkins*, Wreck Cove, Cape Breton Island, Breton Books.

McBriar A.M. 1962, *Fabian Socialism and English Politics 1884-1918*, Cambridge University Press.

McBriar A.M. 1987, *An Edwardian Mixed Double — the Bosanquets versus the Webbs: A Study in British Social Policy 1890-1929*, Oxford, The Clarendon Press.

MacCarthy F. 1989, *Eric Gill: A Lover's Quest for Art and God*, New York, E.P. Dutton.

MacCarthy F. 1994, *William Morris: A Life for Our Times*, London, Faber & Faber.

McCarthy J.P. 1978, *Hilaire Belloc: Edwardian Radical*, Indianapolis, Liberty Press.

MacEachern D.J. 1937, *It Happened in Judique*, St. John's, Newfoundland, Department of Rural Reconstruction.

Mackail J.W. 1899, *The Life of William Morris* (Two Volumes), London, Longmans, Green & Co.

Mackenzie N. & J. 1977, *The First Fabians*, London, Weidenfeld & Nicolson.

MacLeod G. 1997, *From Mondragon to America: Experiments in Community Economic Development*, Sydney, Nova Scotia, University College of Cape Breton Press.

MacLellan M. 1985, *Coady Remembered*, Antigonish, Nova Scotia, St Francis Xavier University Press.

MacPherson I. 1979, *Each for All: A History of the Co-operative Movement in English Canada, 1900-1945*, Toronto, The Macmillan Co.

Mairet P. 1966, *A.R. Orage: A Memoir*, New York, University Press.

Markel M. H. 1982, *Hilaire Belloc*, Boston, Twayne Publishers.

Marquand D. 1997, *The New Reckoning: Capitalism, States and Citizens*, Cambridge, Polity Press.

Mathews J. 1989, *Age of Democracy: The Politics of Post-Fordism*, Oxford University Press.

Mathews J. 1994, *Catching the Wave: Workplace Reform in Australia*, Sydney, NSW, Allen & Unwin.

Mathews R. 1994, *Australia's First Fabians: Middle-Class Radicals, Labour Activists and the Early Labour Movement*, Cambridge University Press.

Mathews R., Evans G. & Wilenski P. 1981, *Labor's Socialist Objective: Three Perspectives*, Victorian Fabian Pamphlet 34, Melbourne, The Victorian Fabian Society.

Melnyk G. 1985, *The Search for Community: From Utopia to a Co-operative Society*, Montreal-Buffalo, Black Rose Books.

Molony J. 1991, *The Worker Question: A New Historical Perspective on Rerum Novarum*, North Blackburn, CollinsDove.

Morrison R. 1991, *We Build the Road as We Travel*, Philadelphia, New Society Publishers.

Morton J.B. 1955, *Hilaire Belloc: A Memoir*, London, Hollis & Carter.

Mowatt C.L. 1961, *The Charity Organisation Society 1869-1913: Its Ideas and Work*, London, Methuen & Co.

Moye M. 1996, *Financing the Industrial Co-operatives of the Mondragon Group*, Economic and Social Research Council Centre for Business Research Working Paper 25, Cambridge, Cambridge University Department of Applied Economics.

Murray R. 1970, *The Split: Australian Labor in the Fifties*, Melbourne, F.W. Cheshire Publishing.

Murtagh J.G. 1944, *The Story of Antigonish: The Extension Movement for Adult Education and Economic Co-operation of St Francis Xavier University, Nova Scotia*, Melbourne, The Australian Catholic Truth Society.

Nearing P. 1975, *He Loved the Church*, Antigonish, Casket Printing & Publishing Co.

Newsome D. 1966, *The Wilberforces and Henry Manning: The Parting of Friends*, The Belknap Press of Harvard University Press.

Newsome D. 1993, *The Convert Cardinals: John Henry Newman and Henry Edward Manning*, London, John Murray.

Oakeshott R. 1978, *The Case for Workers' Co-ops*, London, Routledge & Kegan Paul.

Ormonde P. 1972, *The Movement*, Melbourne, Nelson.

Pearce J. 1996, *Wisdom and Innocence: A Life of G.K. Chesterton*, San Francisco, Ignatius Press.

Pierson S. 1979, *British Socialists: The Journey from Fantasy to Politics*, Harvard University Press.

Pelling H. (ed.) 1954, *The Challenge of Socialism*, London, Adam & Charles Black.

Pelling H. 1965, *The Origins of the Labour Party 1880-1900*, Oxford, The Clarendon Press.

Pelling H. 1960, *Modern Britain 1885-1955*, Edinburgh, Thomas Nelson and Sons.

Pimlott B. (ed.) 1984, *Fabian Essays in Socialist Thought*, London, Heinemann.

Preston P. 1995, *Franco*, London, Fontana Press.

Pugh P. 1984, *Educate, Agitate, Organise: 100 Years of Fabian Socialism*, London, Methuen and Co.

Purcell E.S. 1896, *Life of Cardinal Manning Archbishop of Westminster* (Two Volumes), London, Macmillan & Co.

Rawls J. 1971, *A Theory of Justice*, Cambridge, Mass., The Belknap Press of Harvard University Press.

Reckitt M. 1932, *Faith and Society: A Study of the Structure, Outlook and Opportunity of the Christian Social Movement in Great Britain, and the United States of America*, London, Longmans, Green and Co.

Reckitt M. (ed.) 1968, *For Christ and the People: Studies of Four Socialist Priests and Prophets of the Church of England*, London, Society for the Propogation of Christian Knowledge.

Rentoul J. 1995, *Tony Blair* (Revised Edition 1996), London, Warner Books.

Sandel M. J. 1996, *Democracy's Discontent: America in Search of a Public Philosophy*, Cambridge, Mass., The Belknap Press of Harvard University Press.

Sassoon D. 1996, *100 Years of Socialism: The West European Left in the Twentieth Century*, New York, The New Press.

Schlesinger A. 1978, *Robert Kennedy and His Times*, Boston, Houghton Mifflin Co.

Schmunde K.G. 1974, *The Man Who Was Chesterton: A Centenary Essay 1874-1974*, Australia Catholic Truth Society Publications No. 1661, 15 May 1974.

Sewell B. 1976, *Cecil Chesterton*, Faversham, Kent, Saint Albert's Press.

Semmell B. 1960, *Imperialism and Social Reform: English Social-Imperial Thought 1895-1914*, Harvard University Press.

Smith D.M. 1981, *Mussolini*, London, Weidenfeld & Nicolson.

Sole J. 1989, *Questions of the French Revolution: A Historical Overview*, New York, Pantheon Books.

Speaight R. 1957, *The Life of Hilaire Belloc*, London, Hollis & Carter.

Speaight R. 1966, *A Life of Eric Gill*, London, Methuen & Co.

Stack J. 1992, *The Great Game of Business*, New York, Currency Doubleday.

Sullivan J. (ed.) 1974, *G.K. Chesterton: A Centenary Appraisal*, London, Paul Elek.

Sylvester Smith W. 1967, *The London Heretics 1870-1914*, London, Constable & Co.

Taylor A.J.P. 1972, *Beaverbrook*, New York, Simon & Schuster.

Thomas H. 1961, *The Spanish Civil War*, London, Eyre & Spottiswood.

Thomas H. and Logan C. 1982, *Mondragon: An Economic Analysis*, London, George Allen & Unwin.

Thompson E.P. 1963, *The Making of the English Working Class*, London, Victor Gollancz.

Torr D. 1956, *Tom Mann and His Times*, London, Lawrence & Wishart.

Tsuzuki C. 1961, *H.M. Hyndman and British Socialism*, Oxford University Press.

Valentine F. 1955, *Father Vincent McNabb, O.P.: The Portrait of a Great Dominican*, London, Burns & Oates.

Vanek J. (ed.) 1975, *Self Management: Economic Liberation of Man*, Harmondsworth, Middlesex, Penguin Education.

Ward M. 1944, *Gilbert Keith Chesterton*, London, Sheed & Ward.

Ward M. 1952, *Return to Chesterton*, London, Sheed and Ward.

Warren D. 1996, *Radio Priest: Charles Coughlin the Father of Hate Radio*, New York, The Free Press.

Watkins W.P. 1970, *The International Co-operative Alliance 1895-1970*, London, The International Co-operative Alliance.

Weigel G. and Royal R. (eds) 1993, *Building the Free Society: Democracy, Capitalism and Catholic Social Teaching*, Grand Rapids, Michigan, William B. Eerdmans Publishing Co.

Whyte W.F. & K.K. 1991, *Making Mondragon: The Growth and Development of the Worker Co-operative Complex* (Revised Edition), Ithaca, ILR Press.

Wills G. 1961, *Chesterton: Man and Mask*, New York, Sheed and Ward.

Wilson A.N. 1984, *Hilaire Belloc*, London, Hamish Hamilton.

ENDNOTES

Author's Preface

1   For the contribution of the Antigonish Movement to credit unionism in Australia, see Lewis G. 1996, *People Before Profit: The Credit Union Movement in Australia*, Kent Town, South Australia, The Wakefield Press.

2   Mathews R. 1993, *Australia's First Fabians: Middle-Class Radicals, Labour Activists and the Early Labour Movement*, Cambridge University Press.

3   Mathews R. 1992. 'Back to the Future' in *Eureka Street*, Vol. 2. No. 2. March, 1992, pp. 38–9. The books reviewed were Duncan B. 1991, *The Church's Social Teaching: From Rerum Novarum to 1931*, Melbourne. CollinsDove, and Malony J. 1991, *The Worker Question: A New Historical Perspective on Rerum Novarum.*, Melbourne, CollinsDove.

4   See Mathews R. 1994, 'Shaw and Chesterton: The Reconciliation' in Hogan M. (ed) 1994, *Australian Politics: Catholic Perspectives*, Kings Cross, NSW, Uniya Christian Centre for Social Research and Action Sponsored by the Australian Jesuits. pp. 13–22.

5   Ward M. 1944, *Gilbert Keith Chesterton*, London. Sheed & Ward, p. 447. For the social thought of the Australian hierarchy of the day, see Hogan M. (ed) 1990, *Justice Now! Social Justice Statements of the Australian Catholic Bishops 1940-1966*, Sydney, University of Sydney Department of Government and Public Administration. For accounts of bodies seeking to give effect to Social Catholicism see Henderson G. 1983, *Mr Santamaria and the Bishops*, Sydney, Hale & Iremonger and Ayers T. 1986, *The National Catholic Rural Movement 1939-1955*, Unpublished Honours Thesis, University of Melbourne.

6   For accounts of the origins of the long-running fracas, see Murray R. 1970, *The Split: Australian Labor in the Fifties*, Melbourne, F.W. Cheshire Publishing Pty Ltd. and Ormonde P. 1972, *The Movement*, Melbourne, Nelson.

Chapter 1

1   Marquand D. 1997, *The New Reckoning: Capitalism, States and Citizens*, Cambridge, Polity Press, pp. 3-5.

2   Mounier E. 1938, *A Personalist Manifesto*, London, Longmans, Green & Co, p. 167.

3   Chesterton G.K. 1935, 'Conversion and Conquest' in *G.K.'s Weekly*, Vol. XXII, No. 566, 28 November 1935, pp. 143-4.

4   Tompkins J.J. 1938. The passage is from a draft in a notebook used by Tompkins for the preparation of his sermons.

Tompkins Papers, Beaton Institute Archives, University College of Cape Breton.

5   Ward M. 1944, *Gilbert Keith Chesterton*, London Sheed & Ward, pp. 445-6.

6   Webb T. 1996. Conversation with the author, Antigonish, 7 June 1996. Attempts to obtain further details of the link during my stays with the Otalora Institute in Mondragon the following month and again in 1997 were unsuccessful.

7   Coady M.M. 1939, *Masters of Their Own Destiny*, New York, Harper & Row.

8   Lerner L. 1963, 'Organisation Formed to Aid Antigonish Movement' in the *Boston Sunday Globe*, 2 June 1963. Details of the Institute are in Smyth F.F. 1960, 'The Coady International Institute' in *The Casket*, 27 October 1960. As quoted in Laidlaw A.F. 1961, *The Campus and the Community: The Global Impact of the Antigonish Movement*, Montreal, Harvest House Limited, pp. 159-60.

9   Boyle G. 1953, *Father Tompkins of Nova Scotia*, New York, P. J. Kennedy & Sons, p. 26.

10 Quoted in Fowler B.B. 1938, *The Lord Helps Those ... : How the People of Nova Scotia Are Solving Their Problems Through Co-operation*, New York, The Vanguard Press, p. 145.

11 Laidlaw A.F. 1971, *The Man from Margaree: Writings and Speeches of M.M. Coady*, Toronto, McClelland and Stewart, p. 13.

12 Quoted in Whyte W.F. & Whyte K.K. 1991, *Making Mondragon: The Growth and Dynamics of the Worker Co-operative Complex* (Revised Edition), Ithaca, New York, ILR Press, p. 257.

13 Donahue J.D. 1989, *The Privatisation Decision: Public Ends, Private Means*, New York, Basic Books, p. 43.

14 See, for example, Donahue, 1989, p. 39.

15 A report by the Queensland Criminal Justice Commission sees workplace crime arising from 'growing job insecurity, lax corporate morals and dislike of the boss' as having an average annual cost for Australia of about $A13 billion. *The Age*, 13 March 1997, p. 8.

16 Donahue, 1989, p. 38.

17 Jensen M. and Meckling W. 1976, 'The Theory of the Firm: Managerial Behaviour, Agency Costs and Ownership Structure' in *The Journal of Financial Economics*, No. 3, p. 309.

18 For a useful extended discussion of co-operatives and other mutualist bodies as social movements, see Develtere P. 1992, *Co-operative Development: Towards a Social Movement Perspective*, Saskatoon, University of Saskatchewan Centre for the Study of Co-operatives.

19 Belloc H. 1925, *The Cruise of the Nona* (Penguin Edition 1958), Middlesex, Penguin Books, p. 123.

20 Barker D. 1973, *G.K. Chesterton: A Biography*, London, Constable and Co, p. 275.

21 Thorn M.J. 1997, 'Towards a History and Interpretation of the Distributist League' in *The Chesterton Review*, Vol. XXIII. No. 3, August 1997, p. 317.

22 Corbett E.A. 1951, Letter to Boyle G, 24 August 1951. As quoted in Boyle 1953, p. 153.

Chapter 2

1 Most notably by the late, great labour historian E.P. Thompson. See for example Thompson E.P. 1967, 'The Political Education of Henry Mayhew' in *Victorian Studies*, 1967, p. 43.

2 Disraeli B. 1845, *Sybil*, Wordsworth Editions Limited 1995, Ware, Hertfordshire, p. 58.

3 Anonymous 1883, *The Bitter Cry of Outcast London: An Inquiry into the Condition of the Abject Poor*, London, p. 5.

4 MacKenzie N. & J. 1977, *The First Fabians*, London, Weidenfeld & Nicolson, p. 38.

5 Rowntree S. 1901, *Poverty: a Study of Town Life*, London, Macmillan & Co, p. 133.

6 This is not to deny that the extent of poverty was to some extent disguised by the division between the East and West Ends of London, but as the Booths will be seen to have discovered to their cost, the significance of the separation could be exaggerated. See Booth C. 1891, *Life and Labour of the People of London*, Vol. II., Revised Edition 1902, London, Macmillan & Co. Reprinted 1969, New York, Augustus M. Kelley, pp. 18-24.

7 Chesterton C. 1903, 'The Soul of Kensington' in *Outlook*, 20 June 1903.

8 Booth, 1891, p. 23.

9 Williams R. 1969, Introduction to Fried A. and Elman R. 1969, *Charles Booth's London: A Portrait of the Poor at the Turn of the Century*, drawn from his 'Life and Labour of the People in London', Hutchinsons, p. xxi.

10 Hynes S. 1968, *The Edwardian Turn of Mind*, Princeton University Press, p. 55.

11 Hobsbawm E. 1968, *Industry and Empire: An Economic History of Britain Since 1750*, London, The History Book Club, p. 137.

12 Barnett C. 1972, *The Collapse of British Power*, London, Eyre Methuen, p. 103.

13 Charles R. 1993, 'Review of *The Spirit of Democratic Capitalism*' in *The Chesterton Review*, Vol XIX, No. 4, November 1993, p. 537.

14 Hobsbawm, 1968, p. 137.

15 Himmelfarb G. 1991, *Poverty and Compassion: The Moral Imagination of the Late Victorian*, New York, Alfred A. Knopf, p. 4.

16 Mackenzie N. & J. (ed.), *The Diary of Beatrice Webb, Volume I. 1873-1892: Glitter Around and Darkness Within*, London, Virago, p. 115.

17 Himmelfarb, 1991, p. 71.

18 For a comprehensive account of the Charity Organisation Society and its differences of opinion with socialists such as Beatrice and Sidney Webb, see McBriar A.M. 1987, *An Edwardian Mixed Double — the Bosanquets versus the Webbs: A Study in British Social Policy 1890-1929*, Oxford, Clarendon Press.

19 Green and Lloyd George would not necessarily be pleased to be bracketed with one another even under so broad a label as 'New Liberal', but their views on the point in question are sufficiently similar for the link to be valid.

20 *The Christian Socialist* was published jointly by the Land Reform Union and the Guild of St Matthew. Champion was the Treasurer of the Land Reform Union and edited *The Christian Socialist* in conjunction with J.L. Joynes and R.P.B. Frost. Frost had been one of his contemporaries at Marlborough, and Joynes was a master at Eton. The comprehensive biography which Champion so richly merits and has so inexplicably been denied is at long last being undertaken by Professor John Barnes of the School of English at La Trobe University in Melbourne, Australia. For an account of Champion's later political activities in Australia, where he died in 1928, see Mathews R. 1994, *Australia's First Fabians: Middle-Class Radicals, Labour Activists and the Early Labour Movement*, Cambridge University Press.

21 Colloms B. 1982, *Victorian Visionaries*, London, Constable, p. 237. For Christian socialism more generally, see in particular Jones P. d'A. 1968, *The Christian Socialist Revival, 1877-1914: Religion, Class and Social Conscience in Late-Victorian England*, Princeton, New Jersey, Princeton University Press, and also Binyon G.C. 1931, *The Christian Socialist Movement in England: An Introduction to the Study of Its History*, London, The Society for Promoting Christian Knowledge.

22 Shaw G.B. 1949, *Sixteen Self-Sketches*, London, Constable, p. 58.

23 Shaw G.B. 1933, *The Political Madhouse in America and Nearer Home*, London, Constable & Co, p. 61.

24 Shaw, 1949, p. 58.

25 Pease E.R. 1916, *The History of the Fabian Society*, London, Cassell, pp. 19-21.

26 Champion H.H. 1907, '"*Quorum Pars Fui*": An Unconventional Autobiography' in Henderson L.M. 1973, *The Goldstein Story*, Melbourne, Stockland Press, p. 107.

27 *Nineteenth Century*, January, 1891. Quoted in MacKenzie N. & J. 1977, p. 19. Characteristically, Hyndman failed to acknowledge his debt to Marx and so estranged himself from both Marx and Marx's most important disciple, Engels, in a long-running feud which the nascent socialist movement could ill-afford. At the 1880 elections, Hyndman nominated as an independent against two Gladstonian Liberals in the Marylebone electorate, but withdrew his candidature when Gladstone denounced him as a Tory.

28 MacKail J.W. 1899, *The Life of William Morris*, Vol. II., London, Longmans, Green & Co, p. 244.
29 Laurence D.H. (ed.) 1965, *Bernard Shaw: The Collected Letters, 1874-1897*, London, Max Reinhardt, p. 351.
30 Frost had attended Marlborough with Champion and Joynes was a schoolmaster at Eton, who resigned his position after he and Henry George were arrested as suspected Fenian organisers during George's 1882 lecture tour of Ireland.
31 For a comprehensive account of the establishment of the Fabian Society, see MacKenzie N. & J. 1977, Chapter 1, in conjunction with MacKenzie N. 1979, 'Percival Chubb and the Founding of the Fabian Society', in *Victorian Studies* 23, No. 1, 1979.
32 Holroyd M. 1988, *Bernard Shaw, Volume I, 1856-1898: The Search for Love*, London, Chatto & Windus, p. 132.
33 Quoted in Brandon R. 1990, *The New Women and the Old Men: Love, Sex and the Women Question*, London, Secker & Warburg, p. 29.
34 Quoted in Tsuzuki C. 1961, *H.M. Hyndman and British Socialism*, Oxford University Press, p. 64.
35 Champion H.H. 1887, *Social-Democracy in Practice*, London, Swan Sonnenschein & Co, p. 5.
36 As opposed to standing candidates for the SDF, whose contesting of three constituencies at the 1885 elections was a conspicuous failure.
37 Pelling H. 1953, 'H.H. Champion: Pioneer of Labour Representation', in *The Cambridge Journal*, Vol. VI, October 1952-September 1953, Cambridge, Bowes & Bowes, p. 238.
38 Shaw G.B. 1884, *A Manifesto*, Fabian Tract No. 2, London, The Fabian Society, p. 4.
39 'The Old Gang' and 'the Great Fabians' are terms used for the inner circle of the Fabian Society respectively by Shaw and the British historian Robert Skidelsky, and Gilbert Chesterton singles out Shaw in his turn as 'the great Fabian'. For 'Old Gang' see Shaw G.B. 1892, *The Fabian Society: Its Early History*, Fabian Tract No. 41, London, The Fabian Society, p. 24; for 'Great Fabians' Skidelsky R. 1979, 'The Fabian Ethic' in Holroyd M. (ed.) 1979, *The Genius of Shaw*, New York, Holt, Rinehart and Winston, p. 126; and for 'the great Fabian' Chesterton G.K. 'Bernard Shaw and the Three Witnesses' in *The New Witness*, Vol. VIII, No. 186, 25 May 1916, p. 111.
40 See, for example, Webb S. 1894, *Socialism: True and False*, Fabian Tract No. 51, London, The Fabian Society.
41 Chesterton C. 1916, 'The Rise and Fall of the Fabian Society' in *The New Witness*, Vol. VIII, No. 185, 18 May 1916, p. 87.
42 Cole G.D.H. 1955, *Beatrice and Sidney Webb*, Fabian Tract 297, London, The Fabian Society, p. 35.
43 Cole M. 1961, *The Story of Fabian Socialism*, London, Heinemann, p. 1.
44 Cole M. 1961, p. 1.

45 Webb S. & B. 1920, *A Constitution for the Socialist Commonwealth of Great Britain*, London, Longmans, p. 174.
46 Pimlott B. (ed.) 1984, *Fabian Essays in Socialist Thought*, London, Heinemann, p. vii.
47 Cole M. 1961, p. 328.
48 Quoted in Mackenzie & Mackenzie, 1977, pp. 281-2.
49 Cole M. 1961, p. 338.
50 Shaw G.B. 1931, 'Preface to the 1931 Reprint' in Shaw G.B. (ed.) 1950, *Fabian Essays in Socialism 1889*, London, George Allen & Unwin, p. v.
51 MacKenzie N. & J. (ed.) 1983, *The Diary of Beatrice Webb, Volume 2, 1892-1905, All the Good Things of Life*, London, Virago, p. 132.
52 Shaw, 1892, p. 19.
53 Cole G.D.H. & Postgate R. 1938, *The Common People*, London, Methuen & Co, p. 423.
54 Cole M. 1961, p. 107.
55 See Mathews, 1993.
56 Cole M. 1961, p. 139.
57 Beveridge. W. 1953, *Power and Influence*, London, Hodder and Stoughton, p. 86.
58 Cole M. 1961, pp. 171-2.
59 Cole M. 1961, p. 339.
60 Shaw G.B. 1889, 'The Transition to Social Democracy' in Shaw G.B. (ed.) 1889, *Fabian Essays in Socialism*, London, The Fabian Society, p. 200.
61 Chesterton C. 'Guilds and Utopias' in *The New Witness*, Vol IV, No. 84, 11 June 1914, p. 176.
62 Cole M. 1971, *The Life of G.D.H. Cole*, London, Heinemann, p. 81.
63 Mairet P. 1966, *A.R. Orage*, New York, University Books, pp. 25-6.
64 'Gild' is Penty's preferred spelling, and appears throughout his work.
65 Orage to Wells, 23 July 1906. Quoted in Britain I. 1982, *Fabianism and Culture: A Study of British Socialism and the Arts c. 1884-1918*, Cambridge University Press, p. 11.
66 Orage to Wells, 9 June 1907. Quoted in Mackenzie N. & J. 1977, p. 344.
67 Eric Gill to *The New English Weekly*, 15 November 1934. Quoted in Britain, 1982, p. 12.
68 Britain, 1982, p. 168. None of this is to suggest that the criticisms of the society by Orage and Penty and their fellow dissidents were necessarily correct. For a compelling argument to the contrary, see, for example, Britain 1982, Chapter 7.
69 Sewell B. 1975, *Cecil Chesterton*, Faversham, St Albert's Press, p. 26.
70 Quoted in Sewell, 1975, p. 26.
71 Corrin J.P. 1981, *G.K. Chesterton and Hilaire Belloc: The Battle Against Modernity*, Ohio University Press, p. 79.

72 Belloc H. 1934, Obituary for A.R. Orage in *G.K.'s Weekly*, 15 November 1934. Reprinted in *The Chesterton Review*, Vol. XX. No. 1, February 1994, pp. 120-2.

73 Mackenzie J. & N. 1977, p. 345.

74 For a useful meditation on parallels in the rather different experience and aspirations of American bodies such as the Knights of Labor (1869-1902) and their relevance to current debate on citizenship and civil society issues, see Sandel M. J. 1996, *Democracy's Discontent: America in Search of a Public Philosophy*, Cambridge, Massachusetts, The Belknap Press of Harvard University Press, Chapter 5.

75 Glass S.T. 1966, *The Responsible Society: The Ideas of Guild Socialism*, London, Longmans, p. 5.

76 Mairet, 1966, p. 67.

77 Quoted in Mairet, 1966, p. 69.

Chapter 3

1 Johnson P. 1993, review of Newsome D. 1993, *The Convert Cardinals: J.H. Newman and H.E. Manning*, in the *Sunday Telegraph*, 26 December, 1993. Re-printed in *The Chesterton Review*, Vol. XX, No. 1, February 1994, p. 127.

2 See Newsome D. 1966. *The Wilberforces and Henry Manning: The Parting of Friends*, Cambridge, Massachusetts, The Belknap Press of Harvard University Press, pp. 147-8.

3 Manning was formally received into the Church in April 1851. It is interesting that, like his no less distinguished fellow convert, Cardinal Newman, he was, in the Anglican phase of his career, notably intolerant of measures for Catholic Emancipation. See, for example, Jenkins R. 1996, *Gladstone*, London, Papermac, pp. 48-9.

4 Ultramontane — literally 'beyond the mountains' — opinion within the Church upheld increasing Roman control and centralisation in policy and the appointment of bishops, as against those seeking to be wholly or in part free from papal direction. See Duncan B. 1991, *The Church's Social Teachings: From Rerum Novarum to 1931*, North Blackburn, Victoria, CollinsDove, pp. 7-8.

5 Manning H.E. 1947, *What One Work of Mercy Can I Do this Lent: A Letter to a Friend*, London, p. 10.

6 Manning H.E. 1880, Lenten Pastoral Letter quoted in McClelland V.A. 1992, 'Manning's Work for Social Justice' in *The Chesterton Review*, Vol. XVIII, No. 4, November 1992.

7 Duncan, 1991, p. 54.

8 Quoted in Mathews R. 1981, 'Democratic Socialism: An Ethic for the Eighties' in Mathews R., Evans G. & Wilenski P. 1981, *Labor's Socialist Objective: Three Perspectives*, Victorian Fabian Pamphlet 34, Melbourne, The Victorian Fabian Society, p. 14.

9 Duncan, 1991, p. 41.

10 Quoted in Kohler T.C. 1993, 'In Praise of Little Platoons: *Quadragesimo Anno* (1931)' in Weigel G. and Royal R. (eds) 1993, *Building the Free Society: Democracy, Capitalism and Catholic Social Teaching*, Grand Rapids, Michigan, William B. Eerdmans Publishing Company, p. 35.

11 Quoted in Kohler, 1993, p. 35.

12 Quoted in Kohler, 1993, p. 35.

13 Council of Fribourg, 1886, report to Pope Leo XIII, as quoted in Duncan 1991, p. 54.

14 Mermillod G. 1897, letter to Pope Leo XIII, as quoted in Duncan 1991, p. 48.

15 McClelland, 1992, p. 533.

16 Gilley S. 1992, 'Manning and Chesterton' in *The Chesterton Review*, Vol. XVIII, No. 4, November 1992, p. 491. Arch's recently formed National Agricultural Labourers' Union was effectively brought to its knees when an eighteen-week lockout in Suffolk in 1874 cost it nearly £25,000 and caused many of the 2400 of its members involved to emigrate or move to other parts of England. Stead — a crusading journalist — challenged the practice of trafficking in children for prostitution by openly committing the offence and writing an article, 'The Maiden Tribute of Modern Babylon', which documented and denounced it. His three-month prison sentence was instrumental in bringing about the Criminal Amendment Act of 1885. Efforts by the Catholic Archbishop of New York, Patrick Corrigan, to ban the Knights of Labour — a largely mutualist body of working people with a strong commitment to establishing co-operatives as a means of bringing about a fairer social order — on the grounds of their socialist and Georgist sympathies were frustrated when Manning and Cardinal Gibbons of Baltimore convinced Leo XIII that to do so would be unjust and counter-productive. Gibbons and Manning were less successful in dissuading Leo from having George's works placed in the Index of Forbidden Books, although it was decided that the decision should be kept secret.

17 Quoted in Reckitt M. 1932, *Faith and Society: A Study of the Structure, Outlook and Opportunity of the Christian Socialist Movement in Great Britain and America*, London, Longmans, Green & Co, p. 101.

18 Champion H.H. 1986, 'Men I Have Met: II. Henry Edward Manning' in *The Champion*, Vol. 2, No. 48, 16 May 1896, p. 1.

19 Champion, 1907, p. 125.

20 Champion, 1907, p. 126.

21 Quoted by Archbishop, later Cardinal, Hinsley in an address at a dinner honouring the Dock Strike leader Ben Tillett, in London on 21 October 1936. Reprinted in *The Chesterton Review*, Vol XVIII, No. 4, November 1992, p. 624. See also the letter by Francis Bywater in *The Chesterton Review*, Vol. XIX, No. 4, November 1993, p. 579.

22　Mann T. 1923, *Tom Mann's Memoirs*, Melbourne, The Labour Publishing Company, p. 65.

23　Reckitt, 1932, p. 101.

24　Hinsley, 1936, p. 622.

25　See, for example, the differing views of contributors to the Cardinal Manning Special Issue of *The Chesterton Review*, Vol. XVIII, No. 4, November 1992. The drafting of *De Rerum Novarum* was substantially delegated, most notably to the Jesuit priest, Matteo Liberatore, but also to Cardinals Zigliara and Mazzella. For a useful account of the drafting process, see Molony J. 1991, *The Worker Question: A Historical Perspective on Rerum Novarum*, Melbourne, CollinsDove.

26　Pius XI 1931, *Encyclical Letter on Social Reconstruction*, Boston, Mass, St Paul Editions, p. 40.

27　Manning H. E. 1891, 'A Pope on Capital and Labour, the Significance of the Encyclical *Rerum Novarum*' in *The Dublin Review*, July 1891, pp. 153-67.

28　Straiton M. 1990, 'The Cockney's Cardinal', Opening Address at an Exhibition in Honour of the Centenary of the death of Cardinal Manning and the Tenth Anniversary of the Papal Visit to Britain, Westminster Cathedral, London, in *The Chesterton Review*, Vol. XVIII, No. 4, November 1992, p. 586.

29　Chesterton G.K. 1935, p. 144.

30　Penty joined the Distributist League, and Orage told Titterton before he died that he too was a distributist. See Titterton W.R. 1936, *G.K. Chesterton: A Portrait*, London, Alexander Ousley, pp. 63-5.

31　Chesterton, Mrs C. 1941, *The Chestertons*, London, Chapman & Hall, p. 22.

32　Chesterton, Mrs C. 1941, p. 9.

33　Titterton, 1936, p. 13.

34　Titterton, 1936, p. 10.

35　Valentine F. 1955, *Father Vincent McNabb, O.P.: The Portrait of a Great Dominican*, London, Burns & Oates, pp. 276-7.

36　Chesterton, Mrs C. 1941, p. 57.

37　Ransome A. 1976, *The Autobiography of Arthur Ransome*, London, Jonathan Cape, p. 100. When Cecil published his anonymous — albeit largely laudatory — biography of Gilbert, *G.K. Chesterton: A Criticism*, in 1908, it was Ransome who signed the contract, so that Cecil's identity could be protected. Ransome is perhaps best remembered less as a journalist than as a children's writer whose 'Swallows and Amazons' books are still widely read.

38　See Chesterton G.K. 1919, 'Biographical Note on the Author' in Chesterton C. 1919, *A History of the United States* (Everyman Edition 1943), London, J. M. Dent and Sons, p. xviii.

39　Chesterton G.K. 1937, *Autobiography*, London, Hutchinson & Co, p. 198.

40　Quoted in Wilson A.N. 1984, *Hilaire Belloc*, London, Hamish Hamilton, p. 237.

41 See, for example, O'Donnell F.H. 1913. 'The Child Murder and Mutilation in Kiev', 'The Horror at Kiev and the Revelations of *The Golden Bough*' and 'A Jew Cinema Film Shows Christians Killing the Little Christian Child in Kiev' in *The New Witness*, Vol. II, No. 50, 16 October 1913, pp. 749-51; Vol. II, No. 51, 23 October 1913, pp. 778-80; Vol. III, No. 63, 15 January 1914, pp. 336-8; and Vol. III, No. 65, 29 January 1914, pp. 339-40.

42 Streicher was among the senior Nazis convicted and hanged for their war crimes at Nuremburg after the Second World War.

43 Wilson, 1984, p. 184.

44 Quoted in Coren M. 1990, *Gilbert: The Man Who Was Thursday*, New York, Paragon Press, p. 216.

45 See, for example, the denial that Gilbert Chesterton was anti-semitic in Heseltine G.G. 1974. 'G.K. Chesterton — Journalist' in Sullivan J. (ed.) 1974, *G.K. Chesterton: A Centenary Appraisal*, London, Paul Elek, pp. 133-4; and an acerbic rebuttal by Bernard Levin in Levin B. 1974, 'The Case for Chesterton' in *The Observer*, 26 May 1974, reprinted in Conlon D.J. (ed.) 1987, *G.K. Chesterton: A Half Century of Views*, Oxford University Press, pp. 314-6.

46 See Hobsbawm E. 1964, *Labouring Men: Studies in the History of Labour*, London, Weidenfeld & Nicolson, p. 268.

47 As in the case of Champion, no biography of Marson has so far been published, but the Melbourne historian Hugh Anderson has recently located the manuscript of an account of his life prepared by his fellow clergyman in the neighbouring parish of Minehead, the Reverend Francis M. Etherington, in conjunction with Dr Maud Karpelis. For some details of his career, see Reckitt M.B. 1968, 'Charles Marson, 1859-1914 and the Real Disorders of the Church' in Reckitt M.B. (ed.) 1968, *For Christ and People: Studies of Four Socialist Priests and Prophets of the Church of England between 1870 and 1930*, London, Society for the Propagation of Christian Knowledge. For details of his Fabian activities in Australia, see Mathews, 1993.

48 Cole M. 1961, p. 56.

49 Sewell, 1975, p. 19.

50 Chesterton C. 1916, 'The Rise and Fall of the Fabian Society' in *The New Witness*, Vol. VIII, No. 185, 18 May 1916, p. 86.

51 Chesterton, Mrs C. 1941, p. 59.

52 Chesterton, Mrs C. 1941, pp. 59-60.

53 Chesterton, Mrs C. 1941, p. 60.

54 Quoted in Bettany F.G. 1926, *Stewart Headlam: A Biography*, London, John Murray, p. 128.

55 Quoted in Bettany, 1926, p. 91.

56 Chesterton, Mrs C. 1941, p. 58. Edith Nesbit was later a frequent contributor to Cecil's distributist weekly, *The New Witness*.

57 Sewell, 1975, p. 21.

58 Chesterton C. 1916, p. 86.

59 Chesterton C. 1912, 'Some Church Socialists and Their Views: IV. Cecil Chesterton' in *The Church Socialist Quarterly*, Vol. 1, No. 4, April 1912, p. 6. Membership dates for various Fabians including Cecil are in Pugh P. 1984, *Educate, Agitate, Organise: 100 Years of Fabian Socialism*, London, Methuen & Co, pp. 32-6.
60 Titterton, 1936, p. 51.
61 Chesterton G.K. 1919, p. xxix.
62 See, for example, Titterton 1936, pp. 51-2.
63 Chesterton C. 1912, 'The Servile State' in *The Eye Witness*, Vol. III, No. 20, 31 October 1912, p. 631. Italics added.
64 Chesterton C. 1912. 'Ultimus Romanorum' in *The New Witness*, Vol. I, No. 7, 19 December 1912, p. 215.
65 Chesterton G.K. 1919, p. xxv.
66 Chesterton, Mrs C. 1941, p. 123.
67 See, for example, Titterton 1936, p. 99, and Chesterton, Mrs C. 1941, p. 221.
68 Chesterton, Mrs C. 1941, p. 207.

Chapter 4

1 Chesterton G.K. 1923, as quoted in Pearce J. 1996, *Wisdom and Innocence: A Life of G.K. Chesterton*, San Francisco, Ignatius Press, p. 63.
2 Quoted in Wilson A.N. 1984, *Hilaire Belloc*, London, Hamish Hamilton, p. 90.
3 Later, as Marie Belloc Lowndes, an author in her own right, with over forty crime novels to her credit.
4 Belloc Lowndes M. 1943, *I, Too, Have Lived in Arcadia*, London, Readers Union Limited, p. 95.
5 Wilson, 1984, p. 113.
6 Gilley S. 1992, 'Manning and Chesterton', in *The Chesterton Review*, Vol. XVIII, No. 4, November 1992, p. 489.
7 Quinn D. 1992, 'Manning, Chesterton and Social Catholicism' in *The Chesterton Review*, Vol. XVIII, No. 4, November 1992, p. 512.
8 Wilson, 1984, p. 49.
9 Smith F.E. 1923, Rectorial Address on 'Idealism in International Politics', Glasgow University, 7 November 1923, as quoted in Campbell J. 1983, *F.E. Smith: First Earl of Birkenhead* (Pimlico Edition 1991), London, Jonathan Cape, p. 636.
10 Speaight R. 1957, *The Life of Hilaire Belloc*, London, Hollis & Carter, p. 92.
11 Six Oxford Men, 1897, *Essays in Liberalism by Six Oxford Men*, London, Cassell & Co, pp. vii-viii.
12 Wilson, 1984, p. 50.
13 Quoted in Speaight, 1957, p. 282.
14 Speaight, 1957, p. 118.
15 Belloc H. 1897, 'The Liberal Tradition' in *Six Oxford Men*, 1897, p. 8.
16 Belloc, 1897, p. 8.

17 Belloc, H. 1911, *The French Revolution*, London, Williams and Norgate, p. 17.
18 Belloc, H. 1901, *Robespierre*, London, James Nisbet & Co, p. 29.
19 Belloc, 1911, p. 218.
20 Belloc H. 1920, *Europe and the Faith*, London, Constable & Co, p. 2.
21 Belloc, 1920, pp. 23-4.
22 Belloc, 1920, p. 13.
23 Belloc, 1920, p. 13.
24 Belloc, 1920, p. 13.
25 Belloc, 1920, p. 191.
26 Corrin J.P. 1981, *G.K Chesterton and Hilaire Belloc: The Battle Against Modernity*, Athens, Ohio University Press, p. 18.
27 Belloc H. 1899, *Danton.* Reprinted 1972, London, Tom Stacey, p. 3.
28 Belloc, 1899, p. 4.
29 Belloc, 1911, p. 74.
30 Belloc, 1899, p. 28.
31 Corrin, 1981, p. 19.
32 'In 1789, 40 per cent of the kingdom's population depended on charity, two out of every five men, women and children'. Weber E. 1989, Foreword to Sole J. 1989, *Questions of the French Revolution: An Historical Overview*, New York, Pantheon Books.
33 Belloc, 1911, p. 222.
34 Belloc, 1911, pp. 79, 82.
35 Speaight, 1957, p. 135.
36 Belloc, 1911, p. 21.
37 Speaight, 1957, p. 97.
38 Wilson, 1984, p. 258.
39 McCarthy J. 1957, *Hilaire Belloc: Edwardian Radical*, Indianapolis, Liberty Press, p. 261.
40 Baring, 1932, p. 171.
41 Speaight, 1957, p. 97.
42 Speaight, 1957, p. 121.
43 Wilson, 1984, p. 90.
44 Wilson, 1984, p. 258.
45 Wilson, 1984, p. 188.
46 Speaight R. (ed.) 1958, *Letters from Hilaire Belloc*, London, Hollis & Carter, p. 116.
47 Belloc H. 1922, *The Jews*, London, Constable & Co, p. 305.
48 Speaight R. 1970, *The Property Basket: Recollections of a Divided Life*, London, Collins & Harvill Press, p. 373.
49 Belloc, 1922, p. 304.
50 McCarthy, 1978, p. 21.
51 Belloc, 1897, p. 9.
52 Belloc, 1897, p. 8.
53 Belloc, 1897, p. 29.
54 Belloc, 1920, p. 192.
55 Quoted in Markel M.H. 1982, *Hilaire Belloc*, Boston, Twayne Publishers, p. 11.

56 For useful discussions of why such a conclusion might have been reached, see Markel, 1982, p. 10 and Wilson, 1984, p. 62.
57 Quoted in Speaight, 1957, p. 218.
58 Quoted in Speaight, 1957, p. 258.
59 Belloc concluded characteristically that Ware was getting rid of him because he had written articles 'disrespectful of the wealthy'. Wilson, 1984, p. 175.
60 Markel, 1982, p. 153. Belloc's close friend and fellow writer, Desmond MacCarthy, once asked him what was the greatest number of words he had produced in a day. Belloc replied '23,000 — and they were quite good words too'. Cecil H. & M. 1991, *Clever Hearts: Desmond & Molly MacCarthy*, London, Victor Gollancz, p.119.
61 For an account of manuscript material held in the Belloc Collection at Boston College, see Markel M.H. 1986, 'The Manuscript Poetry of Hilaire Belloc' in *The Chesterton Review*, Vol. XII, No. 2, May 1986, pp. 221-9.
62 Quoted in Speaight, 1957, p. 207.
63 Quoted in Wilson, 1984, p. 139.
64 Quoted in Speaight, 1957, p. 211.
65 McCarthy, 1978, pp. 131-4.
66 McCarthy, 1978, p. 113.
67 Belloc H. 1907, 'The Recess and the Congo' in *The New Age*, 8 August 1908, p. 284.
68 Wilson, 1984, p. 91.
69 Belloc H. and Chesterton C. 1911, *The Party System*, London, Stephen Swift, p. 29.
70 Quoted in Wilson, 1984, p. 171.
71 Quoted in Speaight, 1957, pp. 314-5.
72 Wilson, 1984, p. 152.
73 Sewell, 1975, p. 33.
74 Belloc & Chesterton, 1911, p. 33.
75 Belloc & Chesterton, 1911, p. 33.
76 Belloc & Chesterton, 1911, pp. 41-2.
77 Belloc & Chesterton, 1911, p. 37.
78 Chesterton G.K., 1937, pp. 213, 210.
79 Belloc & Chesterton, 1911, p. 103-4.
80 Belloc & Chesterton, 1911, p. 110.
81 Belloc & Chesterton, 1911, pp. 110-1.
82 Belloc & Chesterton, 1911, p. 34.
83 Reckitt M. 1941, *As It Happened*, London, J.M. Dent & Sons, pp. 107-8.
84 Belloc H. 1912, *The Servile State* (Third Edition) 1927, London, Constable & Co, p. 57.
85 Belloc, 1912, p. xi.
86 Belloc, 1912, p. 6.
87 Chesterton G.K. 1937, p. 297.
88 Belloc, 1912, p. 31.
89 Belloc, 1912, pp. 49-50.
90 Belloc, 1912, p. 57.

91 Belloc, 1912, p. 52.
92 Belloc, 1912, p. 15.
93 Belloc, 1912, p. viii.
94 Belloc, 1912, p. 69.
95 Belloc, 1912, p. 5.
96 Belloc, 1912, pp. 5, 105.
97 Belloc, 1912, p. xv.
98 Belloc, 1912, p. 85.
99 Belloc, 1912, p. 113.
100 Belloc, 1912, p. 143.
101 Belloc, 1912, p. 6.
102 Belloc, 1912, p. 183.
103 Belloc H. 1936, *An Essay on the Restoration of Property*, London, The Distributist League, p. 5.
104 Belloc, 1912, p. 138.
105 Belloc, 1936, p. 5.
106 Belloc, 1936, p. 40.
107 Belloc, 1936, p. 83.
108 Belloc's sister, Maria Belloc Lowndes, sees him as having had a wonderful life 'for, say 15 years — perhaps only 10 years, if one leaves out the first war'. Lowndes S. (ed.) 1971, *Diaries and Letters of Marie Belloc Lowndes 1911-1947*, London, Chatto & Windus, p. 278.
109 McCarthy, 1978, p. 15.
110 Wilson, 1984, p. 254.
111 An aberration in which he was not alone. Bernard Shaw and Winston Churchill also admired Mussolini, and Beatrice and Sidney Webb admired Stalin.
112 Corrin J.P. 1985, 'G.K. Chesterton and the Corporate State' in *The Chesterton Review*, Vol. XI, No. 3, August 1985, p. 292.
113 Speaight, 1957, p. 306. For comprehensive and devastating accounts of how cynically and comprehensively Belloc and those of his fellow distributists who shared his admiration for the dictators were deceived, see Smith D.M. 1981, *Mussolini*, London, Weidenfeld and Nicolson, and Preston P. 1993, *Franco*, London, HarperCollins.
114 Warren D. 1996, *Radio Priest: Charles Coughlin the Father of Hate Radio*, New York, The Free Press, pp. 104-5.

Chapter 5

1   Quoted in Ward M. 1944, *Gilbert Keith Chesterton*, London, Sheed & Ward, p. 113.
2   Chesterton G.K. 1937, *Autobiography*, London, Hutchinson & Co, p. 118.
3   Quoted in Ward, 1944, p. 113.
4   Titterton W.R. 1936, *G.K. Chesterton: A Portrait*, London, Alexander Ouseley, p. 47.
5   Quoted in Ward, 1944, p. 526.

6   Canovan M. 1977, *G.K. Chesterton: Radical Populist*, New York, Harcourt Brace Jovanovich, p. 109.

7   Chesterton G.K. 1924. 'Apologia' in *G.K.'s Weekly*, Vol. I, Friday, 24 November 1924, p. 2. Gilbert ultimately put on so much weight that, when he wanted to see Robert Speaight as Beckett in Eliot's *Murder in the Cathedral* in 1935, he was unable to do so because none of the seats in the theatre were big enough to hold him. Speaight R, 1970, *The Property Basket: Recollections of a Divided Life*, London, Collins & Harvill Press, p. 177.

8   Quoted in Conlon D.J. (ed.) 1987, *G.K. Chesterton: A Half Century of Views*, Oxford University Press, p. xxiv.

9   Canovan, 1977, p. 85.

10 Chesterton G.K., 1937, p. 111.

11 Quoted in Ward, 1944. pp. 71-2.

12 Quoted in Ward, 1944, p. 74.

13 MacKail J.W. 1899, *The Life of William Morris*, Vol. II, London, Longmans, Green & Co, p. 244.

14 Titterton W.R. 1926 (2), 'Revolutionary Days' in *G.K.'s Weekly*, 3 July 1926, p. 281.

15 Titterton W.R. 1926 (1), 'The Webb and the Spider' in *G.K.'s Weekly*, 23 January 1926, p. 476.

16 Titterton, 1926 (2), p. 281

17 Titterton, 1926 (2), p. 476.

18 Ward, 1944, p. 76.

19 Chesterton G.K., 1937, p. 111.

20 Gilley S. 1995, 'Chesterton's Politics' in *The Chesterton Review*, Vol. XXI, Nos. 1 & 2, February & May 1995, p. 33.

21 Quoted in Ward, 1944, p. 120.

22 Quoted in Jones P. d'A. 1968, *The Christian Socialist Revival 1877-1914: Religion, Class, and Social Conscience in Late-Victorian England*, Princeton University Press, p. 241.

23 Jones, 1968, pp. 240-1.

24 See Hetzler L.A. 1981, 'Chesterton's Political Views 1892-1914: With Comments on Chesterton and Anti-Semitism' in *The Chesterton Review*, Vol. VII, No. 2, Spring 1981, p. 123.

25 For example, see Chesterton G.K. 1908, 'Why I am not a Socialist' in *The New Age*, 4 January 1908, as reprinted in *The Chesterton Review*, Vol. VII, No. 3, August 1981, pp. 189-95.

26 Ensor R.C.K. 1936, *England 1870-1914*, Oxford, The Clarendon Press, p. 391.

27 Lloyd George — newly appointed as President of the Board of Trade by the incoming Liberal Prime Minister, Sir Henry Campbell-Bannerman — presciently summarised what a Liberal failure might look like and its likely consequences, in an address to the Welsh National Liberal Council in Cardiff on 11 October 1906. See Gilbert B.B. 1987, *David Lloyd George: A Political Life, Vol. I, The Architect of Change 1863-1912*, London, B.T. Batsford, p. 290.

28 Chesterton G.K., 1908, p. 249.

29 Ensor, 1936, p. 438.

30 Gilley S, 1995, 'Chesterton's Politics' in *The Chesterton Review*, Vol. XXI, Nos. 1 & 2, February & May 1995, pp. 40-1.

31 Quinn D. 1992, 'Manning, Chesterton and Social Catholicism' in *The Chesterton Review*, Vol. XVIII, No. 4, November 1992, p. 513.

32 Chesterton G.K. 1910, *What's Wrong with the World*, in Marlin G.J., Rabatin R.P. and Swan J.L (eds), *The Collected Works of G.K. Chesterton*, Vol. IV, San Francisco, Ignatius Press, p. 66.

33 Chesterton G.K., 1924, 'Apologia' in *G.K.'s Weekly*, Vol. I, 24 November 1924, p. 1.

34 Quoted in Gilley, 1995, pp. 39-40.

35 Chesterton G.K. 1926, p. 6.

36 Chesterton G.K. 1926, p. 23.

37 Chesterton G.K. 1926, pp. 27-9. Italics added.

38 Chesterton G.K. 1910, *What's Wrong with the World*, in Marlin G.J., Rabatin R.P. and Swan J.L. (eds.) *The Collected Works of G.K. Chesterton*, Vol. IV, San Francisco, Ignatius Press, p. 213.

39 Chesterton G.K. 1919, 'Biographical Note on the Author' in Chesterton C. 1919, *A History of the United States* (Everyman Edition 1940), London, J.M. Dent & Sons, p. xxviii.

40 Chesterton G.K. 1934, *G.K.'s: A Miscellany of the First 500 Issues of G.K.'s Weekly*, London, pp. 15-6, as quoted in Quinn D. 1994, 'Distributism, Democratic Capitalism and the New World Order' in *The Chesterton Review*, Vol. XX, Nos. 2 & 3, May and August 1994, p. 168.

41 Chesterton G.K., 1926, pp. 108, 151, 148.

42 Quinn D. 1995, 'The Historical Foundations of Modern Distributism' in *The Chesterton Review*, Vol. XXI, No. 4, November 1995, p. 464.

43 Quoted in Mueller J. 1991, 'Chesterton and Distributism' in *The Chesterton Review*, Vol. XVII, No. 2, May 1991, p. 282.

44 Chesterton G.K., 1910, p. 224.

45 Quoted in Furlong W.B. 1970, *Shaw and Chesterton: The Metaphysical Jesters*, The Pennsylvania State University Press, p. 7.

46 Chesterton G.K. 1937, *Autobiography*, London, Hutchinson & Co, p. 181.

47 Shaw G.B. 1908, 'Belloc and Chesterton' in *The New Age*, 15 February 1908, p. 309.

48 Shaw, 1908, p. 310.

49 Quoted in Furlong, 1970, p. 126.

50 Quoted in Ward M., 1952, *Return to Chesterton*, London, Sheed & Ward, p. 4.

51 Quoted in Furlong, 1970, p. 184.

52 Chesterton G.K. 1909, *George Bernard Shaw*, London, John Lane, The Bodley Head, pp. 11-12.

53 Chesterton G.K. 1908. 'Why I Am Not a Socialist' in *The New Age*, 4 January 1908, pp. 189-90.

54 Chesterton G.K. 1909, p. 71.
55 Wells H.G. 1908, 'About Chesterton and Belloc' in *The New Age*, 11 January 1908, p. 209.
56 Furlong, 1970, p. 67.
57 Titterton W.R. 1936, *G.K. Chesterton: A Portrait*, London, Alexander Ousley, p. 194.
58 Quoted in Ward, 1952, p. 225.
59 Barker D. 1973, *G.K. Chesterton: A Biography*, London, Constable, p. 276.
60 Titterton, 1936, p. 194.
61 Belloc H. 1908, 'Not a Reply' in *The New Age*, 8 February 1908, pp. 289-90.
62 Chesterton C. 1917, 'Shaw and My Neighbour's Chimney' in *The New Witness*, 3 May 1917, p. 13.
63 Shaw G.B. 1935, 'Provocations' in *G.K.'s Weekly*, 21 March 1935, p. 8.
64 Chesterton G.K., Shaw G.B. & Belloc H. 1928, *Do We Agree?*, London, Cecil Palmer, pp. 46-7.

Chapter 6

1 Chesterton G.K. 1926, *The Outline of Sanity*, London, Methuen & Co, p. 9.
2 Chesterton, Mrs C. 1941, *The Chestertons*, London, Chapman & Hall, pp. 114-5, 127.
3 Titterton W.R. 1908, 'The Great Child' in *The New Age*, 10 October 1908, p. 471.
4 Quoted in Ward M. 1952, *Return to Chesterton*, London, Sheed & Ward, p. 228.
5 Sewell B. 1974, 'Devereux Nights: A Distributist Memoir' in Sullivan J. (ed.) 1974, *G.K. Chesterton: A Centenary Appraisal*, London, Paul Elek, p. 150.
6 Sewell, 1990, p. 21.
7 Quoted in Thorn J.M. 1997, 'Towards a History and Interpretation of the Distributist League' in *The Chesterton Review*, Vol. XXIII, No. 3, August 1997, p. 309.
8 Quoted in Sewell, 1990, p. 22.
9 The records have been destroyed. Sewell, who has the advantage of first-hand knowledge, gives the figure of 2000, but Thorn believes it was no more than 500. See Thorn, 1997, p. 325.
10 In 1995 the Bergengren Credit Union had more than 12,000 members and assets in excess of $C70 million. *Annual Report 1995*, Antigonish, Bergengren Credit Union.
11 Doyle I. 1998, Letter to the author, 12 January 1998.
12 Doyle I. 1996, Interview with the author, Antigonish, 9 June 1996.
13 Quoted in Ward, 1952, p. 209.
14 Titterton, 1936, p. 186.

15 Sewell B. 1966, *My Dear Time's Waste*, Aylesford, St Dominic's Press, p. 47.

16 Distributist League, 1932, 'Research Committee Report' in *G.K.'s Weekly*, Vol. XIV, No. 364, 5 March 1932, p. 419.

17 Quoted in Thorn, 1997, pp. 315-6. For the Birmingham Plan in full see Robbins H. 1948 (1), 'The Last of the Realists: G.K. Chesterton and His Work' Part IV, Appendix A, in *The Cross and the Plough*, Vol. 15, No. 4, Christmas 1948, p. 10.

18 Robbins H. 1948 (2), 'The Last of the Realists: G.K. Chesterton and His Work' Part II, Appendix A, in *The Cross and the Plough*, Vol. 15, No. 2, Saints Peter and Paul, 1948, p. 10.

19 Chesterton, Mrs C. 1941, p. 123.

20 Quoted in Heseltine G.C. 1927, 'Distributism in the North', *G.K.'s Weekly*, 2 July 1927, p. 476.

21 Thorn, 1997, p. 318.

22 Quoted in Chesterton G.K. 1933, 'A Web of Homespun' in *G.K.'s Weekly*, 10 August 1933.

23 Valentine F. 1955, *Father Vincent McNabb, O.P.: The Portrait of a Great Dominican*, London, Burns & Oates, p. 144.

24 Chesterton G.K. 1955, 'Introduction' in McNabb V., *Francis Thompson and Other Essays*, London, Blackfriars Publications, as reproduced in *The Chesterton Review*, Vol. XXII, Nos 1 & 2, February & May 1996, p. 6.

25 Quoted in Pepler H. 1943, 'Handwork or Landwork', *Blackfriars*, August 1943, p. 294.

26 Robbins H. 1933, 'A Land Movement' in *G.K.'s Weekly*, 3 August 1933, p. 349.

27 Quoted in Robbins H. 1948 (3), 'The Last of the Realists: G.K. Chesterton and His Work' Part III, in *The Cross and the Plough*, Vol. 15, No. 3, Michaelmas 1948, p. 16.

28 Robbins, 1948 (2), p. 17.

29 Quoted in Attwater D. 1969, *A Cell of Good Living: The Life and Works and Opinions of Eric Gill*, London, Chapman, p. 59.

30 Quoted in MacCarthy F. 1989, *Eric Gill: A Lover's Quest for Art and God*, New York, E.P. Dutton, p. vii.

31 Quoted in Speaight R. 1946, *The Life of Eric Gill*, London, Methuen and Co, pp. 88-9.

32 What Gill's original biographer, Robert Speaight, dismisses perhaps too lightly in his memoirs as 'one or two skeletons in Eric Gill's cupboard' is presumably a reference to the extensive sexual irregularities which are discussed in detail in a later study by Fiona MacCarthy. See Speaight R. 1970, *The Property Basket: Recollections of a Divided Life*, London, Collins & Harvill Press, p. 376. and MacCarthy, 1989, p. 376.

33 Thorn, 1997, p. 316.

34 Quoted in Ward, 1952, pp. 226-7.

35 Gleeson, 1952, p. 223.

36 Robbins, 1933, p. 349.

37 Macdonald G. 1927. Letter to *G.K.'s Weekly*, 16 July 1927, p. 506.

38 Robbins, 1948 (3), p. 12.
39 Quoted in Chesterton G.K. 1916, 'Bernard Shaw and the Three Witnesses' in *The New Witness*, Vol. VIII, No. 186. 25 May 1916, p. 110.
40 Chesterton G.K. 1920, 'The Problem of the "New Witness"' in the *The New Witness*, Vol. XVI, No. 405, 13 August, 1920, p. 293.
41 Sewell B. 1990, *G.K.'s Weekly: An Appraisal*, Aylsford, The Aylsford Press, pp. 18, 23.
42 Aiken M. (Lord Beaverbrook), 1927, Letter to Harmsworth H.S. (Lord Rothmere), as quoted in Taylor A.J.P. 1972, *Beaverbrook*, New York, Simon & Schuster, p. 229.
43 Corrin J.P. 1981, *G.K. Chesterton & Hilaire Belloc: The Battle Against Modernity*, Athens, Ohio, Ohio University Press, p. 204.
44 Belloc H. and Chesterton C. 1911, *The Party System*, London, Stephen Swift, p. 194.
45 Quoted in McCarthy J.P. 1978, *Hilaire Belloc: Edwardian Radical*, Indianapolis, Liberty Press, p. 262.
46 Belloc H. 1920, 'An Appeal for *The New Witness*' in *The New Witness*, 13 August 1920, p. 293.
47 Chesterton G.K. 1920. 'The Problem of *The New Witness*' in *The New Witness*, 13 August 1920, p. 292.
48 Chesterton G.K. (ed.) 1918, 'Comments of the Week' in *The New Witness*, 19 April 1918, pp. 564-5.
49 Chesterton G.K. 1917, 'The Jew and the Journalist' in *The New Witness*, 11 October 1917, p. 282.
50 O'Donnell F.H. 1913, 'Mr Baring's Error' in *The New Witness*, 13 November 1913, p. 52.
51 Figes O. 1996, *A People's Tragedy: The Russian Revolution 1891-1924.* (Pimlico Edition 1997), London, Random House, pp. 13, 242-4.
52 See, for example, Sparkes R. 1997, 'Review of *Wisdom and Innocence: A Life of G.K. Chesterton*' in *The Chesterton Review*, Vol. XXIII, No. 3, August 1997, p. 339.
53 Chesterton G.K. (ed.) 1920, 'Comments of the Week' in *The New Witness*, 5 March 1920, p. 285.
54 Gleeson D. 1952 '*G.K.'s Weekly* — What Led Up To It' in Ward, 1952, p. 213.
55 Chesterton 1924, p. 1.
56 Quoted in Ward 1952, p. 229.
57 Reckitt M. 1941, *As It Happened*, London, J.M. Dent & Sons, p. 185.

Chapter 7

1 Coady M.M. 1939, *Masters of Their Own Destiny: The Story of the Antigonish Movement of Adult Education Through Economic Co-operation*, (Paperback Edition 1980), Antigonish, Nova Scotia, Formac Publishing Company, p. 68.
2 Doyle I. (also known in her Antigonish Movement days as Sister Anselm) 1964, *The Antigonish Idea and Social Welfare*,

Antigonish, Nova Scotia, St Francis Xavier University Press, p. 3.

3   Royal Commission Investigating the Fisheries of the Maritime Provinces and Magdalen Islands 1928, *Report*, Ottawa, The Kings Printer, p. 102.

4   The Canadian scholar R. James Sacouman notes in a 1979 study that 'Average *annual* incomes in the fisheries in 1933 ranged from $C160 ($C110 from line fishing, $C50 from lobster fishing) at Canso to about $C200 at Queensport in Guysborough County; $C100 in Richmond County at Arichat and Petit de Grat; $C75 in Cape Breton at Glace Bay and $C100 at L'Archeveque, North Sydney, Gabarouse, Grand River and Forchu; and $C175 at Louisburg'. Sacouman R.J. 1979, 'Underdevelopment and the Structural Origins of Antigonish Movement Co-operatives in Eastern Nova Scotia' in Brym R.J. and Sacouman R.J. (eds) 1979, *Underdevelopment and Social Movements in Atlantic Canada*, Toronto, New Hogtown Press, pp. 118-9.

5   MacSween R.J. 1953, 'The Little University of the World' in *The Universities Review*, Vol. XXV, No. 2, February 1953, pp. 91-8, As quoted in Laidlaw A.F. 1961, *The Campus and the Community: The Global Impact of the Antigonish Movement*, Montreal, Harvest House, p. 58.

6   Boyle G. 1953, *Father Tompkins of Nova Scotia*, New York, P.J. Kennedy & Sons, p. 45.

7   So named to distinguish him from Dr H.P. MacPherson, who became the rector of the university.

8   O'Dwyer E.T. 1900, *A University for Catholics in Relation to the Material Interests of Ireland*, Dublin, Catholic Truth Society, p. 7. As quoted in Boyle 1953, p. 49.

9   Tompkins J.J. 1945, Letter to Father Peter Nearing, 28 November 1945. As quoted in Boyle, 1953, p. 49.

10 Boyle, 1953, p. 51.

11 MacInnes D.W. 1978, *Clerics, Fishermen, Farmers and Workers: The Antigonish Movement and Identity in Eastern Nova Scotia 1928-1939*, Unpublished PhD dissertation, McMaster University.

12 MacInnes, 1978, p. 161.

13 Later renamed 'For Social Betterment' with separate sections for 'Agriculture' and 'Education'. Alexander A. 1997, *The Antigonish Movement: Moses Coady and Adult Education Today*, Toronto, Thompson Educational Publishing, p. 67.

14 Laidlaw, 1961, p. 64.

15 Tompkins J.J. 1921, *Knowledge for the People: A Call to St Francis Xavier's College*, Antigonish, Nova Scotia.

16 As quoted in Lotz J. and Welton M.R. 1997, *Father Jimmy: The Life and Times of Jimmy Tompkins*, Wreck Cove, Cape Breton, Breton Books, pp. 45-6.

17 Quoted in Lotz and Welton, 1997, p. 46.

18 Quoted in Boyle, 1953, p. 90.

19 So named for its authors, Dr Kenneth C.M. Sills and Dr William S. Learned. Sills was the president of Bowdoin

College, and Learned a member of the Carnegie Foundation staff.

20 Quoted in Boyle, 1953, p. 108.
21 Quoted in Boyle, 1953, p. 126.
22 Royal Commission Investigating the Fisheries of the Maritime Provinces and Megdalen Islands 1928, p. 81.
23 Quoted in Lotz and Welton, 1997, p. 93.
24 Laidlaw, 1961, p. 65.
25 Quoted in Laidlaw, 1961, p. 66.
26 Coady M.M. 1957, 'My Story', Interview for CBC TV, Antigonish, Extension Department, St Francis Xavier University, p. 1.
27 Coady, 1957, p. 1
28 Coady, 1957, p. 2.
29 Boyle, 1953, p. 30.
30 Coady, 1957, p. 2.
31 Quoted in MacLellan M. 1985, *Coady Remembered*, Antigonish, Nova Scotia, St Francis Xavier University Press, p. 47.
32 Coady, 1957, pp. 4-5.
33 Coady, 1957, p. 6.
34 Quoted in MacLelland, 1985, p. 51.
35 Coady, 1957, p. 6.
36 Laidlaw A.F. 1971, *The Man from Margaree: Writings and Speeches of M.M. Coady*, Toronto, McClelland and Stewart, p. 22.
37 Delaney I. 1985, *By Their Own Hand: A Fieldworker's Account of the Antigonish Movement*, Hantsport, Nova Scotia, Lancelot Press, p. 31.
38 Coady M.M. 1958. In Laidlaw, 1971, pp. 33-4.
39 Coady M.M. 1949. In Laidlaw, 1971, p. 44.
40 Laidlaw, 1971, p. 95.
41 Coady M.M. 1953. In Laidlaw, 1971, p. 27.
42 Coady M.M. 1953. In Laidlaw, 1971, p. 29.
43 Laidlaw, 1971, p. 22.
44 Laidlaw, 1971, p. 95.
45 Coady M.M. 1956. In Laidlaw, 1971, p. 129.
46 Coady M.M. 1951. In Laidlaw, 1971, p. 185.
47 Coady M.M. 1949. In Laidlaw, 1971, p. 172.
48 Laidlaw, 1971, pp. 36-7.
49 Australian readers will recognise in the 'the Big Picture' a phrase much used by the former Labor Prime Minister of Australia, Paul Keating. Did he perhaps pick it up unconsciously from references to the Antigonish Movement overheard in the course of a Catholic boyhood?
50 Coady M.M. 1945. In Laidlaw, 1971, p. 109.
51 Coady M.M. 1950. In Laidlaw, 1971, pp. 104-5.
52 Quoted in Delaney, 1985, p. 29.
53 Coady M.M. 1956. In Laidlaw, 1971, p. 53.
54 Quoted in Laidlaw, 1961, p. 92.
55 Laidlaw, 1971, p. 75.

Chapter 8

1   Fowler B.B. 1938, *The Lord Helps Those Who Help Themselves: How the People of Nova Scotia Are Solving Their Problems Through Co-operation*, New York, The Vanguard Press, p. 31.

2   Fowler, 1938, p. 39.

3   Fowler, 1938, pp. 40-1.

4   MacLellan M. 1935. 'The St Francis Xavier University's Extension Department' in Coady M. (ed.) 1935, *How St. F.X. University Educates for Action: The Story of the Remarkable Results Achieved by the Extension Department of the University of St Francis Xavier*, New York, The Co-operative League, p. 17.

5   MacLellan, 1935, p. 17.

6   For a particulary detailed and useful case study of the Grand Etang experience, see LeBlanc U. and Teaf H.M. Jnr, not dated, *The Rehabilitation of a Nova Scotia Fishing Village*, Haverford, Pa., Haverford College Graduate Program in Social and Technical Assistance. For Little Dover see MacLellan 1935, pp. 15-8, and for Judique, MacEachern D.J. 1937, *It Happened in Judique*, St. John's, Newfoundland, Department of Rural Reconstruction. See also the accounts of Larry's River, Petit de Grat, Havre Boucher and Ballantyne's Cove in Coady, 1953, pp. 46-52, 104-5.

7   Coady, 1957, p. 6.

8   MacSween R.J. 1953, 'The Little University of the World' in *The Universities Review*, Vol. XXV, No. 2, February 1953. As quoted in Laidlaw A.F. 1961, *The Campus and the Community: The Global Impact of the Antigonish Movement*, Montreal, Harvest House, p. 69.

9   Figures as quoted in Lotz J & Welton M.R. 1987, '"Knowledge for the People": The Origins and Development of the Antigonish Movement' in Welton M.R. (ed.) 1987, *Knowledge for the People*, Toronto, Oise Press, p. 107.

10 Delaney I. 1985, *By Their Own Hands: A Fieldworker's Account of the Antigonish Movement*, Hantsport, Nova Scotia, Lancelot Press, p. 145.

11 MacDonald J.D.N. 1986, *Memoirs of an Unorthodox Clergyman*, Truro, Nova Scotia Co-operative Resources, p. 45.

12 Arsenault E., not dated, *How the Credit Union Movement Came to Canada*, Antigonish, Nova Scotia, University of St Francis Xavier Extension Department. As quoted in Laidlaw, 1961, p. 85.

13 Delaney, 1985, p. 69.

14 Quoted in Lotz J. & Welton M.R. 1997, *Father Jimmy: The Life and Times of Jimmy Tompkins*, Wreck Cove, Cape Breton Island, Breton Books, p. 107.

15 Lotz & Welton, 1997, p. 95.

16 Doyle I. 1998. Letter to the author, 14 April 1998.

17 Quoted in Laidlaw, 1961, pp. 97-8. Italics in the original.

18 Delaney, 1985, p. 23.

19 Delaney, 1985, pp. 24-30.
20 Coady M.M. 1938, 'Adult Education in Action'. Radio Address over the CBC, February 10 1938, pp. 3-4.
21 For a useful account of the activities of the Movement in the province of Prince Edward Island — adjacent to Nova Scotia — see Croteau J.T. 1951, *Cradled in the Waves: The Story of a People's Co-operative Achievement in Economic Betterment on Prince Edward Island, Canada*, Toronto, The Ryerson Press.
22 Lotz J. & Welton, 1987, p. 107.
23 Doyle I. 1995, 'The Antigonish Movement Beyond the Atlantic Region', research paper, 4 October 1995, Antigonish, University of St Francis Xavier Extension Department, p. 3.
24 Quoted in Laidlaw, 1961, p. 92.
25 Quoted in Laidlaw, 1961, p. 92.
26 Quoted in Smyth F.J. 1960, 'The Coady International Institute' in *The Casket*, 27 October 1960. In Laidlaw A.F. 1961, *The Campus and the Community: The Global Impact of the Antigonish Movement*, Montreal, Harvest House, p. 160.
27 Coutinho B. 1966, *Community Development through Adult Education and Co-operatives: The Story of the Antigonish Movement*, Rome, C.I.S.I.C. Institutum Sociologiae Pastoralis, p. xiv.
28 For a first-hand observer's account of organisations beyond the Atlantic region that emerged through individual and institutional links with the Antigonish Movement, see Doyle, 1995.
29 Boyle G. 1953, *Father Tompkins of Nova Scotia*, New York, P.J. Kennedy & Sons, p. 196.
30 Delaney, 1985, p. 141. The implication of Delaney's account is that Arnold and Read were readily accepted in the movement and the wider community. For an interesting alternative reading from a feminist perspective, see Neal R. 1996, 'The Work of Mary Arnold, Nova Scotia, 1937-1939: Accommodating Anomalies and Explaining Exceptions', conference paper for the Canadian Association for Studies in Co-operation, June 1996.
31 Arnold M.E. 1951, letter to Boyle G., 26 September 1951. In Boyle, 1953, p. 195.
32 Delaney, 1985, p. 141.
33 Boyle, 1953, p. 198. For a detailed account of the co-operative housing program in its formative stage, see Arnold M.E. 1940, *The Story of Tompkinsville*, New York, The Co-operative League.
34 Boyle G. 1953, p. 199. Italics in the original.
35 Boyle, 1953, p. 178.
36 Boyle, 1953, p. 181.
37 Anonymous, 1937, 'The Restoration of Property by Hilaire Belloc' in *The Extension Bulletin*, 27 March 1937, p. 5.
38 Corbett E.A. 1937, letter to Tompkins J.J., 18 December 1937, Beaton Institute Archives MC 10-2, University College of Cape Breton.
39 Tompkins J.J. 1938, speech given at the Antigonish Co-operative Conference, 16 August 1938. In Boyle 1953, p. 230.

40 The grant was conditional on matching grants from the provincial government over a five-year period. In the event, only the first $10,000 was paid over. 'The Second World War', write Jim Lotz and Michael R. Welton in their 1997 study of Tompkins, 'diverted interest away from libraries'. Lotz & Welton, 1997, p. 133.

41 Coady M.M. 1950. In Laidlaw, 1971, p. 108.

42 Details of the failed bid for the CWS are from Birchall J. 1998 'The Lanica affair: an attempted takeover of a consumer co-operative society' in *The Journal of Co-operative Studies*, Vol. 31, No. 2, 1998, pp.15-32, and I gratefully acknowledge Dr Birchall's kindness in making an advance copy of his article available to me.

43 Seaman D.K. 1998, '"Momentous Times" for the UK Co-operative Retail Sector' in Hurp W. (ed.) 1998, *The World of Co-operative Enterprise 1988*, Oxford, The Plunkett Foundation, p. 179.

44 Hyland A. 1997, 'Trumbull Set to Earn Huge Money as Chief', Melbourne, *The Age*, 8 October 1997, p. B. 1. Other reports assess the shares as having a substantially higher value.

45 Smith A. W. 1999, 'Mutual Societies are Going, Just When We Need Them Most' in the *Independent*, 18 Jan 1999, p. 4.

46 For details of the demutualisation of the Sunstate Credit Union in Australia in 1997, see Mathews R. 1998, 'Re-invigorating Credit Union Mutuality', paper presented at the Australasian Credit Union Directors Ltd 1998 Northern Regional Seminar, Brisbane, 16 May 1998.

47 Fukuyama F. 1995, *Trust: The Social Virtues and the Creation of Prosperity*, New York, The Free Press, p. 7.

48 Laidlaw A.F. 1971, *The Man from Margaree: Writings and Speeches of M.M. Coady*, Toronto, McClelland and Stewart, p. 163.

49 Delaney, 1985, pp. 86-7.

50 Delaney, 1985, p. 59.

51 Melnyk G. 1985, *The Search for Community: From Utopia to a Co-operative Society*, Montreal-Buffalo, Black Rose Books, pp. 116-7.

52 Coady, 1957, p. 9.

53 Hogan A. 1981, 'Moses Coady: His Contribution to Co-operative Ideology and His Role as a Co-op Leader', Antigonish, unpublished paper for Co-op Week, 14 October 1981, p. 15.

54 Most of the local consumer co-operatives initially chose to affiliate with ECS, but three of them amalgamated with it, and it is likely that, if ECS had survived, more amalgamations would have occurred. MacDonald A.A. 1998, e-mail to the author, 4 March 1998.

55 'The co-operatives which own Co-op Atlantic have sales of over a billion dollars, more than 5000 workers, assets in excess of $300 million, and are owned by more than 168,000 families representing over 500,000 people ... Common interest exists with over 250 credit unions and caisses populaires having more than 475,000 member-owners, $1.3 billion in savings, and $1.4 billion in assets and with co-operative insurance

organisations having over 500 workers and an business volume in excess of $90 million per year'. Anon. 1991, *A Proposal for Renewal*, draft resolution 11, proposed for submission to the Annual General Meeting of Co-op Atlantic, 5 March 1991.

56 Delaney, 1985, p. 103.

57 MacDonald A.A. 1998. *The Antigonish Movement: Adaptation and Sustainability*, paper presented at The People's School on the Economy, 26 March 1998, Antigonish, St. F.X. Extension Department.

Chapter 9

1 MacLeod G. 1997, *From Mondragon to America: Experiments in Community Economic Development*, Sydney, Nova Scotia, University College of Cape Breton Press, p. 11.

2 Statistics for performance indicators are from Mondragon Corporacion Cooperativa 1997, *MCC Annual Report 1996*, Mondragon, MCC Corporate Centre.

3 'A report on absenteeism "due to illness" for 2500 workers shows that this is about twice as high in capitalist enterprises as in co-operative firms. For 1965 a percentage of 2.05 in ULARCO compares with 4.33 per cent in capitalist enterprises, this relative position being maintained up to 1976 when the percentages were 3.63 for the co-operatives versus 8.65 for others'. Thomas H. & Logan C. 1982, *Mondragon: An Economic Analysis*, London, George Allen & Unwin, p. 50. More recent reports suggest that absenteeism in the co-operatives is currently just over 5%. Greenwood D.J. & González J.L. et al. 1992, *Industrial Democracy as Process: Participatory Action Research in the Fagor Co-operative Group of Mondragon*, Stockholm, The Swedish Centre for Working Life, p. 168.

4 Bradley K. & Gelb A. 1983, *Co-operation at Work: The Mondragon Experience*, London, Heinemann Educational Books, p. 58.

5 For a full account of the Valencia group — as in Mondragon, a community bank, a string of co-operative retail stores (now linked with the Mondragon Eroski consumer co-operatives), an insurance company, employee-owned factories and a professional school — see MacLeod, 1997, Chapter 6.

6 Current practice is for senior managers to earn to within '30% of market' which could equate to a 13:1 ratio. It is also reported that the new MCC president, Antonio Cancelo, has a 12 million peseta salary ($US90,000-100,000), which is 7.5 times the lowest theoretical *anticipo*, but in reality a lesser multiple, given that few if any workers are actually rated at 1.0 on the scale. By contrast, the average CEO of a 'Fortune 500' company in the US was paid 41 times as much as the average factory worker in 1960, and 157 times as much in 1995.

7 For a detailed discussion of the Basic Principles see Ormaechea J.M. 1993, *The Mondragon Co-operative Experience*, Mondragon, Mondragon Corporacion Cooperativa, pp. 139-86.

8   A fourth historically Basque province, Navarra, has remained outside the regional government, and there are a further three Basque provinces in France.

9   Quoted in MacLeod, 1997, p. 47.

10   For a useful account of the anarcho-syndicalist tradition in the Basque region and adjacent areas, and its influence on the Mondragon co-operatives, see Long M. 1996, 'The Mondragon Co-operative Federation: A Model for Our Times?' in *Libertarian Labor Review*, Number 19, Winter 1996, pp. 19-36.

11   Quoted in Whyte W.F. & Whyte K.K. 1991, *Making Mondragon: The Growth and Dynamics of the Worker Co-operative Complex*, Second Edition, Ithaca, New York, ILR Press, p. 242.

12   Quoted in Whyte & Whyte, 1991, p. 243.

13   Quoted in Whyte & Whyte, 1991, p. 253.

14   Quoted in Whyte & Whyte, 1991, p. 254.

15   Quoted in Whyte & Whyte, 1991, p. 255.

16   Quoted in Whyte & Whyte, 1991, p. 244.

17   Quoted in Whyte & Whyte, 1991, p. 260.

18   Quoted in Whyte & Whyte, 1991, p. 258.

19   Quoted in Whyte & Whyte, 1991, p. 256.

20   Quoted in Whyte & Whyte, 1991, p. 245.

21   Mounier E. 1938, *A Personalist Manifesto*, London, Longman, Green & Co, p. 281. Italics as in the original.

22   Quoted in Whyte & Whyte, 1991, p. 258.

23   Oakeshott R. 1978, *The Case for Workers' Co-ops*, London, Routledge & Kegan Paul, p. 173. For a full list of Arizmendiarrieta's books, see Azurmendi J. 1984, *El Hombre Cooperativo: Pensamiento de Arizmendiarrieta*, Mondragon, Caja Laboral Popular/Lan Kide Aurrezkia, pp. 832-7.

24   Whyte & Whyte, 1991, p. 247.

25   Quoted in Whyte & Whyte, 1991, p. 266.

26   Quoted in Whyte & Whyte, 1991, p. 247.

27   Quoted in Whyte & Whyte, 1991, p. 245.

28   Quoted in Whyte & Whyte, 1991, p. 254.

29   Quoted in Whyte & Whyte, 1991, pp. 259-60.

30   Kasmir S. 1996, *Co-operatives, Politics and Working-Class Life in a Basque Town*, Albany, State University of New York Press, pp. 65-73.

31   'Bishop Mújica of Vitoria angrily told Cardinal Gomá that it would have been better if Franco and his soldiers had kissed Father Arín's feet instead of shooting him'. Morrison R. 1991, *We Build the Road as We Travel*, Philadelphia, New Society Press, p. 43. Total deaths resulting from the Civil War are estimated at approximately 600,000. Some 320,000 are thought to have died in action, 220,000 from disease or malnutrition and 100,000 by murder or summary execution. Two million people are estimated to have passed through Franco's prisons and concentration camps prior to 1942, and 340,000 were exiled. Thomas H. 1961, *The Spanish Civil War*, London, Eyre

& Spottiswood, pp. 606-8.
32 Whyte & Whyte, 1991, p. 248.
33 The definitive account of Arizmendiarrieta's thinking is in Azurmendi, 1984. For the best account so far available in English, see MacLeod, 1997.
34 Whyte & Whyte, 1991, p. 28.
35 Whyte & Whyte, 1991, p. 242.
36 Whyte & Whyte, 1991, p. 266.
37 Whyte & Whyte, 1991, p. 267.
38 *Maestria* is roughly equivalent to secondary school technical course, and *peritaje industrial* to the course for a first degree.
39 Whyte & Whyte, 1991, p. 256.
40 Thomas and Logan, 1982, p. 18.
41 Whyte & Whyte, 1991, p. 32.
42 There is a notable irony in the fact that, while the co-operatives grew and prospered, employment in the Unión Cerrajera declined between 1955 and 1991 from 1350 to 370, and the steelworks has subsequently been closed. Long, 1996, p. 34.
43 Thomas & Logan, 1982, p. 20.
44 Whyte & Whyte, 1991, p. 34.
45 Thomas & Logan, 1982, p. 20.
46 Larrañaga J. 1998, letter to the author, October 1998.
47 Whyte & Whyte, 1991, p. 268.
48 While the Mondragon co-operatives owe their origin to Arizmendiarrieta and the Church, they are today explicitly secular, non-political bodies, where members from a wide range of religious and political persuasions are able to work harmoniously for their common objectives.

Chapter 10

1 Morrison R. 1991, *We Build the Road As We Travel*, Philadelphia, New Society Press, p. 73.
2 For a useful discussion of 'open book' management, see Stack J. 1992, *The Great Game of Business*, New York, Currency Doubleday.
3 The ban on unions was lifted after Franco's death, and members of the co-operatives are free to join or remain outside their unions as they see fit. Union membership is widespread and stoppages have been held on national issues in solidarity with the union movement.
4 Quoted in Whyte W.F. & Whyte K.K. 1991, *Making Mondragon: The Growth and Dynamics of the Worker Co-operative Complex* (Second Edition), Ithaca, New York, ILR Press, pp. 39-40.
5 In legal terms, members do not have a claim on collective reserves, either collectively or individually. Were a co-operative to go bankrupt and need to liquidate its assets, such of the collective reserves as remained after settling its liabilities would transfer to the Confederation of Co-operatives of Euskadi.

6   The committees can obtain advice from a Remuneration Studies Section within the MCC, which also advises on remuneration for senior managers. See note 6 of Chapter 9.

7   By 1990, members of the co-operatives had had an estimated increase in their purchasing power since 1956 of around 250 per cent. Ormaechea J.M. 1993, *The Mondragon Co-operative Experience*, Mondragon, Mondragon Corporacion Cooperativa, p. 167.

8   The entry fee represents roughly 10 per cent of the estimated average capital requirement for the creation of a new job. The level of the fee in real terms fell by half between 1960 and 1990. Ormaechea 1993, p. 157.

9   Whyte & Whyte 1991, p. 265.

10   Morrison, 1991, p. 50.

11   Whyte & Whyte, 1991, p. 50.

12   Whyte & Whyte, 1991, p. 51.

13   MacLeod G. 1997, *From Mondragon to America: Experiments in Community Economic Development*, Sydney, Nova Scotia, University College of Cape Breton Press, p. 16.

14   MacLeod, 1997, p. 17.

15   Ellerman D. 1982, *The Socialisation of Entrepreneurship: The Empresarial Division of the Caja Laboral Popular*, Boston, Industrial Co-operative Association, p. 4.

16   Whyte & Whyte, 1991, p. 179.

17   Ormaechea 1993, p. 101. For example, Copesca was established in 1965 as a secondary support co-operative in order to make available fishing boats to twenty-four fishing co-operatives. Copesca's capital structure was a departure from the usual Mondragon arrangements, in that 71 per cent of its funds were provided by the government in the name of job creation, as against 24 per cent from the Caja and only 5 per cent by the fishermen themselves. Rather than pay off the capital debt, the fishermen chose instead to increase their incomes. When further capital was required to keep the co-operative afloat, they refused to supply it, and the business closed down in 1973. Its eight-year history is an object lesson in the wisdom of Mondragon's insistence that adequate capital stakes should be held by both co-operatives and their members.

18   Ellerman D.P. 1984, *The Mondragon Co-operative Movement*, Harvard Business School Case No. 1-384-270, Boston, Harvard Business School, p. 18.

19   Mondragon Corporacion Cooperativa, 1995, p. 14.

20   Long M. 1996, 'The Mondragon Co-operative Federation: A Model for Our Times? in *Libertarian Labor Review*, Number 19, Winter 1996, p. 28.

21   Long, 1996, p. 28.

22   Quoted in Whyte & Whyte, 1991, p 265.

23   Ikerlan is the only Spanish research firm that has met NASA technical specifications and consequently secured permission for a project on the Columbia space shuttle. MacLeod, 1996, p. 8.

24 Caja Laboral Popular, 1994, *Annual Report 1993*, Mondragon, p. 112.

25 The group changed its name to Fagor in 1986.

26 Morrison, 1991, p. 208.

27 *TU/Lankide*, December 1996, p. 25.

28 *TU/Lankide*, January 1998, p. 21.

29 Grupo Cooperativo Mondragon, 1989. *Congreso del Grupo Cooperativo Mondragon: compendio de normas aprobadas*, Mondragon. Quoted in Whyte & Whyte 1991, p. 201.

30 Freundlich F. 1998, 'The Inverted Conglomerate: The Mondragon Co-operative Corporation', paper presented at the conference on 'Shared Capitalism: Mapping the Research Agenda', Washington, 22-23 May 1998.

31 In 1997 a major expansion of Saiolan was said to be envisaged, but had not so far eventuated.

32 Moye M. 1996, *Financing the Industrial Co-operatives of the Mondragon Group*, Economic and Social Research Council Centre for Business Research Working Paper 25, Cambridge, Cambridge University Department of Applied Economics, p. 28.

33 Caja Laboral, 1993, *Annual Report 1992*, Mondragon, Caja Laboral, p. 71.

34 Respectively, Greenwood D.J. & González J.L.G. 1991, *Industrial Democracy as Process: Participatory Action Research in the Fagor Co-operative Group of Mondragon*, Stockholm, The Swedish Centre for Working Life; Lezamiz M. *et al* 1990, *Estudio Sociologico Sobre Grado De Aceptacion De La Sociedad Co-operativa*, Mondragon. Ikasbide Hezkuntzetxea: Centro de Formacion; and Kasmir S. 1996, *The Myth of Mondragon: Co-operatives, Politics, and Working-Class Life in a Basque Town*, Albany, State University of New York Press.

35 For a useful account of one aspect of the change process, see Whyte W.F. & Whyte K.K. 1991, *Making Mondragon: The Growth and Dynamics of the Worker Co-operative Complex*, Ithaca, New York, ILR Press, Chapter 12, 'Sacrificing for Collective Survival', pp.131-49.

36 Greenwood & González, 1991, p. 119.

37 Greenwood & González, 1991, p. 106.

38 Kasmir, 1996, p. 182.

39 Kasmir, 1996, p. 166.

40 Greenwood & González, 1991, p. 133.

41 Greenwood & González 1991, p. 111. Emphasis in the original.

42 Kasmir 1996, p. 153.

43 It is not clear whether the question about ownership was in all cases understood as the designers of the survey intended. Subsequent qualitative research indicated that some strongly co-operativist respondents meant that they, as individuals, did not feel they owned the means of production of their co-operative, which more properly belonged to the membership as a whole.

44 Greenwood & González, 1991, p. 133.

45 Quoted in Moye M. 1993, *Lean Production in the Mondragon Co-operatives*, working paper, p. 11.
46 Kasmir, 1996, p. 122.
47 Greenwood & González, 1991, p. 108.
48 Figures made available to the author in Mondragon in 1996.
49 See Kasmir, 1996, p. 54.
50 Quoted in Moye M. 1996, *Financing the Industrial Co-operatives of the Mondragon Group*, ECRC Centre for Business Research Working Paper No. 25, Cambridge University, p. 31.
51 Quoted in Whyte & Whyte, 1991, p. 265.
52 Moye, 1996, p. 33. It is unclear whether Moye's comparison between the two aggregates is wholly valid, in that her 1992 figure may not take into account all the sources from which aid is in reality available. For example, debt forgiveness is said to still be an option for co-operatives which are experiencing difficulties. The issue may in any case now be less relevant, since resources held in the inter-co-operative aid funds (FCI) have increased substantially since 1992.
53 Cheney G. 1997, 'The Many Meanings of 'Solidarity': The Negotiation of Values in the Mondragon Worker Co-operative Complex under Pressure' in Sypher B.D. (ed.) 1997, *Case Studies in Organisational Communication 2: Perspectives on Contemporary Work Life*, New York, Guilford Press. As posted on the Web site of the University of Wisconsin Center for Co-operatives, p. 6. While concerns over the loss of locational links are seen to have been the main cause of the separation, factors such as personal rivalries may also have been significant.
54 Kasmir, 1996, p. 37.
55 Quoted in Ormaechea J.M. 1993, *The Mondragon Co-operative Experience*, Mondragon, Mondragon Corporacion Cooperativa, p. 7.
56 Greenwood & González, 1991, pp. 149, 153-4.
57 Greenwood & González, 1991, pp. 149, 153.
58 Kasmir, 1996, pp. 190-1.

Chapter 11

1 Pius XI, 1931, *Quadragesimo Anno (On Social Reconstruction)*, Boston, St Paul Editions, pp. 32-3.
2 Pius XI, 1931, p. 41.
3 John Paul II, 1998, Homily delivered at a Mass in Havana, Cuba, on 25 January 1998, in *Osservatore Romano*, 26 January 1998, p. 1.
4 Preece G. 1995, *Changing Work: A Christian Response*, Melbourne, Acorn Press, p. 202.
5 Mongelos J. 1994, as quoted in Parry J.N. 'Mondragon Pushed to the Peak of Success', *The European*, 28 October 1994, p. 12.

6   Belloc H. 1937, *The Crisis of Our Civilisation*, London, Cassell & Co, p. 205. Italics as in the original.

7   Kohler T.C. 1993, 'In Praise of Little Platoons: *Quadragesimo Anno* (1931)' in Weigel G. and Royal R. 1993, *Building the Free Society: Democracy, Capitalism and Catholic Social Teaching*, Grand Rapids, Michigan, William B. Eerdmans Publishing Company, pp. 47, 49.

8   Marquand D. 1997, *The New Reckoning: Capitalism, States and Citizens*, Cambridge, Polity Press, p. 4.

9   Hirst P. 1994, *Associative Democracy: New Forms of Economic and Social Governance*, Cambridge, Polity Press, p. 2.

10 Hirst P. 'Associative Democracy' in *Dissent*, Vol. 41, Spring 1994, p. 244.

11 Rawls J. 1971, *A Theory of Justice*, Cambridge, Mass., The Belknap Press of Harvard University Press, pp. 14-15.

12 Belloc H. 1924, *Economics for Helen*, Bristol, Arrowsmith, p. 124.

13 For useful accounts of the impact of ESOPs and ESOP legislation in the US, see Blasi J.R. 1988, *Employee Ownership: Revolution or Ripoff?*, New York, Harper Business, and Gates J. 1998, *The Ownership Solution: Toward a Shared Capitalism for the 21st Century*, Reading, Massachusetts, Addison-Wesley.

14 Hirst, 1994, p. 13.

15 Quoted in Rentoul J. 1996, *Tony Blair*, London, Warner Books, p. 39.

16 Rentoul, 1996, p. 42.

17 Quoted in Rentoul, 1996, p. 44.

18 Quoted in Rentoul, 1996, p. 290.

19 Quoted in Rentoul, 1996, p. 291.

20 Quoted in Rentoul, 1996, p. 296.

21 Le Grande J. 1998, 'Blair's Third Way: Community, Opportunity, Responsibility and Accountability' in *The Australian Financial Revew*, 20 March 1998, Review Section, pp. 1-2.

22 Quoted in Le Grande, 1998, p. 2.

23 Quoted in Schelesinger A. 1978, *Robert Kennedy and His Times*, Boston, Houghton Mifflin Company, p. 886.

INDEX

93; and distributism 17, 42, 59, 92, 99, 107-110,119,124, ; and poverty 22; and the Fabian Society 31, 54-56; and collectivism 36; and his family background 51-52; and Gilbert Chesterton 52; and Arthur Ransome 52; and Robert Blatchford 52; and his journalism 53, 58; and anti-Semitism 53, 73, 127 and the Church of England 53; and the Christian Social Union 54, 96; and Bland, Shaw, Conrad Noel and Charles Marson 54; and the Anti-Puritan League 54; and the Guild of St Matthew 55; and *The Church Socialist Quarterly* 56; and the Church Socialist League 56, 96; and Belloc 53, 57, 127; and *The New Age* 57; and *De Rerum Novarum* 57; and conversion 57; and debates between socialists and distributists 57, 103-110; and becomes a Catholic 57; and the distributist weeklies 58, 125-132; and his books 58-59; and military service 59; and Ada Jones 59; and his death 59; and the party system 81-82; and the Marconi Affair 127; and worker ownership 108-109, 124,176

Chesterton, Edward 51

Chesterton, Frances (Frances Blogg) 93, 105

Chesterton, Gilbert Keith And debates with socialists ix,103-110, 115; and Shaw ix 104-105; and socialism 6, 93-97, 100; and distributism 17, 92, 99-103, 107-110, 111, 179; and the Leeds Arts Club 37; and the Fabian Nursery 50; and Cecil Chesterton 52, 125-126; and anti-Semitism 53, 73; and

Hitler 53; and the Anti-Puritan League 54-55; and Belloc 57, 90-92, 103-104; and becomes a Catholic 57; and *The Servile State* 83;as a writer 91; and the BBC 91-92, 107; and the First World War 92; and Christianity 93-94 and William Morris 93; and liberalism 95-98; and the Christian Social Union 93, 96; and associative and communitarian attitudes 95-96; and the Church Socialist League 96; and the National Committee for the Breakup of the Poor Law 97; and communism 100-101, 102; and *De Rerum Novarum* 97, 101; and parliament 98; and capitalism 99-102, 105; and *What's Wrong with the World* 100-101; and property 101-102; and poverty 105; and *The Outline of Sanity* 111; and the Distributist League 114, 119and Gordon Selfridge 115; and McNabb 120; and the distributist weeklies 125-132; and press lords 126; and the Marconi Affair; and fascism 131-132; and leadership 113; and Chaim Weizmann 130; and Israel Zangwill 130

Chesterton, Marie Louise 51

Chestertons, The x

Cheticamp 156

Christian socialism ix, 26-27; and social Catholicism 26; and distributism 237; and the Church Socialist League 96-97; and Peter Thomson 245; and Tony Blair 245

Christian Socialist, The 26

Christian Socialist League, The 25

Christian Social Union, The 25, 96

Christian Worker Movement, The 189

Chubb, Percival, 30

Church and the Land, The 121

Church Reformer, The 26

Church Socialist League, The 25, 96

Church Socialist Quarterly, The 96

Common Sense 26

Clarion, The 26, 94

Coady International Institute, The 9, 165, 177

Coady, Father Moses 7; and papal commendations 8, 153; and co-operation 8, 134, 148, 150-152, 168-169; opposition to sectarian and discriminatory practices 8; and adult education 18, 134, 147-148, 151, 161-163, 193-194; and distributism 116, 132, 148; and regional economic development 134; early life and education 145-146; and Tompkins 145-146; and St Francis Xavier University 146, 147; and the Antigonish Movement 147; and the Extension Department 147; and the Royal Commission 147; and the United Maritime Fishermen 147; and property 148-149; and the environment 149-150; and democracy 150; and the Rochdale Pioneers 152, and social Catholicism 152, 236; and Bergengren 158-159; and credit unions 159; and death of 177; and Mondragon 185

Cole, G.D.H 33, 40, 169

Cole, Margaret 32

Collège Stanislas 62, 71

Colloms, Brenda 26

Communism 100-101, 236

Communist Party of Great Britain, The 31

Communitarianism viii, 4, 237

Congo Reform Association, The 78

Consum 203-204

Consumer Affairs Council (Brussels) 203

Consumer co-operatives 13-14

Commonweal 26

Coop Atlantic 175

Co-operatives And mutualism 4; and Rochdale consumer co-operatives 5, 168-171; and distributism 8, 102; and the Antigonish Movement 8, 34-35, 142-143, 163; and Raiffeisen credit unions 13, 102, 132, 150-152; and the Rochdale cul-de-sac 14,168-173, 178; and Sweden 135; and Nova Scotia 142; and the Royal Commission on the fisheries of the Maritime Provinces and the Magdalen Islands 143; and Coady 150-152; and housing 166-167, 241; and co-operative education177; and libraries 167-168; and member loyalty 173-174; and re-invention 242

Co-operative Bank, The 170

Co-operative Insurance Society, The 170

Co-operative League of the United States, The 150, 164, 166

Co-operative Party, The x

Co-operative Services Inc 241

Co-operative Wholesale Society, The 159, 170-171

Copresci 214

Corbett, E.A 168

Corrin J.P 39, 69-70

Coutinho, Father Boavida 165-166

Credit Unions And Australia viii-ix; and mutualism 4, 13-14; and distributism 4; and the Antigonish Movement 158-159, 163; and Tompkins159;

Also in the Radical Writing series

The Armour Plated Ostrich *by Tim Webb*
The Hidden Costs of Britain's Addiction to the Arms
Business.

A witty and well researched expose of Britain's addiction to the arms trade. £9.99

White Nation *by Ghassan Hage*
Fantasies of white supremacy in a multicultural society.

Essential reading for everyone anxious to understand the basis of modern racism. £12.99/$24.95

Celebrities, Culture and Cyberpace *by McKenzie Wark*
Britain's New Labour has echoes of the
Australian Experience.

The author, a media expert examines the Cultural Revolution of Australia's 13 years of Labor rule – time when policies very similar to Britain's New Labour were being applied. £12.99/$24.95

Comrades and Capitalists *by Rowan Callick*
Hong Kong since the handover.

Much has been written about Hong Kong before the handover. Of more historic importance was the first year under Chinese rule. Nothing turned out as expected. Capitalism, not communism, caused the problems that nearly wrecked the economy. £9.99

Radical Writing – *books to stretch your mind*
is an imprint of Comerford and Miller
and Pluto Press Australia

Available from all good booksellers, or
in the United Kingdom from Central Books
99 Wallis Rd. London E 11 5LN Tel: 0181 986 4854
(Visa and Master cards accepted)